God's Fools

God's Fools

SAINTS, PROPHETS, MARTYRS, AND THE MAKING OF MODERN COMEDY

JASON CRAWFORD

BLOOMSBURY ACADEMIC
NEW YORK · LONDON · OXFORD · NEW DELHI · SYDNEY

BLOOMSBURY ACADEMIC

Bloomsbury Publishing Inc, 1359 Broadway, 12th Floor, New York, NY 10018, USA
Bloomsbury Publishing Plc, 50 Bedford Square, London, WC1B 3DP, UK
Bloomsbury Publishing Ireland, 29 Earlsfort Terrace, Dublin 2, D02 AY28, Ireland

BLOOMSBURY, BLOOMSBURY ACADEMIC and the Diana logo are trademarks of Bloomsbury Publishing Plc

First published in the United States of America 2026

Copyright © Jason Crawford 2026

For legal purposes the Acknowledgments on **p. ix** constitute an extension of this copyright page.

Cover design: Devin Watson
Cover images © iStock.com/sedmak; iStock.com/sjingel

All rights reserved. No part of this publication may be: i) reproduced or transmitted in any form, electronic or mechanical, including photocopying, recording or by means of any information storage or retrieval system without prior permission in writing from the publishers; or ii) used or reproduced in any way for the training, development or operation of artificial intelligence (AI) technologies, including generative AI technologies. The rights holders expressly reserve this publication from the text and data mining exception as per Article 4(3) of the Digital Single Market Directive (EU) 2019/790.

Bloomsbury Publishing Inc does not have any control over, or responsibility for, any third-party websites referred to or in this book. All internet addresses given in this book were correct at the time of going to press. The author and publisher regret any inconvenience caused if addresses have changed or sites have ceased to exist, but can accept no responsibility for any such changes.

Library of Congress Cataloging-in-Publication Data Available

ISBN:
HB: 978-1-4930-8059-5
ePDF: 979-8-7651-6134-0
eBook: 978-1-4930-8060-1

Typeset by Deanta Global Publishing Services, Chennai, India
Printed and bound in the United States of America

For product safety related questions contact productsafety@bloomsbury.com.

To find out more about our authors and books visit www.bloomsbury.com and sign up for our newsletters.

for James, Eliza, and Cate

Contents

Acknowledgments   ix

Introduction: What Is a Comedian?   1

I: Saints

1. The Patron Saint of Laughter: Francis of Assisi   25
2. Unlucky Winners: From an Orphan Queen to an Awkward Black Girl   47

Interlude: A Joke Is a Prophecy   63

II: Prophets

3. The Prophet in Agony: From Snuff the Clown to Shakespeare's Fool   73
4. The Prophet Confesses: Richard Pryor   91

Interlude: Comedy is a Carnival   107

III: Martyrs

5. Hilarious Martyrs: From Perpetua of Carthage to Lawrence of Rome   115
6. Holy Fools: From Thecla in the Desert to Symeon in the City   131

Interlude: Rites of Renewal   155

IV: INNOCENTS

7. The Child Everlasting: Charlie Chaplin   163

8. Apocalyptic Comedy   191

Notes   203
Index   216

Acknowledgments

People sometimes ask me what comedians I like, and what I really want to say is: James, Eliza, and Cate. They are hilarious. They make the world bright. Whatever is true, innocent, or beautiful in this book is for them.

The best conversations I've had about many of the figures in this book, from Perpetua and Symeon to Saint Francis and Robert Armin, have been with my students at Union University. They have a way of asking questions I haven't thought to ask. Their voices are here in much of what I've written.

I wish I could name all the people at Union who have made themselves friends to me as I've worked on this book. I'm grateful especially to my colleagues in the Department of Languages, Literature, and Writing and in the Honors Community here. The members of my former writing group—Jay Beavers, Jeremy Blaschke, Phil Davignon, Joy Moore, and Jacob Shatzer—offered particular help and camaraderie in the early stages of my work, and some of them stepped in again in the end. John Netland and Scott Huelin have been friends to me and my writing from the moment I landed at Union, as generous and steadfast as friends can be.

Jason Strandquist has good taste in many of the things that matter in this book: jokes, monks, Peoria, dogs. He has been a co-conspirator like no other, in writing and much more. Sally Swanson has been a wise interlocutor and fellow traveler as I've wrestled my way through. Leah Buturain Schneider and Ed Schneider gave me extraordinary gifts of welcome, and a place to write and rest, as I was getting started.

I'm grateful to the colleagues and fellow writers, far and wide, who have offered help along the way. Daniel Swift in 2019, and Daniel Pollack-Pelzner and Elizabeth Tavares in 2021, were welcoming hosts at conference workshops where I experimented with early ideas for this book. Christopher Hodgkins has been fun to collaborate with on our essay about biblical laughter. David Aers, Sarah Beckwith, Michael Cornett, and James Simpson are always fun to collaborate with, and they helped greatly as I wrote about comic retribution for a special issue of the *Journal of Medieval and Early Modern Studies*. James Parker and Andrew McConnell Stott have both been wonderfully hospitable, including at the moments when I knocked on their respective doors as a stranger and asked if they wanted to talk about comedy. Van Partible welcomed me into his studio and creative process. Melanie East, Laurie Camp Hatch, and T. M. Moore offered perceptive feedback on two of these chapters in CCL summer writing workshops. Chad Schrock was there for those workshops, too, and for much more along the way. I wouldn't enjoy writing nearly as much if he weren't out there to read what I've done and send good things in return. My colleagues in the Lilly Network are always encouraging; Mark Schwehn has cheered and nourished my writing since long before I started thinking about comedy.

All these folks, of course, will find plenty of things here to dislike. That makes their generosity all the more remarkable.

In my work on this book, I've been grateful for the librarians and resources at the Huntington Library, Harvard's Houghton Library, Duke's University Libraries, and Union's Logos Library. I was supported along the way by a William A. Ringler Short-Term Fellowship at the Huntington Library and by Pew Research Grants here at Union. I'm grateful to the *Los Angeles Review of Books* for publishing my work on comedy and for permission to reprint material that appeared there in earlier forms.

I'm grateful to my agent, Andrew Stuart, for taking this project on and for his tireless work to see it into the world. I'm grateful to my editor, Chris Chappell, for taking the care to know this book so well and for his perceptive thoughtfulness about questions both creative and practical. I'm grateful to the folks at Bloomsbury who have worked so skillfully on the book's production and design.

I once again don't have the words to acknowledge the debts that matter most. My family and my friends, in Jackson and far off, are extraordinary. They have loved me beyond all belief. Especially to my people in Baton Rouge and in Charlotte—and in Columbus, Greensboro, and Atlanta—I am grateful.

And then there's Chelsy. How would I even start? She is good to laugh with and good to wonder with. She, more than anyone, has made this book better. But that's only the beginning. She makes everything better.

surely goodness and mercy

Introduction

What is a Comedian?

Long ago, by a lake somewhere in Russia, there lived three holy hermits. These three hermits were famous for their mystical devotion and charitable acts, but they didn't know a thing about the teachings of the Christian church: not one creed or prayer, not one feast day or fast day, not one council or controversy or point of doctrine. So one day the bishop of their region sailed across the lake to their little hut and spent an afternoon teaching them how to say the Lord's Prayer: "Our Father, who art in heaven," and so forth. That evening the bishop was sailing home, and out on the lake he saw the three hermits hurrying toward him. They were walking on the water. "Sorry to disturb you, father bishop," they called out, "but we seem to have forgotten that prayer you taught us. Could you remind us of the part about the daily bread?" And the bishop sighed. "Never mind," he called down from his boat. "Just go home and do whatever you were doing before."

*

I got this story from the great sociologist of religion Peter Berger.[1] He doesn't say where he got it from. Even if you aren't a great sociologist of religion, you probably know more or less what the story means. It's a spiritual parable, built around a tension at the heart of the Christian tradition to which it belongs. These three hermits are both scandalously ignorant and beatifically good. They don't know any of the things they are supposed to know, but that very deficiency is a sign of their special purity or innocence. They are straight out of Eden—the embodiment of Jesus's teaching that "unless you turn and become like children, you will never enter the kingdom of heaven"—and their walk across the water enacts an upside-down order of things in which fools turn out to be wise and the small turn out to be strong.[2] They therefore confront the bishop not just with a miracle but with what many Christian writers have called an *apocalypse*: a revelation (the Greek word *apokalyptein* means to reveal or uncover). They seem to live in a future that the rest of us, with our book learning and our boats, can hardly imagine.

But there's also something more to this story. Read it in the right way, and it comes across as something like a joke. It has a punchline. It's structured like a comic scene. And it looks like a lot of other comic scenes, from well beyond the world of religious teaching and apocalyptic vision. American pop culture (for instance) is full of comedies in which a weirdo comes to our world from some other place. Buddy the Elf travels to Manhattan from the North Pole. Alf and E. T. travel to California from their own far-off galaxies. Ancient queens, stone-age warriors, friendly ghosts, and top-hatted presidents come crashing into the suburbs and high schools of contemporary life, while everyone here gapes in surprise and scrambles to contain the damage.

Who are these strange pilgrims? They come swinging their swords, talking in funny accents, eating cotton balls and family pets, ambassadors to a world in need of help from somewhere else. In one subset of these fish-out-of-water comedies—*The Bishop's Wife*, *Michael*, *It's a Wonderful Life*—the stranger is an angel, sent down from heaven to say something true or set something right on earth. In another subset—*Barbie*, the 1995 *Brady Bunch* movie, the 2004 *Fat Albert* movie—the stranger comes from the myth-world of pop culture, a traveler from the parallel universe of our own collective imagination. The story isn't new: Shakespeare's clowns and fools all have the quality of otherworldly visitors who don't quite fit in the skins that ordinary mortals wear. So do Charlie Chaplin's many iterations of his Tramp persona. And in all these versions of the story, the visitor is an agent of redemption, renewing the weariness and sadness of our world with the preternatural vitality of that other place.

It could be, then, that my spiritual parable and the stories of comedy have something in common. Those stories, too, represent a far-off order of things, an alternative world that turns this world upside down. They tend to feature reversals and enchantments, magical twists of fate in which moms and daughters switch bodies, regular kids become princesses or CEOs, and respectable people get turned into shaggy dogs. And they tend to move from those weird fantasies to final visions of a world made new. Comedies conventionally end with moral awakenings, unlikely weddings, miracles of reconciliation and resurrection. They tend to conclude by looking ahead to a story that will be better than the stories we have lived before. Wesley in *The Princess Bride* rises from deadness (or from *mostly dead*-ness, as Miracle Max says) to new life. Mr. Portokalos, who has finally come around to accept his new in-laws, stands up at the end of *My Big Fat Greek Wedding* and pronounces, "We all different, but in the end, we all fruit." There's an apocalyptic spin in these episodes, a gravitational center that lies outside the present age.

And what about the three hermits in my little parable? Do they share anything with the otherworldly visitors of comedy? Perhaps they do. In a certain way, they are like the Three Stooges or the Three Amigos, fumbling the script delivered to them by the big people in charge. They are like Sally, Linus, and Pigpen, little philosophers on the loose in an all-too-grown-up world. It isn't hard, in fact, to imagine the performers of the comic stories I've mentioned playing the parts of these holy strangers. Chaplin could execute their walk across the water exquisitely, tipping his hat and shrugging sheepishly as the waves lap around his floppy shoes. Will Ferrell as Buddy the Elf and Margot Robbie as Barbie could play their exchange with the bishop. They would wave up at the boat with magical buoyancy, exasperating and life-giving in their infinite exuberance.

Those resemblances are no accident. Chaplin's lover Pola Negri once commented that "it was as if a part of Chaplin had never grown up," and comedians at a certain level are always acting out a kind of perpetual childhood.[3] It's easy to see when they have names like Pee-Wee Herman or vocal affectations like Andy Kaufman's "Foreign Man" warble. But even in our most provocative comedians—in, say, the tradition of taboo-breaking stand-up performers from Lenny Bruce and Richard Pryor to Maria Bamford and Sarah Silverman—there seems to be something of the petulance and innocence, the vulnerability and wonder, of children. Bruce plays the part of a mischievous boy, pulling pigtails and making eyes at his mother. Silverman bills herself as "The Bedwetter," eternally the little girl waking up in her own damp embarrassment. Pryor had the best puppy-dog eyes in the history of the business. And much of the work these comedians do revolves around their collisions with the grown-up world in which we all live. The encounter of the three hermits with the bishop could be a blueprint for Barbie's encounter with the Mattel C-suite or Ted Lasso's with the British press, or for Philomena Cunk's encounters with every expert she interviews in her absurdist historical documentaries. All these overgrown children have a preternatural ability to exasperate, interrupt, and confuse. But all of them also come bearing a truth that the grown-ups of this world can't understand and don't acknowledge. They seem in their own way to be emissaries of Eden, touched with an innocence that lifts them above the ordinary world's laws of gravity.

Is it possible, then, that comedians share something with the three hermits walking on the water? Could it be that those holy fools and these modern performers respond to a common spiritual hunger or belong to a common history? These are strange questions to contemplate. When you think of holiness, Richard Pryor might (let's boldly propose) not be the first thing that comes to mind. But the resemblances between the world of the three hermits and the world of comedy are worth contemplating. It could be that Buddy the Elf, too, is a walking apocalypse, made incarnate in this world so that he can bring some grace from the world beyond. It could be that performers such as Pryor, too, have some sort of spiritual charisma, rooted in their ability to inhabit a reality far off from our own. This book is about these performers, and about that charisma.

*

I'm a literature professor by trade. I spend a lot of time thinking about Shakespeare, and about the emergence of modern culture in the sixteenth and seventeenth centuries. And I spend a lot of time thinking about how ancient forms of sacred experience and ritual—what some people call "enchantment"—continue to have power in our secular age.

A few years ago, I started thinking about comedians. I was trying in those days to write a book about the history of comedy, from the Greek festivals where comic theater was born to the contemporary world. I wanted to understand why comedy tends to flourish at moments of culture war, of cataclysmic change and social conflict. I wanted to understand why comedy, in our own moment, is so interested in violence and artistic risk, in the boundaries between laughter that degrades and dehumanizes and laughter that reveals and heals. And I wanted to understand how the power of comedy is related to its roots in sacred ritual: in the fertility dances of ancient Greece, in the Christmas revels and Carnival mischief of medieval Christianity, in the wedding toasts and funeral roasts that have been used for millennia to confer blessing and ward off evil. I had a sense that right now, in the thick of our own culture wars, comedy is playing out some surprisingly ancient forms of ritual violence and sacred laughter. I wanted to sort that out, with the hope that I could say something about how comedy matters to our lives right now.

I was musing on all those questions when, in 2019, I went to Los Angeles for a few weeks to do some research at the Huntington Library. I was paying a lot of attention to contemporary comedy in those days, and I decided it was time to get out into LA and do some field work. By day I camped out in the Huntington reading room, poring over old accounts of feasts of fools, carnivalesque lynch mobs, and ceremonies of ritual mockery. And in the evenings I ventured out to comedy venues and improv studios all over the city. In those various venues, I saw famous comedians and obscure comedians, old comedians and young comedians. I saw stand-up performers working out the same bits again and again, for different audiences and in different contexts, fine-tuning the balances of risk and response. I saw performers failing on purpose, committing and confessing sins, telling jokes that they knew would turn their audiences hostile. I saw Esther Povitsky in what looked like pajama pants and Christina P in an old track suit. I saw Pauly Shore in middle age. I watched all these performers interrogating and condemning audience members, dispensing judgement and forgiveness. And I watched at one show, in West Hollywood, as Argus Hamilton got the sort of laughter he'd been looking for and so pronounced, like a priest speaking a blessing, "*Now* you're a crowd!"

So it came about that I started to think seriously about the *performers* of comedy. I came to suspect more and more, as I watched these comedians, that there was a ritual quality, something prophetic or priestly, in a lot of the work they did onstage. What sorts of rituals were they orchestrating as they presided over their crowds? What were they inviting or daring us to do, and what gave them their peculiar aura of social and spiritual authority? I began to wonder, too, about where these performers come from. Of course you can track the genealogies of contemporary comedians back through a lineage of twentieth-century performers: Bamford and Pryor, Joan Rivers and Lenny Bruce, Groucho Marx and Sophie Tucker. You can even track those genealogies back to the vaudeville emcees, music-hall clowns, and Yiddish *tummlers* from whom the emerging comedians of the early twentieth century learned much of their art.[4] But by the time you get to the jugglers and minstrels of the nineteenth century, the trails have become pretty faint. Where do you go from there? Does the comedian have a history older than the theaters in which Charlie Chaplin and Sophie Tucker got their start?

As I searched, I found that the history of the comedian leads back to the characters known in pre-modern Europe as "fools," the carnival jesters, weird healers, and prophesying vagrants who haunted the town squares and respectable houses of that older world. And I came to suspect that the history both of modern comedians and of pre-modern fools has roots in the places where comedy itself began, in the realms of sacred ritual and religious experience. I started digging up stories of saints, rabbis, martyrs, and hermits, and I started to see that those ancient figures were themselves performers. The early Christian martyrs took their stands in vast Roman arenas, billed as entertaining spectacles. Holy fools such as the fake prostitute Maria and the desert saint Symeon Stylites drew jostling and jeering crowds to the city squares and desert pillars where they staged their acts. These sacred performers developed many-layered stage identities, played mind games with the crowds who gathered around, acted out extreme forms of human abasement and ecstasy. In their weird displays, they made visible the same upside-down kingdom that the three hermits prophesied when they walked out onto the water. Like those hermits, they were apocalyptic figures, irruptions into the present age of something secret and strange.

This book tells the stories of those sacred fools, and of the modern comedians who carry on their work. It's a book of portraits more than a book of arguments, but the great motleyness of the crew I've assembled here itself amounts to a kind of argument. I'm going to propose that modern performers and ancient saints might really share something. I'm going to put third-century martyrs alongside silent film icons, desert prophets alongside stand-up provocateurs. And I'm going to claim that we have to put these figures together if we want to understand who comedians are and what comedians do. In telling the stories of these figures, I'm going to claim that the work of comedians matters in special ways in times of culture war and social division, and that their aim has often been not just to make us laugh but to make us whole. We might need the antics of these figures—of Charlie Chaplin and Lenny Bruce in their particular moments, or of Issa Rae and Philomena Cunk in theirs—in much the same way that the communities of thirteenth-century Italy needed the mischief-making of Francis.

Which is, I know, a lot to claim about Lenny Bruce and Philomena Cunk. So before I get down to business, let me put a few things in place. Here, now, comes one definition (of "comedian"), another definition (of "comedy," by Mel Brooks), a small complaint (by me, about that definition of "comedy"), a distinction (between moralists and prophets), a bold claim (that comedians are one of these things and not the other), a frank admission (that comedy is awful), and a kind of benediction, with help from

G. K. Chesterton: blessed are those who have seen the kingdom, and laughed out loud.

*

When we use the term "comedian," in the contemporary English-speaking world, we generally use it to mean a particular thing. A comedian is not the same as a clown or a humorist. A comedian is not the opposite of a tragedian. A comedian is not anyone who's funny. Winston Churchill and Yogi Berra are funny, but they aren't comedians. The term, for us, names something specific and distinctive.

Let's start with this simple fact: comedians are themselves works of art. If painters make canvases, poets make poems, and dramatic actors make representations of other lives, comedians, more than anything, make representations of themselves. They cross the borders between art and reality, always playing themselves, always making themselves the primary object of our attention. Groucho Marx or Charlie Chaplin might pass into various roles—a gold miner, a constable, the president of a small nation—but they carry into those roles their own unmistakable identities, their own scene-stealing charisma. It's exactly this charisma that determines whether, in contemporary parlance, we call a comic performer a "comedian" or an "actor." We find actors at work in repertory comedies, such as the plays of Shakespeare, that circulate from one cast to the next, and in the ensemble-driven screen comedies we associate with Robert Altman or John Hughes. But we find a *comedian* at work when the performer's identity is the product: when it's a Bob Hope or a Cheech and Chong movie, or when it's a show such as *Roseanne, Martin, Ellen, Seinfeld, Louis, The Cosby Show, Mr. Iglesias, The Mindy Project, I Love Lucy, Everybody Loves Raymond,* or *Everybody Hates Chris,* in which the performer's name, reduced to single word, becomes the icon of a whole dramatic world. In some of those shows, the comedian's alter ego shares her first name but not her last. Mindy Kaling, Roseanne Barr, and Andy Griffith play Mindy Lahiri, Roseanne Conners, and Andy Taylor. If the last name suggests a formal distinction between the comedian and her persona, the shared first name indicates a more intimate identification, a tearing down of the distinction between the performer and the role. Sometimes the names of the comedian and the character indicate no distinction at all: Jerry Seinfeld plays "Jerry Seinfeld," living a life that is "Jerry Seinfeld"'s life but not Jerry Seinfeld's life.

This magical ability to cross the lines of reality and unreality explains why there's such a close relationship between stand-up comedy and cinematic comedies like *City Lights* or *Horse Feathers*. To watch Lenny Bruce or Richard Pryor onstage is to enter an invented world built of dreams and nightmares, to see the living man refracted into images of himself. Watching Chaplin onscreen as the Tramp or the Great Dictator, or Groucho as Quincy Adams Wagstaff or Hugo Z. Hackenbush (or Pryor himself as Sharp Eye Washington or Daddy Rich), invites us into the same sort of border-crossing experience. At the end of the performance, a comedian like Pryor, unlike a dramatic actor, still bears the weight of everything he has just shown us on stage or screen. His calling, after all, is not just to enact something but to *be* something. When he says or does outrageous things, we are left to wonder: was that Richard Pryor talking, or was it "Richard Pryor" talking? Where does the one identity end and the other begin?

The propensity of comedians to offer themselves as their own most important creations has a lot to do with one of the core purposes of comedy. More than most other art forms, comedy orchestrates danger. Comedians make it their business to break taboos, to disrupt the everyday order of things, to test the extreme limits of social transgression. Artists like Bruce and Pryor do their work on the verge of real danger—Bruce, famously, kept getting himself arrested for the things he did onstage—and in their enactments of their various decadent selves they take a risk, venturing out to the places where the public, or the justice system, might turn against them. This flirtation with danger explains the spectacles of Curly Howard getting whacked with a mallet, Joan Rivers kvetching about her husband, and Milton Berle flouncing around in a dress. These are all activities that could, in our world, get you hurt, or cancelled, or killed. And this experimentation with danger drives even broadly likeable comedians like Seinfeld, Nate Bargatze, and Jim Gaffigan out to the boundaries beyond which their audiences might finally snap. Gaffigan plays a slovenly and regressive American dad, blathering about what he just cooked in the microwave plenty loud enough for everyone to hear. Seinfeld plays a know-it-all motor-mouth schoolboy, the schmucky nephew who won't stop talking about that thing on your nose or why he doesn't like chocolate sprinkles. How much farther would either of them have to go before we, the audience, started booing or reaching for our mallets?

*

These games of self-exposure will matter to almost all the stories I have to tell in this book. And they will matter because comedy is always preoccupied with sin and consequences, with the laws of moral judgment. Moral judgment is so central to comedy, in fact, that we could build a definition of comedy around it.

There's no one canonical statement about what comedy is or does. For tragedy, we've got Aristotle in the *Poetics*—"tragedy, then, is a representation of an action which is serious, complete, and of a certain magnitude... and through the arousal of pity and fear effecting the *katharsis* of such emotions"—and so we've got a founding claim about what tragedy is good for, how it matters to human life.[5] It's the opening move in a long critical tradition. For comedy, we've also got Aristotle—"the comic is one species of the shameful. For the comic is constituted by a fault and mark of shame, but lacking in pain and destruction"—but this isn't nearly as useful.[6] *Lacking in pain and destruction*: I'd guess there are some stooges and obscenity trial defendants who would beg to differ. The definition certainly hasn't stuck.

Better than Aristotle in the *Poetics*, perhaps, is Mel Brooks in a 1966 interview: "Tragedy is when I cut my finger. Comedy is when you fall into an open sewer and die."[7] That might be only marginally better than Aristotle: the bit about tragedy and cutting your finger, clearly, is just a setup for the open sewer punchline. And of course it isn't quite right that dying in an open sewer equals comedy. If you fall into an open sewer and die because you lost your eyesight to cancer as a child, it's not comedy. If you fall into an open sewer and die because an officer is throwing everyone in your ethnic group into open sewers to die, it's not comedy. If you fall into an open sewer and die because you're leaping heroically to save someone from an oncoming truck, it's not comedy. So Brooks's definition seems to be missing something; that's my small complaint.

But there's also something interesting here. The definition, at least sometimes, might hold up perfectly well. Let's venture a few scenarios. If you fall into an open sewer and die because you're turning your nose up at someone who smells like sewage, then it might be comedy. If you fall into an open sewer and die because you've vainly chosen to wear shoes that look dazzling but have terrible traction, it might be comedy. If you fall into an open sewer and die because you're the genocidal officer and you've just dug this open sewer to throw other people into, it might be comedy. And if you fall into an open sewer and die because you in particular, pathetic and helpless *you* in particular, *just would* fall into an open sewer and die, then you might just be in the neighborhood of comedy.

What's the difference of these latter scenarios? It's the same, really, as the actual difference (because there is a difference) between tragedy and cutting my finger: the one involves moral catastrophe and moral recognition, and the other does not. The sewer deaths that seem potentially comic involve morally significant consequences for morally significant actions. The moment you turned your nose up or put on those ridiculous shoes, you began to *deserve* to fall into an open sewer and die. And so your stinky death is an apocalypse, a revelation of a moral order that governs our lives and directs our ends. Even the scenario in which you fall into a sewer because you *just would* is an apocalypse, because it discloses something about who you are. And comedy loves apocalypse. It loves consequences, and the more gruesomely humiliating, the better. It loves to see those who deserve it falling into open sewers, meat grinders, the domineering embraces of ugly sexual partners. And it loves these humiliations because it loves to overthrow pride, to leave preening, powerful characters looking stupid and smelling bad. So much for Aristotle's *lacking in pain and destruction*. Mel Brooks, the comedian, knows that comedy has to hurt.

Brooks reflected on this reality more openly in a 1975 interview:

> The greatest comedy plays against the greatest tragedy. Comedy is a red rubber ball and if you throw it against a soft, funny wall, it will not come back. But if you throw it against the hard wall of ultimate reality, it will bounce back and be very lively.[8]

Against what ultimate reality does the ball of comedy bounce? Brooks goes on in this interview to say that the ultimate reality, for him, is death: his father's death when he was a child; the death of passing from childhood to adulthood; the deaths of millions of Jews in gas chambers and labor camps; his own inevitable disappearance from life and from this earth. He practices his comic art in the face of death, and his red rubber ball is an act of defiance, a way of insisting that death is not the only thing that's real. His laughter, in this way, has a miraculous quality, a bounce that the hard walls of mortal existence can't themselves offer. But his comedy also depends on his embeddedness, his participation in the suffering against which he hurls the rubber ball. He knows that there's no escape from that participation, because in this world of open sewers, the comedian is often the one doing the falling.

*

Because comedians embed themselves in a world of suffering—because they make their own vulnerable selves the material of their art—their performances often have the quality of an offering, a sacrifice rendered on this world's altars of pain.

It's easy to misunderstand this particular quality of comic laughter. When we talk about comedians, we often imagine them as moralists, confronting the world with blazing social commentary. The laughter they provoke, we tend to say, is like a spoonful of sugar to help the medicine of truth-telling go down. But there's a difference between moralists and prophets. Moralists speak from a place of critical distance. They speak their truths with the authority of their own moral uprightness, and they know that their authority depends on their difference from the idiots, cowards, and degenerates whose moral failures they expose. Moralists can be funny: and when they are funny, they create satire. Good for them. Satire is a sharp-fanged animal, quick and powerful in its own distinctive ways.

Then there are prophets. In the Hebrew scriptures, the prophet Hosea marries a prostitute; the prophet Ezekiel burns his own hair; the prophet Jeremiah walks around with a yoke on his neck. "Eat your bread with quaking," the Lord says to Ezekiel, "and drink water with trembling and with fearfulness"—because the sinners he has come to condemn are his own people.[9] That's the difference of the prophet. These weeping, wandering figures have authority not because they are morally upright but because they have been *touched*: they've encountered a truth that makes them odd. Because they bear a word that comes from somewhere else, they experience their own condemnations and prophesies as mysterious, truths beyond their own powers of comprehension. And they tend to speak not from the critical distance of the moralist but from a place of moral entanglement. "Woe is me! For I am lost," cries Isaiah, "for I am a man of unclean lips, and I dwell in the midst of a people of unclean lips."[10] When the prophets come, they tell us that they are themselves the idiots, cowards, and degenerates. They confess even as they proclaim, and they invite a wayward community to join them in confronting a message that, though it comes from beyond them, seems also to be written into their very personhood.

Prophets can be funny too. And when they are funny, they create a sort of theater very close to comedy, an enactment of an upside-down kingdom breaking into our world. Some ancient biblical interpreters mused that the prophets of Israel—Jeremiah with his yoke, Isaiah walking around naked—were remarkably like the hilarious vagrants and holy fools who haunted the early Christian communities of Syria, Egypt, Turkey, and Rome. I'll explore the possibility here that Francis of Assisi and the holy fool Symeon of Emesa practiced a prophetic comedy, staging spectacles of their own hilarious shabbiness and attempting to inhabit a holy ignorance or infancy. And I'll explore the possibility that modern comedians practice something similar. I'll ask whether Charlie Chaplin and Linus and Lucy don't practice a kind of prophetic comedy, alchemizing laughter out of their own bewildered experiences of suffering. I'll ask whether provocative stand-up comedians don't sometimes practice their own forms of prophetic comedy, transgressing even as they condemn. I'll entertain the possibility that even the stupidest comedians—the Stooges and Jackasses—might practice something in the general vicinity of prophetic comedy, enduring in their bodies the human degradation and splenetic violence that their comedy forces us to confront. Even for a stooge, perhaps, there's no relief from the travails of moral embeddedness.

But the boundaries between prophets and moralists are also fragile and unstable, and many comedians slip back and forth, teetering on the tightrope between the prophetic agony of embeddedness and the moral necessity of distance. It's almost a cliché that comedians age into moralists. Young Mort Sahl was a comedian; old Mort Sahl was a moralist. He crossed into a different sort of speaking as he became preoccupied with conspiracy theories and political corruption. Lenny Bruce crossed the same boundary in his late performances, when he rebranded himself as a free-speech warrior and bored his audiences by reading legal texts onstage. Dick Gregory crossed the boundary more decisively, giving up comedy altogether for a career in activism. Other comedians—Stephen Colbert, Samantha Bee, John Oliver—have slipped more fluidly back and forth, as if the demands of their particular comic styles ask them to walk right on the border between comic abasement and satirical distance. It's hard to escape the feeling that many comedians live close to that border, or that they have a moralist smoldering volcanically within them, just waiting to erupt.

The uncanny art of comedians depends on that interior pressure. The inner moralist is always just visible, pointing the finger right at the comedian herself. It happens in the comedy of culture-warring comedians like Lenny Bruce, but it also happens in the work of fat comedians, dweeby comedians, neurotic comedians, bed-wetting comedians, dumb comedians, grumpy old comedians, addicted and scandal-shamed and socially tainted comedians. They all embody their own worst selves, and they all embody the worst narratives that a larger society thrusts upon them, and in that embodiment they issue a condemnation that includes both themselves and everyone else. Some commentators have claimed that comedians like Lenny Bruce are essentially conservative figures. Bruce's biographer Albert Goldman wrote that, "The attempt to make Lenny superior to morality, to make him a hippie saint or a morally transcendental *artiste*, was tantamount to missing the whole point of his sermons, which were ferociously ethical in their thrust and firmly in touch with all the conventional values."[11] That's an exaggeration. But it does seem right that, for many comedians, the drive to break taboos and the mania for moral order are linked. And so their art is a paradoxical thing, full of contradiction and danger.

*

That danger is worth acknowledging out loud. A lot of comedy is awful. A lot of comedy is an excuse to be awful. Bad behavior is a feature of comedy, but it's also a bug.

Of course every art form gets done badly. I like jazz, and I like Shakespeare, and I've heard plenty of bad jazz and seen plenty of bad Shakespeare. But when comedy is bad, it's often bad in its own special way, because comedy is so specifically concerned with the boundaries of acceptable and moral behavior. If comedians at their best patrol those boundaries, testing the limits of what we are willing to confess, endure, and forgive, comedians at their worst cross these boundaries just because they can. And so comedy can be abusive, dehumanizing, misogynist, racist, pointlessly loud, pointlessly obscene, and just plain stupid.

Sorting out these divergent possibilities isn't always easy. Sometimes what looks gratuitous and abusive from one line of sight can look revelatory and self-sacrificing from another. Plenty of comedians have made careers by performing acrobatics at just those ambiguous places, daring us to follow them out to the borders that separate apocalyptic speaking from verbal atrocity. And these comedians themselves know perfectly well that the whole thing is dangerous. Dave Chappelle famously walked away from *Chappelle's Show* in 2005, partly because he worried that he himself had crossed the line. Hannah Gadsby caused a global sensation in 2018 by using a stand-up special to renounce comedy altogether, confronting publicly what it costs when we laugh at the pain of others. Sometimes it costs too much. That's my frank admission.

Even so: these comedians keep coming back, searching for a core of innocence at the heart of their own badness. Chappelle and Gadsby both came back, and comedy in fact is often *about* coming back. It specializes in restoration and renewal. Think about the conventional plots of comic plays and movies. They begin with conflict: with a dad who forbids his daughter to marry, a pair of would-be lovers who can't let their guard down enough to accept each other, a lonely kid wandering into some other body or universe. But they end with the world set right: with Josh Baskin back in his twelve-year-old body, with Harry and Sally finally admitting their love, with E. T. going home. Stand-up comedians orchestrate a similar sort of homecoming, performing and confessing their worst sins and then inviting us into an exchange of forgiveness and reconciliation. In staging these scenes of homecoming and restoration, comedians, like the three water-walking hermits, seem to tap into something miraculous. They invite us to believe in an Edenic order of things, a lost innocence, that our fallen world tends to resist and forget. And like those three hermits, they act as prophets of the eschaton, whispering of a restored innocence beyond the present age. That's the apocalyptic spin of comedy. It keeps orchestrating a longed-for return, insisting on the triumph of life even in a world of death.

In making my claims about the sacred and prophetic possibilities of comedy, I don't intend to discuss the actual religious lives of comedians. Some comedians have a religious faith; I find that fascinating. But what I'm after here is not the spiritual life of any one performer but the spiritual possibilities of an art form. And though I explore the religious roots of comic laughter, I don't want to claim any particular comedian for any religious tradition. It can be fun and thought-provoking to do so. Ralph Gleason, the great music critic, called Lenny Bruce "a primitive Christian preaching a moral message"; Thomas Merton, the Trappist monk, commented that "people like Lenny Bruce are really monks in reverse, and hence I feel much closer to them than I do to say the President of General Motors."[12] That's all worth chewing on. But Lenny Bruce, still, was not a Christian saint and didn't want or claim to be. We might get closer to the distinctive charisma of comedians like Bruce if we ask more carefully about their particular sort of strangeness, and about the religious narratives and longings that haunt the margins of their performances.

Writing about these religious longings is an interesting business. I partly want to say something about the history of comedy, to trace the genealogies that actually connect modern comedians to the carnival fools and desert saints of the pre-modern world. But discussing comedy is also like discussing folklore, or myth, or religion itself: it lives at the ground level of human culture and human consciousness, in a territory that no talk of historical connection can fully explain. Why do cultures with no apparent contact tell similar stories about dying gods and the creation of the world? Why do Lenny Bruce and Saint Francis tell the same jokes and act out the same otherworldly fantasies? We're on ground that isn't easy to map out.

But I want to do some mapping. I'll do that, here, by paying attention to the ancient personae that modern comedians tend to put on, to the way they fashion themselves as martyrs, innocents, strangers, prodigals, and prophets. I'll look at the moments when their comic performances begin to look like sacred rituals, or when their unhinged fantasies begin to look like apocalyptic vision. I've limited my explorations of modern comedy mainly to comedians fairly widely known and working in English, and I've limited my explorations of sacred experience mainly to the Jewish and Christian traditions from which modern western comedy derives much of its vitality (there are of course other traditions to explore and other stories to tell).[13] In building a bridge between those two worlds, the comic and the sacred, I hope to say something about what gives comedy its peculiar beauty.

That is my central claim, more or less: that comedy, at its best, is beautiful. The laughter it provokes lives close to the experiences that we need most and understand least—to prayer, festivity, forgiveness, and love. And its beauty is always under threat, especially in cultures that prize systems of measurement to which laughter can't be assimilated.

Back in the early twentieth century, a writer who clearly cared a whole lot about those systems of measurement, someone named "Mr. McCabe," rebuked G. K. Chesterton in print for joking about sane and serious subjects. Chesterton replied: "I should," he wrote, "regard any civilization which was without a universal habit of uproarious dancing as being, from the full human point of view, a defective civilization. And I should regard any mind which had not got the habit in one form or another of uproarious thinking as being, from the full human point of view, a defective mind."[14] Chesterton's jokes, he fumed, weren't frivolous mockeries of serious topics: they were the best language he had for talking about serious topics, because serious topics live beyond our reach, in a world of miraculous life to which laughter and wonder, loud singing and water walking, are some of the best responses.

The parable of the three hermits says, I think, something similar. Their story is an expression of beatitude, a blessing of those who respond to the truth not by attempting to possess it but by entering into its wild and unpredictable life. Blessed are the uproarious, because uproar is the music of a universe blazing with love. Blessed are the festive—the dancers, the banqueters, the lovers of play—because celebration is the acknowledgment of life as an improbable gift. Blessed are the unruly in thinking—the makers of paradox, the lovers of absurdity—because, as Chesterton says, "paradox simply means a certain defiant joy which belongs to belief." And blessed are those who laugh in hope, because in their laughter, the vitality at the heart of all things overcomes the moralistic solemnity, the reductive rationality, the relentless exploitation, and the sheer mind-numbing blandness of a world under tyranny.

W. H. Auden once wrote that laughter is closer to prayer than either of those things is to "the everyday secular world of Work." Both laughter and prayer, after all, put us in touch with something primal and alive, something that defies the everyday world's economy of violence and acquisition. "Those who try to live by Work alone, without Laughter or Prayer," Auden says, "become insane lovers of power, tyrants who would enslave nature to their immediate desires."[15] Could it be that our laughter, at its best, puts us in touch with experiences of holy longing? Could it be that comedy can help us to imagine a world made new? Perhaps so. The comedians we'll meet here will raise the possibility that strangeness can be a form of innocence, that a joke can also be a promise, and that when the red rubber ball of comedy really bounces, it sails up toward realities even more ultimate than death.

I
SAINTS

1

THE PATRON SAINT OF LAUGHTER

FRANCIS OF ASSISI

Francis of Assisi spent the early months of 1225 in total darkness. It was winter, still bitter cold, and Francis had come home to San Damiano, the church outside Assisi that had offered him shelter since the early days of his religious life. This time, he was here because he needed a place to suffer in peace. The disease that afflicted his eyes—apparently some kind of ophthalmia or trachoma, contracted in Egypt five years earlier—had become so excruciating that he could not tolerate even the brightness of a fire at night. His recurring stomach disorder was getting worse, too, and would by the year's end reduce him to a swollen, blood-vomiting invalid, too weak even to speak. A few months before, the early stories say, he had been stricken with the stigmata, the ever-bleeding wounds of Christ on his hands, feet, and side. And he slogged through all these physical ordeals under the weight of crushing spiritual doubts, misgivings about both himself and the movement to which he had dedicated his life.

He lived increasingly in isolation these days, he who had once been so famously and raucously sociable. A handful of his brothers in the Friars Minor (as he called his fraternity) had rigged up a windowless hut for him next to San Damiano, and he now sat in that hut like a subterranean creature, sequestered in the blindness made necessary by his pain. When he lay on the floor at night or felt his way to the little table, the mice that infested the place scurried all over him and made it impossible to sleep or eat or even to pray. The miseries of his sickness were so desperate that within a few months, he would let his religious brothers wrap his head in rags and lead him around central Italy in search of shop-of-horrors medical treatments not likely to succeed. One doctor perforated his ears with a hot iron. Another burned a trench across his face so brutally that the brothers who had brought him couldn't bear to stay in the room while it happened. It's hard to fathom a disease horrible enough that these atrocities could plausibly represent relief. Even more, it's hard to imagine what could have broken a man who had gone barefoot through hard winters, survived massacres on the battlefield, and embraced starvation as one of his deepest pleasures. He once told his companions that three days of his sickness would make torture and martyrdom look like a day at the beach. Which sounds like an outrageous claim—but then again, the *poverello* of Assisi, as he called himself, was of all people pretty well qualified to make it.

Whatever kind of misery it entailed, Francis's sickness unto death was also the incubator of something else. One night his pain became so unbearable that he cried out to God in the darkness of his hut, "Lord, make haste to help me in my illnesses, so that I may be able to bear them patiently." God talked back, and in their exchange he offered what the little poor man himself called "the promise of His kingdom," the assurance of an inheritance beyond all mortal imagination. Francis awoke the next morning with incandescent energy, told his spiritual brothers what had happened, and declared that he was going to write a "praise of the Lord for his creatures." He got right down to work, pouring forth verses that celebrate the earthly and divine beauties of his favorite things—Brother Sun, Sister Moon, Sister Water, Brother Fire, flowers, fruit, herbs, stars, Sister Mother Earth herself—and before long he had composed the song that we call "The Canticle of Brother Sun" or the "Canticle of the Creatures." In this song, he defied his pain, praising the very things that had become his afflictions. Brother Sun, he sang, "is beautiful and radiant with great splendor." Brother Fire "is beautiful and playful and robust and strong."[1]

Francis clearly regarded the Canticle not just as a gift in the midst of his sickness but as a culmination of his life's work. As soon as he had finished composing the verses and their melody, he called for Brother Pacifico, a skilled musician, and said that he wanted him to send a group of brothers into the world, preaching the gospel and singing this new song. As you go out, he directed these brothers, announce to the crowds that "we are the minstrels of the Lord, and this is what we want as payment: that you live in true penance."[2] *The minstrels of the Lord*: the Latin text, in the early biography that tells this story, is *ioculatores Domini*, and the phrase alludes to the medieval entertainers often called by the French name *jongleurs*, traveling purveyors of comic laughter (the word's closest relative in English is "juggler").[3] This, Francis told his brothers, is who you are.

He had in fact been telling them this for years. "What are the servants of God," he liked to ask, "if not His minstrels, who must move people's hearts and lift them up to spiritual joy?"[4] He had insisted throughout his religious career that he himself was not a bishop or prelate, not a philosopher or theological master, but rather a roving song-and-dance man, God's juggler in the field. In the two years he lived after composing the Canticle, he claimed that vocation as boldly as ever. He had his brothers sing the song to him regularly, including in his final night of mortal suffering. It was, among other things, a reminder: they, like him, were called to perform songs of life even in the house of death. They were holy minstrels, comedians of the Lord.

*

By the time Francis wrote the Canticle, his brothers in the Friars Minor knew all too well that he was a born performer. The early *vitae*, biographies written by his companions and other first-generation followers, are filled with stories of his provocative antics. There was the time he strolled naked into Assisi and got right up to preach, the time he had a brother tie a rope around his neck and drag him into the piazza like a thief, the time he rolled in the mud with pigs and then presented himself stinking before the Pope. He was an outrage artist, and he knew perfectly well how ludicrous it was for the leader of a major religious movement to sing loudly in bad French (he did this a lot) or to talk with animals and flowers (also pretty often). When he was seized with righteous anger, his one-man show of carnival mayhem got even wilder. Once, when an inexperienced young brother asked permission to own a prayer book, Francis rubbed ashes on his own head and repeated again and again, "I'm a prayer book! I'm a prayer book!"[5] Another time, when a woman tried to seduce him at an inn, Francis stripped off his clothes, jumped onto the grate in the inn's blazing fireplace, and called out, "Undress! Hurry! Enjoy this splendid, flowery, wonderful bed!"[6]

Those who knew him said that Francis, though not much to look at, possessed a phenomenal charisma. One observer commented that, while he could remember the sermons of other preachers verbatim, he always found the preaching of Francis strangely elusive: "Even if I memorize some of his words," he said, "they don't seem to me like those that originally poured from his lips."[7] The power seems to have been in his presence, his way of bearing the fire of God in his body, "weaving movement," as one early biographer wrote, "with fiery gestures."[8] And Francis seems to have loved being in front of a crowd. He took his circus of holy hilarity on a never-ending tour, turning fields, roads, ditches, churches, leper colonies, city squares, noble houses, hotel fireplaces, and midnight-dark hovels into stages for his theatrical work. Some modern biographers have noticed that his performances grew only more flamboyantly theatrical in his later years, partly because he was receding from daily leadership of the Friars Minor.[9] As he relinquished that administrative work to others, he instead offered himself to his movement as a kind of icon, blazingly visible and irresistibly watchable. His followers certainly regarded him as a gospel text with two feet, a living work of art who set out, as Bonaventure of Bagnoregio wrote in his great thirteenth-century biography, "to carry in his own body the armor of the cross."[10] If we believe biographers such as Bonaventure or Thomas of Celano, who finished his first *vita* just two or three years after Francis's death, the little poor man preached his message not in what he said but rather in what he did and who he was. He "bore Jesus always in his whole body" so utterly, Thomas wrote, that "it seemed he had just been taken down from the cross."[11] It's no wonder that in the end he even came to bear the crucifixion wounds in his hands, feet, and side. A profound, incongruous, hilarious play-actor, he spent his whole adult life dressing up in his Jesus of Nazareth costume, disappearing progressively into the role and inviting anyone who would listen to grab a cross and join the show.

Francis's biographers have always suspected that the roots of his theatrical vocation lay embedded in his own history, in the longings and disappointments of his early years. He was born in Assisi in late 1181 or early 1182, the eldest child of Pietro and Pica Bernardone. One of the early *vitae* reports that his mother named him John, but when his father returned from the business trip that had caused him to miss his son's birth, he insisted on changing the boy's name to Francesco, which means something like "Frenchy." There's no way to know whether that story is true or why his parents gave him this unusual name, but it certainly is true that the family owed much of its fortune and identity to French culture. Pietro was a cloth merchant; he traveled to the markets of Provins and Troyes and brought back expensive fabrics to sell to the noble families of Assisi. At those markets, he would have encountered the best things European money could buy: pearls, ivories, spices, furs, precious metals, gemstones, wines, exquisite tapestries, currencies from far and wide, human slaves set out nearly naked on display.[12]

But those luxe goods were not for him. Pietro Bernardone was a talented businessman, and thanks to his many enterprises he became prominent and rich, an important leader in his city's fast-rising middle class. No matter how much money he made, though, he and his family, at the end of the day, were subservient to the aristocratic families he sold cloth to. Young Francis didn't play with the children of those families. He wasn't educated like those children (his Latin and French were famously terrible), and he couldn't expect to live the lives that his aristocratic neighbors did. Still, that world of fine French things—silks and velvets, courtly manners, heroic romances—got into his bones. The early biographers all write with curmudgeonly glee about what a spoiled and pampered boy young Francesco Bernardone was. He spent his parents' money with such abandon, one of them comments, that "he seemed to be the son of some great prince rather than their son."[13] He raided the high-end fabrics in his father's storehouses and ordered up outfits designed to get everyone in Assisi talking. Sometimes he would take the cheapest cloth and have it sewn together with the most expensive, prancing around town and basking in the buzz that followed him. His reputation as an over-refined dandy was so well known that when, later, he began to pursue his religious calling and committed himself to the care of an impoverished priest at San Damiano, the priest went out of his way to buy Francis special foods.

As an adolescent, Francis became known also for his feats of carnival excess. He was the *signore* of what in late medieval Italy were called "confraternities of youth," groups of young men who performed songs, dances, masquerades, and farces at various festivals throughout the year, and if the accounts of disapproving contemporaries are to be believed, these groups engaged not just in civic festivity but also in plenty of extracurricular drinking and debauchery.[14] In Assisi, young Francis took on the job of throwing, and funding, the party. Fueled by his wild and whirling imagination and by huge sums of his father's money, Francis's fraternity of misrule paraded drunkenly around the streets and *piazze* of the city, singing erotic hymns, sexually accosting young women (and young men, by some accounts), and making themselves as grandly ostentatious as they could manage.

There seems to have been something wondrous in the spectacle of young Francis's prodigal life. Even his pious early biographers often comment that these orgies of spending and dissipation were an expression of his preternatural generosity and charisma. Followers flocked to him, and he went to magnificent lengths to show those followers something special. The most detailed account of his early life, a thirteenth-century *vita* called *The Legend of the Three Companions*, notes that his reputation for dashing good manners spread "throughout almost the entire region" and prompted rumors "that, in the future, he would be something great."[15] This son of a cloth merchant was bursting, it seems, with everything: charm, song, money, whimsy, prancing vanity, amiable high spirits, and a pageantry of self-regard so razzling and dazzling that no one seems to have looked too carefully into its inner workings. Long before the fire of the Lord had touched him, young Francis already looked strikingly, in ways, like the mature saint of the sacred legends: playing at roles, attracting disciples, upending the rules of prudent civic life, and roving around in strange garments the hem of which everyone wanted to touch.

*

This beautiful boy danced his pageant of extravagance against the backdrop of a brutal social world. The aristocratic families who dominated most Italian cities struggled against each other with such ferocious violence that they often had to agree, during the years of Francis's youth, to entrust the government of their cities to outsiders, brought in for one-year terms as neutral mediators among the homicidal factions.[16] This culture of never-ending warfare was exacerbated by the status of these cities as proxies and prizes in the long conflict between the German emperors and the Roman popes. And in the twelfth century, the lines of conflict were made only more complex by populist movements that shifted power from aristocratic families to a rising class of merchants, financiers, and magnates of business. Middle-class houses such as the Bernardone family of Assisi amassed more and more money and power in the decades before Francis's birth, and in one city after the next they banded together and took up arms against the noble clans, dismantling the old structures of feudal power and constituting themselves as communes, with the *popolo* or "people" at their center.

The shift from a feudal to a communal political order wasn't pretty: noble houses who had lived by the sword could die in only one way. The revolutionary bloodletting came to Assisi in 1197–98, when Francis was about sixteen years old. That winter, Conrad of Spoleto, the duke who had kept Assisi under the emperor's thumb, was summoned away on diplomatic business, and as soon as he was out of the city the people of Assisi rose up, expelling Conrad's troops and pulling his hilltop fortress down stone by stone. The violence then metastasized into civil war, as an army of merchants and artisans carried their campaign to the aristocratic houses around Assisi and then finally into the city itself. They invaded the strongholds of battle-hardened feudal lords, tearing down or burning some of the great houses, seizing and occupying others, and sending the privileged classes of the city fleeing in humiliation and terror.

We don't know exactly what role the sixteen-year-old Francis played in this revolutionary carnage. Given his father's status as a wealthy merchant-citizen and his own later involvement in the conflict, there's a good chance that Francis was there already in 1598, storming the citadels with Assisi's populist army. Whether he was in the fray or not, he was, by all indications, cultivating quite a taste for the romance of war. The boy who flounced around Assisi like a prince also steeped his imagination in tales of crusading knights. French romances and *chansons de geste*, with their tales of Charlemagne and Roland and the knights of the Round Table, were all the rage in twelfth-century Italy. Francis with his confraternity probably sang songs about these heroes and about their ideals of transcendent eros and ritualized violence. He might have enacted some of these tales in festival pageants and civic tournaments. By the time he reached the end of his teens, he was possessed with fantasies of riding heroically into battle, transfigured by his exploits from the son of a cloth dealer into a chivalric warrior. Never mind that the feudal order was crumbling to pieces around him, possibly with his help. It's clear from the early biographies that Francis dreamed of going to battle and winning a place in the upper tiers of that order.

He got his chance soon enough. By the beginning of the year 1200, the exiled nobles of Assisi had made their way to the neighboring city of Perugia and were busy securing the support of that city's ruling class. For the next two years, Assisi and Perugia traded provocations, burning crops, ambushing caravans, hoarding supplies, recruiting allies, hiring mercenaries, arming citizens, and generally making ready for the climactic battle that finally came in November 1202. At the Battle of Collestrada, the grievances of many years exploded into an orgy of killing. Chronicles written in the decades that followed record that the battle was, as Thomas of Celano called it, a "great massacre."[17] The Perugian poet Bonifazio described fields dense with mutilated corpses, limbs and entrails strewn gruesomely about, a slaughter so horrific that pity seized the whole region.[18] When it was all over, the armies of Assisi were devastated.

Francis was among those armies, mounted on horseback with a troop of *cavalieri*. If he imagined that this was the moment his new life would begin, his fantasies were shattered fast. By the time the bloodbath ended, Francis had been captured, and he spent the next year as a prisoner of war in Perugia.

His early biographers offer bits and pieces of information about Francis's time in prison. The conditions were squalid. Francis became sick with some kind of grim and protracted illness. Some of the early *vitae* say that he befriended a prisoner who was hated by the others. Some recount the famous story that Francis one day was so strangely jovial that the other prisoners told him he must be insane; how else could he be happy in the midst of such suffering? "What do you think will become of me?" he replied. "Rest assured, I will be worshipped throughout the whole world."[19]

There is a weird contradiction in these stories. Francis is sick and struggling, but at the same time he is buoyant with life, seemingly untouchable. His prediction about his wonderful future, in particular, seems to belong to two histories at once: it's both the jackassy boast of a conceited young fool and the prophecy of something very different to come. This ambiguity might indicate that in this year of his life, Francis was himself a contradiction, a young man at a threshold. He was visibly, for the first time, a man in darkness, an early image of the dying Francis who would later cry out in his hut. And he was, at the same time, still the would-be hero, a fantastic man-child dreaming his way toward an impossible future. In a certain sense, Francis would live his whole life at that threshold. The whimsical child never did disappear; he would still be there in the dying old saint, singing absurdly in the darkness and dispatching his holy *jongleurs* to conquer the world with song.

Perhaps because Francis was so sick, the Perugians finally accepted a ransom from his father in late 1203, about a year after his capture, and he went home. The early accounts don't say much about the exact nature of his sickness, but it seems to have been severe enough that for significant parts of the year 1204 he couldn't even walk or get out of bed. And the disease didn't afflict his body alone. When Francis did finally gain enough strength to venture out with a cane and visit the streets and fields he so loved, he found himself incapable of enjoyment and "wondered," as Thomas of Celano says, "at the sudden change in himself."[20] Something in him was broken. He "began to regard himself as worthless," Thomas reports, and he entered into what looks like a depressive crisis, overcome by emotional numbness, unable to believe in any of the things he had once lived for.

There's no way to know what relationship Francis's sickness had to the traumas of war and imprisonment. But there's also no way to ignore those traumas. This survivor of war and prison would go on, in his later career, to confront warring cities with tearful pleas for peace and to make himself a special friend of prisoners. In one stunning incident, many years after the Battle of Collestrada, Francis was praying in a clifftop cell at Greccio, and he came down fuming so furiously against Perugia that the brothers with him thought he must have had a vision. He spent several days "with his soul on fire" and finally charged off to Perugia, where he burst into the middle of a city festival, confronted the knights who were jousting there, and thundered, "Hear what the Lord tells you through me, a little poor man.... fully armed you attack your neighbors: you kill and pillage. I tell you, this will not go unavenged."[21] Some of these jousting knights might have been the very men he had faced at Collestrada long before. Was it in that battle that this theatrical boy, so zealous for life, began to discover his vocation to a world touched by death?

*

Those terrible couple of years could have been the end of laughter for a young man as sensitive as Francis. He could have retreated into any number of things: his depression, a hollowed-out simulacrum of his former hedonism, his father's expectation that he would pull himself together and get to work in the family business. But instead, he started waking up to a possibility he had not known before, a new life for his old disciplines of play-acting and carnival misrule.

It began in late 1204 and early 1205. As Francis got stronger, he went looking for ways to recover the zest he had lost on the killing fields of Collestrada. With a friend in Assisi, he hatched the plan of joining the French nobleman Walter of Brienne in his campaign to support papal authority in southern Italy. Walter was a dashing, powerful, and widely admired courtier-crusader, and Francis got the idea that if he fought well enough in Walter's armies, he might win knighthood in the bargain. He began preparing with manic enthusiasm ("burning with desire," as one of the early *vitae* says) and with what smells quite a lot like sheer desperate need.[22] He spent as lavishly as ever. He bought armor and weapons, horses and tack. He raided his father's storehouses of luxury cloth once more. When friends asked him about his new exuberance in the days before he departed, he laid it right out: "I know that I will become a great prince."[23] Which is to say, the old Francis is back.

There were signs, as he got ready for this romantic quest, that a new Francis might be emerging. (In one memorable encounter in the spring or summer of 1205, Francis was riding outside Assisi in his fancy new clothes when he met an impoverished knight, stopped right then and there, and gave the poor knight the clothes off his own back.[24]) But for the most part, Francis kept barreling ahead, and in the summer of 1205, along with some others from Assisi, he finally set out on the journey. He and his party got as far as Spoleto on the first day, but Francis was seized by some sort of crippling illness and had to stop there. One night in his sickness, halfway between sleep and waking, he heard a voice asking him where he was going. Francis explained his plan, and the voice then asked him, "Who can do more good for you? The lord or the servant?" Francis replied, "The lord." Then why, the voice asked, are you going off to follow the servant? And Francis replied: "Lord, what do you want me to do?"[25]

It's the same question Paul asked on the road to Damascus, and it's that kind of scene. The early *vitae* treat this encounter as a pivotal moment, a conversion, in which the prodigal finally names aloud and submits to the figure who has been pursuing him.[26] In response to Francis's Pauline question, the voice of God answered that he should go home and wait, so the failed adventurer turned around and trudged back to Assisi, where indeed he waited, less at home than ever.

For some months, he sat around, brooded, partied half-heartedly with his old friends, prayed a lot, and generally got weirder. He started laying out way too much food on the family dinner table, so that he could then go out and give the leftovers to the poor. He began to have fantasies about traveling to other cities where he could pretend to be poor and beg in the streets. In the spring of 1206, he made a pilgrimage to Rome, and there he made a first experiment in living out these fantasies. He traded clothes with a beggar on the steps of St. Peter's, begged for a while in bad French, and then traded back and became himself again. The experiment must have lived up to expectation: his early biographers report that he would have repeated the adventure many times more, had his companions on the trip not told him to knock it off. Coming back to Assisi in his ordinary clothes, he must have felt let down yet again. Once more, by coming home, he was turning his back on another possible Francis, a dressed-up and fantastical Francis, in order to return to a life that no longer seemed his own. Those other

Francises—the knight Francis, the beggar Francis—haunted and beckoned him. He couldn't figure out how to get himself into the dream-kingdom where they lived.

*

But in the inside-outness or upside-downness of these episodes—in their world-inverting folly—there was already something like an answer to Francis's question. Sometime in this period, God spoke that answer to him right out loud. "Francis," the divine voice said to him one day, "everything you loved carnally and desired to have, you must despise and hate," and "what before seemed delightful and sweet will be unbearable and bitter, and what before made you shudder will offer you great sweetness and enormous delight."[27] This paradoxical promise beckoned Francis toward the same sort of reversal that he had perhaps flirted with when he stripped off his clothes to provide for the poor knight and so swapped his fantasies of heroic nobility for fantasies of heroic poverty. Now, the voice of God beckoned him to plunge in all the way, head over heels into a carnival misrule that would turn the whole world on its head.

Francis entered into the baptismal waters of this misrule not long after, on a day when he met a leper in the road. There was one thing in this world that made Francis shudder like nothing else: leprosy. He loathed lepers with a downright pathological fear, a stomach-sick revulsion. Their disfigured flesh and cringing shame terrified him. Even in his new season of pious charity, he hadn't been able to bring himself to give lepers alms; he had to have others carry the food or money for him. And who could have blamed him for his fear, this child of privilege? Lepers, in Francis's world, lived a walking death. They were stripped of their families and possessions, penned up in colonies, forbidden from touching people or drinking from rivers or going into churches. In Assisi, lepers were barred even from entering the city. Those who did were hunted down and driven out.[28]

So here's Francis, carrying a new mandate to do something zany: *Despise what you have loved, and love what you have despised.* And here comes a leper, as Francis rides his horse one day on a road outside Assisi. What would Francis normally have done? Turned around? Waited for the leper to get off the road before galloping by? Today, he dismounted. He walked right up to the man. And then, when the leper extended a hand to receive alms, he took the man's hand, and he kissed it. He actually put his lips on the skin of a leper. According to one of the early *vitae*, he went even further than this and asked the leper to give him a kiss of peace. It was a life-changing moment. When he got back on his horse, says Thomas of Celano, he was "filled with joy and wonder."[29] The promise of God—that "what before made you shudder will offer you great sweetness"—seemed, astonishingly, to hold true. Within a few days, Francis took his plunge into the abyss and moved into San Lazzaro d'Arce, Assisi's hospital for lepers. There he gave the residents money, kissed them on their hands and lips, cleaned pus from their sores, and made himself, as another early *vita* says, "their servant and friend."[30] As he lived with these figures of dying flesh, something changed in Francis. Years later, he himself traced his conversion to his time with the lepers. In his *Testament*, the account of himself he wrote not long before his death, he recounts that "when I left them, what had seemed bitter to me was turned into sweetness of soul and body. And afterwards I delayed a little and left the world."[31]

And left the world: we have liftoff. In the house of living death, Francis has taken his first real step into an upside-down life, a zero-gravity program of social, moral, and spiritual transvaluation. Among the lepers, he already knows that this new life is going to hurt. The good people of Assisi—his partying friends, his former admirers, his father—are going to hate it. But it's also going to be hilarious, and even here, in the leprosarium, Assisi's young lord of festive misrule must feel already the buzzy euphoria of a shock artist about to pull his biggest stunt yet. Wearing bizarre clothes? Singing racy songs past curfew in the streets? That was all child's play. The carnival king of Assisi is now heading into town with a leper on his arm. For the next twenty years, no one will be able to stop watching.

*

Things happened fast now, and it wouldn't be long before Francis mounted his climactic renunciation of his old life and his first public performance of holy folly. In a fateful chain of events, God told Francis to rebuild the dilapidated church of San Damiano, Francis infuriated his father by stealing cloth from the family storehouses and selling it to raise funds, and finally, after weeks of dramatic conflict, the two of them agreed to take their dispute to Assisi's bishop. The bishop counseled the young delinquent to return his father's money and to trust in the Lord's provision for his church-building project, and Francis responded by making his first real announcement of his new life. He cheerfully declared, "My lord, I will gladly give back not only the money acquired from his things, but even all my clothes."[32] Then he stripped off his clothes and presented himself stark naked, right there in front of everyone. Exultant and defiant, he proclaimed aloud, "I return to him the money on account of which he was so upset, and also all the clothing which is his, wanting to say from now on: 'Our Father who are in heaven,' and not 'My father, Pietro di Bernardone.'"[33]

It was a hair-raising, daredevil performance, his first and one of his greatest. You can still hear Bonaventure gasping at the audacity of the thing nearly sixty years later, when he writes in his *Major Legend* that Francis "even took off his trousers, and was completely stripped naked before everyone."[34] The people present actually wept to see it. Pietro Bernardone stormed off in grief and rage. Some servants of the bishop brought Francis a cheap cloak that had belonged to a local farmer. And Francis himself took that cloak and went on his way, dressed like a farmer and singing like a troubadour. He was wholly now the citizen of another kingdom, a man from elsewhere, though the people of Assisi followed wide-eyed as he went.

With this performance, Francis's career as a holy comedian properly began. For the rest of his life, he would keep returning to and developing the elements of this primal scene. In cities, villages, palaces, and cathedrals, year after year, he disrupted official proceedings, tweaked authority figures, made apocalyptic pronouncements, pulled exasperating stunts, jabbed and slashed with his killer wit, and performed his estrangement from the prevailing social order. He made a whole career of self-abasement, taking on "little poor man" as a sort of sobriquet and identifying himself with those who own nothing and are nothing in this world. His life was by many standards a phenomenal success—he founded a fraternity that by the time of his death had attracted thousands of members; he camped with the armies of the Fifth Crusade and met the sultan al-Malik al-Kamil in Egypt; he brokered peace between blood-drunk warlords and wooed rich aristocrats to join him in his poverty—but all along the way, he undermined and ironized himself, turning his wisdom into folly and his power into humiliation. He kept on stripping right down to the end, "left naked," as Bonaventure says of his performance before the bishop, "that he might follow his naked crucified Lord."[35] Standing exposed in the bishop's palace on that first day of his career, Francis did not merely renounce his father. He declared himself a fool, committed to the work of prophetic misrule.

In the medieval tradition to which Francis belonged, to be a saint is to be set apart. The word—derived from the Latin *sanctus*—is connected to holiness, and holiness is difference, a separation from the common stuff of ordinary life. Francis's journey toward sainthood, in other words, was a journey in strangeness. As he performed that strangeness on the stage of this world, Francis tapped into traditions of holy folly that were well over a millennium old, rooted in the Pauline injunction, "If any one among you thinks that he is wise in this age, let him become a fool that he may become wise." And he learned to live at the places where strangeness converges with holiness. This child of the heavenly Father was, in a sense, not from here. His homeland was a kingdom beyond this world, and he was, in a way, like a water-walking hermit, like Barbie or Buddy the Elf arriving from somewhere else. No wonder he dressed funny and had that strange accent. No wonder his life became, all at once, a blazing proclamation of holiness and a jangling roadshow of comic mischief. He had come to know a truth that made him strange.

Francis laid out the comic possibilities of his way of life in a conversation he once had with his companion Brother Leo, recorded in an early text called *True and Perfect Joy*. He begins, in this text, by rattling off some of the things that would *not* bring true joy. If all the Masters of Paris and the kings of England and France entered our order, he says to Brother Leo, we wouldn't have true joy. Likewise if we saw the conversion of all non-believers, or if we had the grace of being able to heal the sick and work miracles, we wouldn't have true joy. Then what on earth, Leo asks, is true joy? Francis answers with a parable:

> I return from Perugia and arrive here in the dead of night. It's winter time, muddy, and so cold that icicles have formed on the edges of my habit and keep striking my legs and blood flows from such wounds. Freezing, covered with mud and ice, I come to the gate and, after I've knocked and called for some time, a brother comes and asks: "Who are you?" "Brother Francis," I answer. "Go away," he says. "This is not a decent hour to be wandering about! You may not come in!" When I insist, he replies: "Go away! You are simple and stupid! Don't come back to us again! There are many of us here like you—we don't need you!" I stand again at the door and say, "For the love of

God, take me in tonight!" And he replies, "I will not! Go to the Crosiers' palace and ask there!"

So? Is *this* true joy? "I tell you this," Francis says. "If I had patience and did not become upset, true joy, as well as true virtue and the salvation of my soul, would consist in this."[36]

This little fantasy of martyrdom is not far off from comedy. The inversions of Francis's parable are kingdom inversions, in which mortification becomes a path to joy, but they are also funny inversions, the standard stuff of a comic theater in which big men are defeated by small bureaucrats and familiar hierarchies collapse. Comic performers have acted out this scene for longer than anyone can remember. In Aristophanes' *Birds*, Peisetairus plays the scene repeatedly, insulting his divine visitor Poseidon ("Shush: I'm slicing pickles") and kicking Iris to the curb. John Cleese plays it as the grumpy Frenchman in *Monty Python and the Holy Grail*, hurling insults and livestock for no good reason at Graham Chapman's hapless King Arthur. In these scenes and a thousand like them, the god or king or great founder becomes a little tramp at the door of the big house, shivering in his rags and holding out his bowler hat to beg. The citizen becomes a stranger.

The comedian of Assisi played variations on this scene again and again. He made himself a stranger, humiliated and despised, when he had Brother Peter drag him naked into the piazza like a thief. He played the stranger when he begged house to house, often unsuccessfully, for crumbs from other people's tables. In one remarkable meeting with the provincial ministers of his order and Cardinal Hugolino of Florence, Francis identified strangeness and abasement as his normative ways of life. His ministers and overseers were pressing him to adopt a monastic rule for his brothers. He fired back:

> I do not want you to mention to me any *Rule*, whether of Saint Augustine, or of Saint Bernard, or of Saint Benedict. And the Lord told me what He wanted: He wanted me to be a new fool in the world. God did not wish to lead us by any way other than this knowledge, but God will confound you by your knowledge and wisdom.[37]

This is a voice crying from the borders, proclaiming a kingdom that upends even the wisdom of cardinals, monastics, and saints. When Francis instructed his brothers to call themselves *jongleurs* of God, he proclaimed this same kingdom. "We are minstrels of the Lord," he told them to announce, "and this is what we want as payment: that you live in true penance."[38] It was partly his way of asking the Lord's people what they came here to see. A great preacher? A monastic eminence? A mighty saint? Francis would not have it. He took the wrecking ball even to his own authority. Nothing to see here, he insisted, but a clown of God, and nothing to do but repent.

*

There is, of course, more than one way to be a stranger. Francis could have uttered his denunciations, asserted his difference, and called it a day. Perhaps his strangeness, in that case, would have been the strangeness of a moralist, the strangeness of critical distance.

But Francis's laughter makes that distance impossible. It makes him paradoxical, and it might be part of what makes him not a moralist but a saint. He and his brothers often preached that "the kingdom of heaven is at hand," but they didn't simply mean by that prophecy that something distant will soon come to reckon with the earth. The prophecy, for them, also included an assurance that, as Thomas of Celano wrote, "the *kingdom of heaven* was established in every *corner of the earth*"—that, in other words, the kingdom is already here.[39] Francis went seeking this kingdom in every place he went, in the conviction that the God of heaven was always and everywhere coming to earth, reconciling himself to the kingdom of mortal flesh.

Francis's comic laughter depends not just on his exile, on his strangeness and renunciations, but also on his charism of reconciliation. There is both a prophetic charisma and a comic panache about the man who extends the titles of Brother and Sister to everything he meets: the sun, the wind, the earth, the human body, water, wolves, lambs, crickets, donkeys, death itself. He actually called worms "Brother Worm" and rescued them from the road. He once took a lost lamb and tried to make it his pet. One time in Gubbio, in a famous (though not necessarily factual) episode, he staged an intervention with a mass-murdering wolf, announcing, "Brother Wolf, I want to make peace between you and them," and sealing the deal in the end with a doggy handshake.[40] All these episodes are marked by Francis's contradictory movements, his moral fire and his bouncing hilarity. At that moment, as the man and the wolf shook on it, some of the people of Gubbio must have snickered—but they must also have perceived that in this handshake, *shalom* had come surging into this world, and that the kingdom was at hand. That's the double-movement of Francis's theatrical folly. He makes real in the present creation what he knows to be real in the new creation. He pulls off the paradox of being both here and there, of inhabiting a kingdom far off even as he lives his earthly life, playing with his pet lamb and shaking hands with wolves.

It's a miraculous feat, but Francis always insisted that he wasn't the first to do it. He wrote in his *Admonitions* that the king Jesus went "from the royal throne into the Virgin's womb."[41] And Francis, in his theater of holiness, always plays the part of Jesus. Thomas of Celano, who tells us about Francis's worm-rescuing habit, explains that he took such care with these creatures because "he had read this text about the Savior: *I am a worm and not a man.*"[42] Which is to say that

Francis identified with worms because he identified with an incarnate God who participates in the life of mortal things. This ethic of identification explains why the early biographies make so much of the claim that Francis received into his own body the stigmata, the five wounds of Christ. In making his body that body, he didn't just enter into a death that separated him from this world—he also made an attempt to enter into every corner of the world. He understood himself to be the worm, the wolf, the wind, the orphan, the leper, the thief, the fool. In his last hours he stripped off his clothes one last time and had himself placed "naked on the naked ground," a brother even of the earth to which he must return.[43]

That might not seem like a starting-point for comedy. But for Francis, laughter always arose from the miracle by which strangeness becomes fellowship and kings become beggars. At the end of his life, a delegation of knights from Assisi found the ailing Francis and carried him home to die. As they passed through a small town on the way, the knights went around searching for someone who would sell them food. No one would do it: there wasn't enough to spare. When they returned and told Francis that there was no food to be had, he sent them again to the same people—but this time, he said, ask for the food as a gift, "for the love of God." And sure enough: this time the townspeople gave.

The knights might not have known it, but they had just played the part of Jesus themselves, clanking from house to house in their armor and holding out baskets like beggars. Did anyone laugh? Who knows—but they all became comedians, players in the theater of the great performer who was dying in their care. This little stunt might have been his last. In it, you can still hear the echoes of all the stunts he had pulled before. It's a comic formula: the big people in charge slam the door; the little saint laughs out in the cold; miracles fall from the sky; and the people gathered around catch a glimpse of something strange, the first glimmer of a world made new.

2

UNLUCKY WINNERS

FROM AN ORPHAN QUEEN TO AN AWKWARD BLACK GIRL

On Richard Pryor's funniest album cover, he is tied to a cluster of wooden stakes against a backdrop of bare rocks and nighttime mist, sticks and logs piled up around his legs and feet. Out of the darkness come four figures in hooded robes, closing in, and in the light of their torches Richard gestures with one hand and looks puppy-dog plaintive as he seems to speak. Above his head, in an all-lowercase font that suggests the meekness of his tone, is emblazoned the title of the album: *Is it something i said?*

He's surprised by this turn of events, clearly. Here is a man who just showed up at the wrong bonfire.

The image, based on Pryor's concept, isn't explicitly of a lynching. The black-robed executioners look more like druidic priests than Klansmen, and Richard in his vaguely ancient-looking tunic looks more like a human sacrifice than a victim of racist violence. But the tug of those other histories on this image is irresistible. We get the idea that whatever's happening here, Richard, it wasn't something you said.

The image is funny partly because the innocent-eyed Richard we see here doesn't seem to know this history, even though we do: it's like the later gag in which he plays a blind man who never figured out before now that he's Black. And the surprise of ending up *here*, the spectacle of the poor schmuck suddenly chosen for something he didn't sign up for, is a classic comic situation. Comedy is full of plots in which an unsuspecting person is sent on a dangerous mission or elected to high office or mistaken for a motorcycle stuntperson. Jefferson Smith, head of the Boy Rangers, happens to catch a political boss's eye just as the boss flips a coin to choose the next US senator; Ted Lasso, American football coach, happens to go viral in a silly dance video just as the owner of an English football club is looking for the worst and stupidest coach she can find; Mia Thermopolis, socially phobic teenager, happens to inherit a European kingdom in need of a princess; Ernest P. Worrell, bank janitor, happens to look just like the dangerous criminal Felix Nash. Next thing you know, the heroes of *Mr. Smith Goes to Washington*, *Ted Lasso*, *The Princess Diaries,* and *Ernest Goes to Jail* have been hauled up out of their ordinary lives and dropped into the middle of an unfamiliar arena, clueless about the forces that brought them here and surrounded by mortal dangers on every side.

In the world of film and TV, there are examples of this comic situation by the thousands, from Chaplin's *The Great Dictator* to Volodymyr Zelensky's *Servant of the People*. Pryor wrote his own version of it in the screenplay for *Blazing Saddles*, where a Black railroad worker named Bart gets sent by a corrupt governor to be the sheriff of a frontier town and arrives to find himself facing a lynch mob. Back behind these comic plots are long traditions of unlucky winners: Shakespeare's Bottom the Weaver happens to stroll into the forest just at the moment when Puck is looking for "some vile thing" to become the new lover of the Fairy Queen. Next thing he knows, there's an ass's head on his shoulders and an otherworldly queen scratching his fuzzy cheeks. How did this happen? Is it something he said?

Pryor's album cover is revealing because it makes explicit a possibility that's always there in these comic plots. It suggests that the unlucky winner is unlucky, and a winner, because he has been chosen out as a human sacrifice. And it isn't alone in making this possibility explicit. Even in mainstream cinematic comedy, the hero is often the victim of some kind of sacrificial ritual. Think about Tom Hanks and Meg Ryan jumping into the volcano in *Joe vs. The Volcano*, Bob Hope eyeing the boiling cauldron in *The Road to Bali*, or Han Solo trying to blow out the fire as he and Luke are roasted by Ewoks as an offering to C3P0, in what might be the first *Star Wars* trilogy's zaniest comic scene. Think about the comic heroes—in films from *Miracle on 34th Street* to *My Cousin Vinny*—who find themselves suddenly starring in legal dramas that seem destined to end in their own ruin. Or think, for that matter, about poor Brian Cohen, Jesus's neighbor, who keeps popping up at the wrong stables, palaces, mob scenes, protests, and interrogations-by-Pilate before he finally ends up on a Roman cross, the puzzledest martyr that ever was. "He's not the Messiah," Brian's mother at one point scolds the adoring crowds. "He's a very naughty boy!"

And that's true. Except that the hero of *Life of Brian* isn't like other very naughty boys. This boy from nowhere has been picked out, gifted with a golden ticket for a ride he never intended to take.

*

Richard Pryor understands this all too well. At some parties, you don't want to be the lucky winner. It will be funny for somebody, but not for you.

This story has a long history. In the biblical saga of King David, its outlines are paradigmatically clear. As the book of 1 Samuel tells it, the Lord tells the prophet Samuel that he'll find the next king of Israel if he invites the sons of a man named Jesse to attend a sacrifice.[1] Samuel goes to Jesse's house and calls out Jesse's seven sons, and when he sees one of them, Eli'ab, who must have been the eldest or the handsomest, he thinks, "Surely the LORD's anointed is before him."² But no: it isn't Eli'ab. And it isn't Abin'adab either, or Shammah, or any of those seven strapping young sons of Jesse. Turns out it's the eighth, the little guy watching the sheep out in the field. Really? It's *him*? Yes: it's *him*, little David with his slingshot and harp. And when Samuel anoints him then and there as his brothers look on, the Spirit of the Lord comes mightily upon him. So there's a surprise: it's not the king we were looking for, and it's not an assignment this boy was looking to get. And why? Was it something he said?

Of course we don't know. Part of the upshot of this unlikely choice is that we *can't* know, as Yahweh reminds Samuel, because "the LORD sees not as man sees." The Almighty One makes his inscrutable choices, and the people do what they do: tremble, wonder, raise their eyebrows, gripe, freak out, laugh. This story plays out again and again in the Hebrew Bible, even when the lucky winner isn't being anointed king of Israel. The funny thing that happens to David also happens to Sarah, Isaac, Joseph, Moses, Samuel, Saul, Job, Esther, Jeremiah. In all these cases, the poor fools in question are minding their own business, herding sheep or sleeping or trying to fit in with the other royal wives, when suddenly a flaming bush starts talking, and life goes off the rails. Often the heroes of these stories are comically obtuse or reluctant, as when the new king Saul tries to hide among the luggage or Samuel thinks the voice of the Lord is actually his teacher Eli. Often they are seized with earth-shattering terror, intimations of a deep violence or atrocity at the heart of their ordeals. "Have pity on me, have pity on me, O you my friends," Job cries out, "for the hand of God has touched me."³ This is not an anointing he was eager to sign up for.

And in many of these stories, there are clues that these unlucky winners, like the Richard Pryor who finds himself tied to the stake, have been brought here to offer themselves as sacrifices. As young

Isaac hauls the firewood up the mountain to the altar, he asks what it is, Dad, that we're going to burn with all this wood? It's an unforgettable question, both sad and funny. Or it's both sad and funny to us, anyway. Isaac isn't laughing. Esther isn't laughing when she gets thrust into the middle of a looming genocide and told that it's up to her to save the day. She is one of the unlikeliest heroes of all, an Israelite orphan in exile. And she finds herself getting snatched up into the unlucky winners' circle again and again. She happens to get chosen to join the Persian king Ahasuerus's harem, and then happens to get chosen from the harem to be Ahasuerus's new queen, and then happens to get recruited by her cousin Mordecai to stop a plot in which Mordecai will be hanged and the Jews in the kingdom slaughtered. "Who knows," Mordecai says, "whether you have not come to the kingdom for such a time as this?"[4] Which is nice to hear, but in order to stop the plot, she will have to commit the capital offense of entering unbidden into the presence of her husband, more or less the equivalent of hauling wood to her own altar of sacrifice. She's going to step between her cousin and his executioners, and in that wild gamble she's going to take upon herself the vulnerability, the shame, and the fate of an entire people. She, barely more than a girl, a foreigner in the Persian court, is going to do this. Everyone's watching. She's Mr. Smith on the Senate floor. She's Coach Lasso in the Premier League title match.

Is it funny yet? It's about to be. But let's not get ahead of ourselves.

*

There's no good name for the kinds of figures I'm describing. I'm calling them unlucky winners or unlikely heroes. In the language of the Bible, they might be called "messiahs" (the Hebrew word *māšîaḥ* means a person anointed or picked out for a special purpose), though that word also has other more particular meanings and connotations that don't get at what's distinctive about these surprising protagonists. But they also bear a striking resemblance to the figures who will later be called "saints." I've said already that to be a saint is to be set apart, that holiness means difference. These unlucky winners, too, are misfits, strangers who don't quite belong in the world they have been sent to help. They are foreigners, like Esther and Joseph, or mere children, like David and Samuel, or old, like Sarah and Abraham. They are out of place, ill at ease. That difference makes them comedic. And it also, against all odds, helps them to win. They are champions of strangeness, called not just to go to a foreign place but to prevail over the strong who rule there.

In some of these stories—in the sagas of Joseph or Esther, of Ted Lasso or Jefferson Smith—the difference or holiness of the unlucky winner is linked with a quality of innocence. Joseph and Esther, Coach Lasso and Mr. Smith, all turn out to be *good*, exemplary in their faithfulness, kindness, and big-hearted courage. There's always some element of mystery in their improbable anointing (and the biblical stories, especially, assert the inscrutability of God's ways), but even so, it's not hard to regard some of these figures as compelling representatives of an upside-down kingdom. Their innocence does at least a little to explain why they have been chosen to enter the arena.

In some of these stories, though, there are whispers of another kind of explanation, an explanation that the unlucky winner probably doesn't want to hear. Take the story of the seven Jewish brothers tortured to death in the second century BCE because they refused to eat pig's flesh sacrificed to Zeus. This story, recorded in the apocryphal books of 2 and 4 Maccabees, presents the brothers as little champions, brave and buoyant as they face down the brutal Seleucid king Antiochus IV Epiphanes (they are splendid favors that you grant us," one of the brothers says brightly to his executioners).[5] But even in this tale of courageous suffering, the real story is not one of the weak overcoming the strong or the good overcoming the wicked. The youngest of the seven brothers says it right out loud. "We are suffering," he declares, near the end, "because of our own sins. And if our living Lord is angry for a little while, to rebuke and discipline us, he will again be reconciled with his own servants."[6] There it is. This dying man's business is not with Antiochus; it's with the "living Lord." And the cause of his ordeal is not the corruption of the Seleucid Empire but instead his own sins and the sins of his people. His death is a sacrifice, and he himself expresses a cheerful hope that the Lord has chosen "through me and my brothers to bring to an end the wrath of the Almighty which has justly fallen on our whole nation."[7] Like Esther, this unlikely hero has been chosen to do something for the rest of us at such a time as this. Unlike Esther, he has been chosen not to claim victory but to bear something awful.

Later Jewish writers often called these deaths-by-persecution *kiddush hašem*, "the sanctification of God's name."[8] The sacrificial victim reckons not with human emperors but with the decrees and standards of a divine judge.[9] Sometimes the victim's sacrifice atones for specific sins, as when the Ten Rabbinic Martyrs are chosen to die to cleanse their people of the sins Joseph's brothers committed when they sold him into slavery.[10] Often it is touched with mystery: why me, and why now? And in this reckoning with the hero's faults and God's mysterious ways, there are the seeds of another kind of comedy. In one episode in the Jerusalem Talmud, Rabbi Akiva laughs under torture, as he explains to his torturer, because he is saying the *Shema* and suddenly sees that his suffering fulfills the clause in the law about loving the Lord with "all your soul."[11] There's something funny here, or so Akiva thinks, some kind of surprising fit between the ordeal of suffering and the unlucky winner who's been chosen to endure it.

This other kind of comedy comes fully into view, in some strains of Jewish culture, in the figure of the *nebbish*. The nebbish is the unluckiest winner of them all: a dingy, hapless, impotent figure, shambling and kvetching through life, a guy (it's usually a guy) for whom nothing seems to go right. Woody Allen, in many of his onstage bits and film roles, is a nebbish. Rodney Dangerfield, with his "no respect" schtick, is in part a nebbish. The protagonist of *A Simple Man*, the Coen brothers' adaptation of the book of Job, is a nebbish, and so are the protagonists of stories like *The Shaggy Dog* and *The Metamorphosis*, turned into dogs and cockroaches for reasons they can't understand. Warren Nefron, Jerry Lewis's protagonist in his 1983 movie *Cracking Up*, is a glorious nebbish, a nebbish of nebbishes, so profoundly ineffectual that even his many suicide attempts end in failure. On a desolate road, in one representative scene, Warren douses himself with gasoline, reaches into his pocket for a match, realizes that he doesn't have one, and then trudges back the way he came, slumping and shivering and clutching his wet blazer around him. That's a nebbish. He's dismal, and he's hilarious.

Why does he suffer in this way? What divine decree or essential personal weakness has set the nebbish apart for this special life of pain? There's an element of mystery in his suffering, just as there is for the biblical Job and the seven Maccabean brothers. But when the nebbish's suffering is funny, there's also, once again, the hint of an explanation: something is wrong with the guy. Perhaps we can't quite name that something or trace its roots. Perhaps his degradation is the work of an inscrutable universe or a generational curse, as it is for Larry Gopnik in *A Simple Man* and for the very nebbishy Yelnats family in Louis Sachar's *Holes*. Whatever the reason, the nebbish is a degraded human specimen. He might be a sniveling prig played by Rowan Atkinson, or a penny-clutching jerk played by Steve Martin, or a money-grubbing narcissist like pretty much everyone in *Arrested Development* or *It's A Mad, Mad, Mad, Mad World*. To be a nebbish—or to play the nebbish—is to take upon oneself not just the unmerited suffering but also the vice, meanness, and stupidity of the human community.

It's back to Mel Brooks and the open sewer. Comedy is when you fall into one, but only if that fall means something—only if, let's be honest, you kind of deserved it. The wholly innocent man burning at the stake isn't funny. Richard Pryor tied to the stake is a different story. "We are suffering because of our own sins," says the youngest Maccabean brother, and when Pryor asks whether it's something he said, we laugh not just because he's so innocent but also because we suspect that he's a little bit guilty. Richard tends to say the kinds of things, after all, that get people tied to stakes.

And so there is something paradoxical about these particular unlucky winners. They are morally deficient, and kind of awful, but the mystery of that deficiency is itself a form of innocence. Poor Warren Nefron, shivering on the highway. Poor Richard Pryor, plaintive at the stake. Do they even know how they got here? The answer seems to be, not really. Something is wrong with them, the poor fools. But they are also strangely heroic, champions of a human community that is always coming to know itself as deficient.

That is perhaps the key distinctive feature of these hilarious sufferers. They are both shabby and heroic, both awful and innocent. And this duality matters to many more stories than the tales of biblical underdogs and sniveling nebbishes. It is right at the heart of what comedians do.

*

Have you ever wondered what's the worst thing you can be in this world? In the first episode of the YouTube show that made her famous, *The Mis-Adventures of Awkward Black Girl*, Issa Rae's character J helps us by providing a handy list of the possibilities: the "WORST THINGS ANYONE COULD BE." As J introduces herself in voiceover, The WORST THINGS catalogue scrolls onscreen with hideous speed: Dirty, Smelly, Angry, Stingy, Pretentious, Dying,

Insatiable, Contagious, Repugnant, Old, Nasty, Gross, Creepy, Whorish, Ugly, Fat, Failed, Self-Righteous, Judgmental, Homosexual, Demonic, Passive-Aggressive, Disabled, and on and on, a high-speed litany of shames. As these labels zip by, J in her voiceover explains that she's "the two worst things anyone could be," and then the image cuts to the two words at the very bottom of the list, just under Poor and Hopeless: Awkward, and Black.

There it is. J announces herself, the Awkward Black Girl. She takes on those labels like a mantle, almost a sobriquet, as if Awkward Black Girl were her stage name or superhero alias. And she suggests right up front that the burden of being Awkward and Black is her special vocation of suffering. It's nebbish life: some deity or fate has marked you out for this inexplicable suffering, and at the same time every instance of the suffering, every excruciating social interaction or professional failure, happens for one very explicable reason—*you*. The bad things happen because there's something wrong with *you*. In *Awkward Black Girl*, J's voiceover threads through episode after episode of her misadventures, and as the situations unfold her narration takes on different qualities, sometimes a complaint, sometimes a plea, sometimes a wry commentary, sometimes a defensive sneer, sometimes an expression of hope, gladness, anger, or lament. In all these modes the show has the quality of a confession, at times of an indiscretion. Having taken these labels upon herself, J now owns them, exposing her Awkward and Black self for everyone else to see.

J's WORST THINGS ANYONE COULD BE could almost be a map of the identities available to modern comedians. At the turn of the twentieth century, Sophie Tucker took up her own Bad Thing You Can Be (it's #16 on J's list) and adopted her persona as "Fat Girl":

> Nobody loves a fat girl,
> But Ohhh, how a fat girl can love!

Nobody seems to want me,
I'm just a truck upon the highway of love!

There's a whole motorcade of Fat comedians on the road behind her, from Oliver Hardy and Curly Howard to John Candy, Roseanne Barr, Chris Farley, and Fortune Feimster. It's Fat Comedy, and this brand of comedy alone has entire ecosystems, traditions and sub-traditions, comedic types that limn a whole array of American cultural stereotypes. Jim Gaffigan plays variations on "dad" Fat, a middle-aged guy looking ambiently intestinal and touching his belly a lot as he goes on about Hot Pockets. Gabriel Iglesias plays variations on "cheery" Fat, and his "Fluffy" persona is a lot like how it sounds, as if it could be the name of a pet or a stuffed animal. Melissa McCarthy fuses the cheery Fat cultural type with various forms of clumsy Fat, quirky Fat, loud Fat, and domineering Fat, pushed often to hysterical excess. Mindy Kaling in *The Mindy Project* plays nuanced variations on Tucker's sexy Fat persona, sneaking sticky buns and taking fart pills but also dressing with dazzling good taste and winning the attention of almost every man she meets.

We could get Linnaean if we wanted to, mapping out genera and phyla, branches and sub-branches in the kingdom of comic fatness. We could put the Fat Boys, who were both a hip-hop group and a comedy troupe, in the taxonomy. We could put Mama Cass in the taxonomy. We could put comedians in the taxonomy who aren't even physically very large. Kaling illustrates that possibility. So does Nate Bargatze, who opens his *Tennessee Kid* Netflix special with a bit in which he's changing his shirt in a parking lot and "this old man walks up and goes, *Olivia?*" This is a fat joke from a guy who looks like he could stand to lose maybe ten or fifteen pounds. No matter: that parking lot encounter is a classic moment of nebbish shabbiness, and Bargatze knows there's material in the Fat Comedy ecosystem that can help him to metabolize the sting of his humiliation.

And that's just one of comedy's many ecosystems of shame. Bargatze, with his "I'm not smart" schtick, belongs mainly to the kingdom of Dumb comedians, which has all sorts of subcultures, from the Dumb and Black racist humor that has inspired and provoked comedians from Stepin Fetchit to Dave Chappelle, to the Dumb Girl humor that has fueled performers from Marilyn Monroe to Diane Morgan, to the Dumb Guy schtick, defiant or complacent, of way too many contemporary male comedians, to the Dumb and Dumber antics of clowns from the Three Stooges and Jerry Lewis to Jim Carrey and the *Jackass* crew. There are even more Dumb comedians than Fat comedians. And just run down that list of WORST THINGS provided by Issa Rae's Awkward Black Girl, and you can probably name comedians of every flavor: there are Angry comedians, Gross comedians, Old comedians, Repugnant comedians, Whorish comedians, Pretentious comedians, Self-Righteous comedians, Failed comedians. I once watched a middle-aged Pauly Shore do a whole set at the Comedy Store about himself as a Failed comedian; he punctuated some of the jokes about his mediocre career by lifting his arm and showing us a rip in the armpit of his sweater, because, you know, even his *sweater* is a failure.

Maria Bamford, in a 2021 special, gives all this failure a kind of motto: *"weakness is the brand!"* That motto, which is also the title of the special, applies in a special way to Bamford's comedy of shockingly honest vulnerability. It applies beautifully to the work of the many comedians who have absorbed her influence, from Neal Brennan, with his onstage discussions of clinical depression, to Kate Berlant, with her dramatizations of her own in-the-moment anxieties as a performer. But the motto also names succinctly what all the shabby comedians I've named are up to. Even when Fatness is the brand or Dumbness is the brand, the point, ultimately, is weakness. The comedian has stood up in front of everyone and confessed that she isn't good enough to be here, that she is a stranger in this world of thin, smart, and successful people. Why does she put that weakness on display? Bamford once commented, on an episode of Mike Birbiglia's *Working It Out* podcast, that "it's such a relief for me if I hear people laugh at something that I found to be shameful."[12] That's one answer to the question. "There's real risk there," as Birbiglia says to Bamford, but exposing her shabbiness offers this comedian a kind of release, a way of acknowledging and metabolizing the shame of not being good enough.

But there's another answer, too. Jeff Foxworthy, who turned Redneck comedy into a national fad for a few years in the nineties, articulated this other answer with crystal clarity. His schtick wasn't just that Jeff Foxworthy is a Redneck: his signature phrase wasn't *I am*. It was, rather, *You might be*. "If your wife's work uniform doesn't have a top, you might be a redneck." "If you've been on TV more than once describing what the tornado sounded like, you might be a redneck." "If you take a nap with at least one hand tucked inside your pants, you might be a redneck." "If you've ever been paid in tomatoes, you might be a redneck."

Well, what do you say, gentle reader? Is it you? Might *you* be a Redneck? And if not a Redneck, which of the WORST THINGS ANYONE CAN BE are you? Are you a little bit fat? A little bit pretentious? A little bit stingy? A little bit self-absorbed? Are you irritable with your kids? Lazier than your go-getting sister-in-law? Secretly, deep down, a little bit racist?

Let's inquire further. Are you not actually doing very much about climate change? Did you only *tell* people you voted in the last presidential election? Do you keep having awkward encounters with an attractive co-worker? Do you wish ill for an obnoxious co-worker? Do you wish ill for your *best friend*?

If so, then *you might be*. You might be one of the unlucky ones: a Dumpy Dad like Jim Gaffigan, or a Self-Absorbed Klutz like Mindy

Kaling's Dr. Lahiri, or an Awkward Black Girl like Issa Rae's J. You, too, have hit the jackpot in the lottery of shabbiness, and these comedians have stood and spoken for you. They have confessed for you, exposed themselves for you. They are representatives of your worst and shabbiest selves, and the laughter they provoke is a laughter of recognition: *me too!* The first words of the first episode of *Awkward Black Girl* are the words of J's voiceover question, "Am I the only one who…?" And those words invite an experience of kinship. *You're not the only one, J! We do that too!* To a certain degree, the confessions of these nebbishes are a form of observational comedy. *Have you ever noticed* that we do this thing or have to put up with that thing? Yes: the crowd *has* noticed, and our laughter has a cathartic power. By naming out loud and laughing at things we thought no one else had noticed or done, we join a community, a fellowship of unlucky winners, trying to make sense of our own shabbiness in this difficult world.

This participatory quality might explain why this particular sort of comedy has made the jump so naturally to our digital lives. Social media has turned a lot of life, for a lot of people, into a DIY pop-up performance of comic shabbiness.[13] Think of the memes, rolling out nonstop from everyday practitioners of Hangry-In-Traffic Comedy, Gloomy-on-Thursday-Morning Comedy, When-Will-My-Kids-Go-Back-to-School Comedy. In the past few months, as I write this paragraph, there has been a moment for "All-Women-Going-Through-Perimenopause-and-Menopause" Comedy, thanks to Melani Sanders and her "We Do Not Care Club." She gets on camera and reads from a list the things about which "We do not care": "if we look pregnant and we're really not pregnant"; "if the cashier at Popeyes automatically gave us the senior discount"; "if the closed captioning is annoying on the TV screen." The world tells us we are supposed to care about these things. But we are strangers, not of this world. We do not care.

There's an old commonplace in literary criticism that tragedy is about moral offenses, where comedy is about social offenses. Tragedy is about sinning before the gods; comedy is about smelling bad or acting awkward at parties. It is, in other words, about strangeness, about the things that might exclude any one of us from the human community. Of course it would be ridiculous, at a certain level, to call these comedians "saints," but they too, in their own way, take up the calling of being set apart. They are different, misfits who don't belong here, and they have been picked out of the crowd to do something hard for the rest of us. By taking our social sins upon themselves and inviting all of us to laugh, they turn what might have been a marker of exclusion into a marker of inclusion. Do *you* smell like that in the mornings too? Do *you* think that unfashionable thing too? It's okay. As we all hear the comedian's confession, the shabbiness becomes *our* shabbiness, and we both offer and receive forgiveness. This hero of Fatness, Dumbness, or Awkwardness becomes something like a priest, welcoming strangers into a community that doesn't need the approval of this world.

When it works, this drama of absolution, inclusion, and kinship can be powerful. But comedy is also paradoxical, and kinship is only half the truth. The image of Richard Pryor at the stake points in the direction of another kind of laughter. The whole scene looks a little too much like the old picture postcards of American lynchings, in which bodies dangle from trees and no one gets to ask whether it was something I said. In its image of a man tied up and about to die, it hints that our laughter at the comedian's suffering might (to put it mildly) signify something other than inclusion. Perhaps Richard's question isn't merely rhetorical: *is* it something he said? Perhaps, in asking it, he means to ask us other questions as well. What do we need to acknowledge about this ordeal of hilarious suffering we've gathered around to watch? That's the question of a prophet. Richard Pryor isn't the first comedian to ask it.

INTERLUDE
A JOKE IS A PROPHECY

Let's have a quiz. Which of the following sayings were written by sages—wisdom writers—and which were written by comedians?

1. A clear conscience is usually the sign of a bad memory.
2. A slip on the pavement is better than a slip of the tongue.
3. An escalator can never break: it can only become stairs.
4. When goods increase, they increase who eat them.
5. There's a fine line between fishing and just standing on the shore like an idiot.
6. Doing nothing is not as easy as it looks.
7. The crabby little girls of today are the crabby old women of tomorrow.
8. Pressing milk produces curds, pressing the nose produces blood, and pressing anger produces strife.
9. The way to a man's heart is through his hanky pocket with a bread knife.
10. Would you know what money is, go borrow some.

Well? How'd we do? The answers, if you want to know, are: comedian, sage, comedian, sage, comedian, comedian, comedian, sage, comedian, sage. Specifically, these bits of wisdom come courtesy of the comedian Steven Wright, the apocryphal sage Sirach, the comedian Mitch Hedberg, the biblical sage Qohelet (a.k.a. the "Preacher" of Ecclesiastes), Steven Wright again, Jerry Seinfeld, Lucy van Pelt, the biblical sage Agur, the comedian Jo Brand, and the seventeenth-century poet George Herbert (who isn't exactly an ancient sage but who collected hundreds of old proverbs, including this one). It's not entirely easy to tell who's who, is it? Because the language of proverbial wisdom is strangely close to the language of the joke.

Or at least, the language of a *certain kind* of proverbial wisdom is strangely close to the language of the joke. Ancient wisdom tends to fall, after all, into two opposed forms. In the Hebrew tradition, there is, on the one hand, the prudential wisdom of Solomon and Sirach, the kind of wisdom that tells you to work hard, heed good counsel, eat your vegetables, find a good spouse, and keep your desires and your kids under control. Do those things, the prudential sages say, and you'll be rewarded with long life and prosperity. These sages can guarantee it, because they know that the world is morally intelligible: we get what we pay for in this life.

But then there are the other sages, the anti-sages, the speakers of Ecclesiastes and the "Proverbs of Agur" and parts of the book of Job. These sages come as prophets of the ironic and the absurd. They preach an order of things that defies intelligibility, a moral universe in which the law of outcomes is involuted and bewildering. Did you think you could train up good children and plan a happy retirement? The anti-sages are here to tell you the truth that your efforts are all vanity. They tell you to spend the nest egg and eat that doughnut, because stock markets crash and skinny people die, too. They tell you that sometimes what looks like success is actually failure and what looks like failure is actually success. They tell you that it doesn't matter what you paid for or what you deserve, because pain makes no distinctions.

In their peculiar brand of wisdom—we might call it negative wisdom—these anti-sages proclaim a secret order of things, a moral economy beyond human understanding. They often begin with assertions of ignorance: "That which is," Ecclesiastes says, "is far off, and deep, very deep; who can find it out?"[1] Their sayings live at the borders of what can be said or comprehended. At the same time, these prophets of unknowing promise that, as the biblical book of Daniel says, "there is a God in heaven who reveals mysteries."[2] Because they want to sound and speak these mysteries, the anti-sages often speak the language of apocalypse. The Greek verb *apokalyptein* means to disclose or uncover, as we know; and the sayings of negative wisdom have a way of disclosing the world's darkest principles and truths. They often depend, for that reason, on surprise. Notice the structure of a proverbial utterance such as this one, from Ecclesiastes: "When goods increase, they increase who eat them." There's a setup—*when goods increase*—and then there's a pause—*yes? what lovely things happen when goods increase?*—and then there's a twist, in which the bitter truth is laid bare—*they increase who EAT them!* That last stroke is like a sudden illumination, or a knife to the side. It's a *click-boom* structure, and the boom is the boom of apocalypse, the disclosure of something we didn't expect to see.

But the *click-boom* structure of this proverb is also a *setup-punchline* structure: the structure of a joke. Theorists of humor have sometimes observed that jokes themselves follow an apocalyptic movement. Freud, in his treatise on jokes, starts from the basic insight that jokes "must bring forward something that is hidden," that they tend to move us from an initial bewilderment to a jolt of recognition, a "second illumination" in which we see the true and deeper meaning of what at first seemed merely absurd.[3] The philosopher Simon Critchley has said that the laughter produced by jokes has "a certain redemptive or messianic power," because jokes have a way of beginning with the world as it is and then swerving into a kind of revelation, a sudden change in perspective. There's a family resemblance between this proverb—*When goods increase, they increase who eat them*—and this joke—*The way to a man's heart is through his hanky pocket with a breadknife*. These one-liners also resemble conventional jokes like this one, which I heard years ago from a source I can't remember:

> A man is driving home from work, and his wife calls him on the phone. "Be careful, dear!" she says. "I just heard on the news that some maniac is driving the wrong way down the freeway!" "Oh, honey," the man replies, "it's worse than you think. It's not just one maniac. It's *everyone!*"

See the structure? The setting is the world of the utterly familiar. In many jokes, including this one, it's the world of the stereotypically or quaintly familiar, like something out of the past. The speakers could be Fred and Wilma, or Ricky and Lucy. The perspective is the man's, the setting his world of middle-class work and rush-hour traffic. But then, in a flash, everything becomes unfamiliar. The man turns out to be the maniac. His understanding of the world turns out to be an illusion. And the perspective we assumed at first gives way, suddenly, to a perspective we didn't anticipate. The joke is designed to deliver a jolt of apocalyptic disorientation.

That might seem like a lot to claim about jokes. But long traditions of absurdist prophets have developed the idioms of Qohelet and the other ancient sages into sayings that walk the line between wisdom and comedy. In a weird set of medieval texts, a wild man called "Marcolf" went toe-to-toe with King Solomon in battles of wisdom and anti-wisdom. (Solomon: "A reverent woman shall be praised." Marcolf: "A cat that hath a good skin shall be flayed.")[4]

The Romantic poet William Blake distilled the hallucinatory wisdom of his visions into what he called his *Proverbs of Hell*. ("The road of excess leads to the palace of wisdom.")[5] These makers of nonsense are comedians of a sort, transgressive and mischievous and bent on orchestrating surprise. They are often vicious, sometimes dirty, carnival scene-spoilers in the theater of good moral discourse. (Solomon: "Of the abundance of the heart, the mouth speakest." Marcolf: "Out of a full womb, the arse trumpeth.")[6] But they also know things that the wisdom of Solomon does not know, truths about the needs, sufferings, and limits of embodied life.

It isn't very far from Marcolf's fart jokes and flayed cats to the anti-wisdom of many modern comedians, from Groucho Marx and Steven Wright to Diane Morgan and Jo Brand. Groucho's apocalyptic utterances have traveled the folkways of twentieth-century culture so extensively that he has become a kind of modern Qohelet, a prophet of hilarious abasement and illuminating surprise. ("Why, a four-year-old child could understand this report. Run out and find me a four-year-old child!") Steven Wright builds entire sets around little apocalyptic speech-bombs, delivered in his signature deadpan register with no explanations or transitions:

> I can levitate birds, but nobody cares.
> Eagles may soar, but weasels don't get sucked into jet engines.
> I intend to live forever. So far, so good.
> I bought some powdered water, but I don't know what to add.
> I went to a place to eat, it said "Breakfast Anytime," so I ordered French toast during the Renaissance.
> The first time I ever read the dictionary, I thought it was a poem about everything.

So does Mitch Hedberg, in his affect of stoned wonder:

> Wearing a turtleneck is like being strangled by a really weak guy.
> Rice is great when you're hungry and you want two thousand of something.
> Dogs are forever in the pushup position.

In every one of these jokes, there's an apocalyptic surprise at the end, a disclosure of something. Often this disclosure reveals something about the comedian himself, his peculiar futility and his lot in life. Look again at the punchlines of these jokes from Wright: *but nobody cares*; *but I don't know*; *so I ordered*; *I thought*. These are confessions. Often these self-disclosures disclose the uncanny logic of the comedian's interior world, so that we have the experience of entering into the visions of a man touched with otherworldly powers of perception. "I put a telescope on the peephole in my door," Wright says in one bit, "so I can see who's coming for two hundred miles." He's like a sage himself, searching the cosmic darkness for figures no one else can see.

These prophetic statements are the territory of many more comedians than just mystically inclined performers such as Hedberg and Wright. In Seinfeld's observational comedy ("What do you do when you get to the bottom of the bowl and you still have milk left? Well, I say, put in more cereal!"), the apocalyptic turns have the quality almost of rabbinic wisdom, a midrash of the everyday.[7] In the hands of an aggressively provocative comedian like Louis C. K. ("Stereotypes are harmful—but the voices are funny"), they have the quality of confessions, disclosures of a degeneracy that might not belong to the comedian alone.[8] In the furrowed-brow philosophizing of *Peanuts* ("I love mankind," Linus says; "It's *people* I can't stand"), they evoke the child's experience of a bewildering world, freighted with more possibilities than any grown-up system of logic can contain.[9] These one-liners, too, are doubly revealing, disclosures both of something in the world and of something in the comedian.

It's no wonder, then, that we want to hear comedians talk, and that they want to hear themselves talk. They are, in this respect, like preachers, pundits, commentators. They have a word to speak. They have a podcast. They make the promise that Qohelet makes in Ecclesiastes—"I have seen everything that is done under the sun"—and they are here to tell us truths that no one else will.

Are you listening? You already know the setup. But the punchline is going to be a surprise.

II

PROPHETS

3

THE PROPHET IN AGONY

FROM SNUFF THE CLOWN TO SHAKESPEARE'S FOOL

It's the summer of 1599, and a stand-up artist has just come on at the Curtain Theatre. He paces downstage, an arresting presence, visibly atypical, numinously strange. The crowd looking on knows already that this bristling figure isn't going to be like the other clowns they've seen on the Curtain stage. He doesn't do jigs or pratfalls. He doesn't smile. He doesn't offer winks or assurances. And he doesn't intend to make this easy, for himself or anyone else. But these two thousand paying customers must also know that Robert Armin, a.k.a. Snuff the Clown, has something else to offer. They are here, after all, for him.

I sometimes try to picture Armin at this moment in his career. He's just past thirty, in 1599, and his name is becoming bankable business in the entertainment districts of north London. Within the year, he'll have partnered with William Shakespeare and will be maturing into one of the most breathtaking performers in the history of comedy. By the time he dies in 1615, his work on stage will have made him rich enough to buy a coat of arms, a working-class kid transformed into a gentleman.

But for now, at this summer afternoon show, Robert Armin stands viscerally, even cruelly, exposed. Fellow characters in his later theatrical productions will mock him for his physical form—they call him a "fragment," a "crusty botch of nature," a "stool for a witch," "the issue of a mangy dog"—and as he approaches his audience today, he telegraphs an aura of pain, cringing and glowering like a frightened animal. His distinctive schtick, we begin to see right away, will depend on his uncanny ability to make himself vulnerable.

Out there, the crowd teems with winos, pickpockets, laborers, government agents, prostitutes on duty, darlings of moneyed society. They scuffle and heckle and buzz, and Armin-as-Snuff stalks watchfully, trolling this sea of faces and noise for his first bit. "What ails that damsel?" someone calls out, gesturing at a distressed-looking young woman in the crowd. That will do. Snuff fires back—"What, is she sick?—and then fires right back at himself—"No, she is lusty and well"—and then erupts into a schizoid fantasy in which a jury of twelve women arrive to investigate this young woman's secret ailment. Snuff ventriloquizes their voices with lunatic zeal. Is she sullen? No! Is she starving? Most definitely not! Has she hurt her foot dancing? Oh no, says one last voice, "yet let me tell you, she hath stepped amiss." Do you see it now? Do you see *her* now? "Then gently judge," the clown concludes, "her sorrow what it is."

What have we just heard? Is it an inquisition? A plea for compassion? A misogynistic atrocity? Is it even funny? No one can quite tell. If you've come to see Snuff the Clown at the Curtain, that's pretty much what you're in for. The questions keep coming: Who's happy? Who's dead? Can that boy read? And the voices of the performer proliferate, swerving wildly between speculative inquiry and leering savagery. There is violence everywhere. In one little freak show of a bit, a guy has fun with his friend by saying, let's play Cain Kills Abel, and you can be Abel. In another, called "What Have I Lost?," various voices try to answer that question until the riddler finally reveals: "I have lost one ear from off my pate." An ear: really?[1] But Armin's clamoring voices love this stuff. He speaks in registers of snarling defensiveness and wounded menace. When one heckler shouts, "Are you there with your bears?" he hisses back: This is a *theater*, not a bear-baiting pit—I'm a *professional*. "When I next see him," he seethes, "I'll make his brains bleed."

Still, Armin finds something transcendent, something beautiful, in the midst of all this freaky humanity. Just listen to him riffing on questions like "Why is he drunk?", and you can hear it. In this bit, Snuff tempts the crowd toward some easy mockery: *Look at that guy stumbling among the groundlings.* Then he makes a hard swerve. *Why is this man drunk?* "I know not why, unless I knew his mind," the comedian declares. Perhaps it's a disguise, or perhaps the guy just tried a liquor he isn't used to, or perhaps he has no tolerance for alcohol. None of us can say unless we *know* this man. Just at the moment when the crowd is ready to unite against a deviant, Armin presents the deviant as an individual, a person with reasons and secrets and a history. And then, when he's got everyone sufficiently bewildered, he brings a punchline: The one thing I know, he says, is that these people "are *all* brained with a brewer's washing beetle."

Brained with a washing beetle—that's to say, bashed in the head with a club. This is a Snuff-Armin production, after all. But the laughter that erupts in the crowd now is not the fatal laughter of a lynch mob but the giddy laughter of a community recognizing itself. The drunk, it turns out, is one of us, a great bunch of characters brain-addled and strange. So is the disgraced young woman, the man with one ear, the man Cain-and-Abeling his friend. That's the world according to Robert Armin: in freakiness, fellowship. And here he stands, the freakiest of us all, holding up a mirror and waiting for the next heckler to step in front of it.

*

The crowds that came to see him in the late 1590s might not have known it, but Robert Armin was inventing a new kind of comedy. He was, even more, inventing a new way of thinking about the *comedian*, of understanding the vocation and identity of the comic performer. By day he was in the trenches as a performer, acting the clown's part in plays and fashioning his Snuff persona. By night he was at his desk, writing up his best bits and working on a book about what he, in the vernacular of the time, called "natural fools," those born atypical or disabled. And all the while, he was crafting a comic art rooted in his own atypical selfhood, his own experiences of strangeness and difference.

Armin occupies a strange place in the history of comedy. Hardly anyone now knows his name (though everyone knows the name of his creative partner). There are no recordings of his performances, and only the merest written clues to what it was like to see him live on stage. His career is more or less a forgotten chapter in the history of modern comedy. But Armin is, as much as anyone, the figure with whom whole stretches of that history begin. He still belongs to the ecosystem of fools and folly that he was writing about in 1599, an ecosystem in which the vocation to laugh belonged to those born different, those touched with special charisms of bodily oddness, mental affliction, and prophetic sight. He could look back, from where he stood, and see a world of holy fools and weird minstrels that was just disappearing from public life. But he also practiced his comic art in a recognizably modern theatrical setting, with paying ticketholders on the ground below and government censors in the stalls above. He helped to initiate traditions of professional clowning that were still alive in the music halls where Charlie Chaplin, Buster Keaton, and Sophie Tucker learned their craft. And he made astonishing experiments in the forms of personhood and pain that contemporary comedians are still exploring. He is, in many ways, the first modern comedian.

When we think of modern comedy, we tend to think of figures whose distinctive selfhood seems to invest them with prophetic power: of Chaplin translating music-hall melodrama into a mythologized representation of his own suffering, or of Lenny Bruce fusing burlesque ribaldry with his own pathologies and revulsions, or of Richard Pryor alchemizing African American folklore into his own private universe of longing and shame. The vulnerable bodies of these performers—Chaplin in rags, Pryor reenacting his heart attack—are icons of a comedy that derives its power from the comedian's own fragile, fissured personhood. The comedy they practice seems modern partly because it's a comedy of the individual, conjured up by one inimitable artist out of old gags and familiar traditions. This sort of comedy always feels like a revelation, a disclosure of the singular personhood of the comic artist. And it often seems to reveal something about who we ourselves are. In the work of all sorts of contemporary comedians, from performers who trade in intimate self-disclosure (Maria Bamford, Neal Brennan, Hannah Gadsby) to performers who trade in knowing self-caricature (Mindy Kaling, Nate Bargatze, Larry David), the performer's revelations are often also prophetic confrontations, attempts to bring to light things we all share but cannot or will not name.

And in the beginning, there was Robert Armin. How to get him into view? He was born in the late 1560s, a few years younger than Shakespeare, and he was, like Shakespeare, the son of provincial tradespeople: Shakespeare's father was a glove-maker in Stratford, Armin's a tailor in King's Lynn. When he was about thirteen, young Robert made the hundred-mile journey to London to start an apprenticeship as a goldsmith. It was an eleven-year commitment, and he stuck it out to the end, but by the time he finished in 1592, he apparently had other things in mind. That year he got himself a gig in a company of players, and he spent the rest of the 1590s earning his stripes as a theatrical clown and putting together the pieces of his comic persona.

We don't know much about his work in those early years. There are shreds of fact: as a teenager he adored Richard Tarlton, the first celebrity clown in London's emerging professional theaters and a living link to folk tradition; he spent years on the road, performing all over rural England; he wrote a lot of ballads. And there are plausible speculations: Did he start out trying to imitate famous clowns like Will Kempe and John Singer, who had made their reputations playing big-hearted bumpkins and rambunctious servants? Did he play the randy horse-keeper Robin in a pirated production of *Doctor Faustus*? We have clues here and there, but not a lot to go on.[2]

Not, that is, until 1600. That year, under the name of Snuff, Armin published a little book called *Quips upon Questions*, which offers a portrait of the artist as a stand-up performer. Each section of this book opens with a question—*What ails that damsel?*— and Snuff responds by catapulting into his verbal acrobatics. He tries to present himself as a writer, crafting these exchanges in his study, but much of the material in *Quips* seems warm with the heat of live performance. Snuff rampages through questions and responses with feral abandon, heaping up piles of underpunctuated text in which individual voices are hard to tell apart and much seems to depend on physical gestures that no reader can see. The book might well reflect something of Armin's work on stage—I've drawn my opening reconstruction of his stand-up act from it—and it might offer a glimpse of this fire-quick performer at a key moment in his development.[3] If he did indeed start out in the mold of the big stars of the early 1590s, with an act built around country-boy antics and silly one-liners, we see him here taking off into new territory, drilling into the chambers of his own volcanic interior. Reading *Quips* is a little like watching Lenny Bruce emerge from his burlesque-emcee phase in 1957, or Charlie Chaplin breaking through the chrysalis of his early Keystone films in 1915. The book captures the comedian at the threshold of an astonishing, vastly ambitious creative endeavor.

That endeavor was close at hand. William Shakespeare and his company, the Lord Chamberlain's Men, had taken notice. Sometime in late 1599 or early 1600, they came calling.

*

The Lord Chamberlain's Men were in crisis when they recruited Armin. They had lost the lease on their home base, the Theatre, in 1597 and had embarked, in early 1599, on the expensive and risky venture of building the Globe, their own theatrical home. Right at that moment, one of their two big stars, the clown Will Kempe, walked out.

No one knows exactly what happened—Shakespeare scholars disagree about the reasons and exact chronology—but something clearly blew up between Kempe and his long-time partners. He bought into the Globe project along with the other shareholding members of the Lord Chamberlain's Men in February 1599. But by summer, when the theater had its grand opening, he was conspicuously absent. The plays Shakespeare and the company brought to their new stage that summer, *Henry V* and *Julius Caesar*, are unusual in having no clown's part, and some scholars think *Henry V* shows signs of having once had a starring role for a clown, stripped out at the last minute. In February 1600, Kempe undertook the great solo performance of his career by morris-dancing a hundred miles from London to Norwich. By the time he published his written account of that famous dance three months later, he was publicly estranged from the Lord Chamberlain's Men and saw fit to address a bitter epilogue to "my notable Shakerags," his friend and creative partner no more. At a time when they very much needed crowds and revenues to pay for their new venture, the company were left without their celebrity clown.

Kempe was the only clown the Lord Chamberlain's Men had ever had, and within the company he had been his own franchise. He and Shakespeare had both been founding members of the company in 1594, and the success of the plays they staged together over the next five years depended on the room Shakespeare gave this great comedian to practice his distinctive art. It was for Kempe that Shakespeare wrote Bottom, Dogberry, Grumio, Costard, Lancelot Gobbo, the Capulet servant Peter, and the gluttonous, garrulous John Falstaff. And the plays that took shape around these characters all bore the marks of Kempe's style, his genial and flush-faced vitality.

The clues we have all suggest that Kempe was a big and athletic man, an irresistible physical presence. The citizens of Norwich long remembered his great leap over the churchyard wall when he came morris-dancing into town, and his famous fifth-act jigs were integral to every play Shakespeare wrote during the years of their collaboration.[4] He played downstage, in reach of the crowd, sometimes talking to the audience directly and often accompanied by an entourage of fellow clowns who came on and off with him, his own little company of hired players. The word "clown" in its earliest senses means a peasant or country bumpkin, and the characters Shakespeare wrote for Kempe tend to be rustics, tradespeople, and servants, plain men with plenty to say and a hearty zest for life. They are short on learning but deep in native wit, and they have a way of zigging and zagging across the main action of the play, graced with a freedom from the appetites and anxieties that drive everyone else. There is something almost Edenic about their guileless, wide-eyed exuberance.[5]

The characters Kempe enacted for Shakespeare are also unmistakably English, common folk uncorrupted by urban and aristocratic sophistication. Even when he popped up in the Athens of *A Midsummer Night's Dream* or the Messina of *Much Ado about*

Nothing, Kempe came supplied with a down-home English charm and even a down-home English name (he was Bottom in Athens, Dogberry in Messina). His presence ensured that the Lord Chamberlain's Men evoked a certain nostalgia for good old red-blooded English values. And he made sure that Shakespeare never strayed too far from his roots in folk culture, in the festive clowning of itinerant hustlers, morality-play pranksters, and May-morning Lords of Misrule. The characters he and Shakespeare created together represent a very familiar kind of comedy, conservative in its sensibilities and popular in its appeal, just the sort of thing many English playgoers wanted and expected to see.

When Kempe left, these characters effectively died. No one else in London could play them the way he did. And Kempe's little crew of hired sidekicks seems to have departed with him. Just like that, the repertory Shakespeare had built around this comedian's gifts became much more difficult to stage. The Lord Chamberlain's Men found themselves with an expensive new theater and a sudden crisis in their capacity to perform there. It was a dire loss.

*

At the same time, Shakespeare must have experienced this loss as an opportunity. In the summer of 1599, when the Kempe crisis began, he was about to start writing *Hamlet*, the play that marks his mid-career dive into a theater of mind-bending difficulty and tortuous interiority. With his company's move to the Globe and the south side of London, he was discovering new reasons to appeal to affluent audiences and to their interests in the cultural avant-garde. It seems to be the case, too, that about this time he was discovering Montaigne's *Essays*, a breathtaking experiment in self-dissection and a book Shakespeare read to pieces.[6] Never mind that there was a new theater to pay for: London's most successful dramatist, in 1599, was on the verge of reinventing himself. It might have seemed the perfect moment to leave Will Kempe behind.

The Lord Chamberlain's Men had probably performed at the Curtain during the period from 1597 to 1599, when they had no permanent home. They would have encountered Armin there, and some scholars have suggested that Armin might even have joined them there as a guest performer, a year or two before he took Kempe's place as a full member of the company.[7] There's no way to know just how or when their relationship with Armin began (or whether it contributed to Kempe's huffy departure), but Shakespeare and company must have figured out fast that this was a different sort of clown. Where Kempe had projected a kind of oversized extrovert simplicity, Robert Armin was a walking labyrinth, involuted and complicated, peering out from behind his many masks. The Shakespeare who was about to create Prince Hamlet must have been fascinated by this riddling philosopher-clown, with his antic riffs on abstract questions and his intimations of a mind out of joint.

By the summer of 1600 at the latest, Armin had joined the Lord Chamberlain's Men as a full shareholder and star player.[8] Shakespeare wasted no time in writing a major role for him, and that role—Touchstone, in *As You Like It*—suggests that the company was eager to celebrate their new clown. The name Touchstone might itself be a Robert Armin joke, an allusion both to his goldsmithing background and to a clown, Tutch, he had played in his own comedy *The Two Maids of More-clacke*. When Touchstone makes his first entrance, the characters on stage inspect and discuss him for a dozen lines before he speaks, playing up the drama of his arrival: here's the new guy at last. And then, when the melancholy nobleman Jaques meets this new clown a few scenes later, he erupts into his ecstatic "A fool! a fool! I met a fool" speech—another indication that what we've got here is a grand entrance. There might even be an Armin-beats-Kempe joke in this play, in the scene where Touchstone outwits a rustic shepherd, stealing his girl, bludgeoning him with nonsense, and finally sneering, "Therefore, you clown... tremble, and depart."⁹ The vanquished shepherd's name? William. No wonder Kempe was fuming across town.

So it was a whole new game now, and the crowds who came to see new plays such as *As You Like It* and *Twelfth Night* must have felt the difference right away. Touchstone and Feste, the key comic figures of these plays, are not clowns but fools, blistering and unsettling in their absurdist wit. They mimic clerics and courtiers and vanquish aristocrats in verbal battle. They have no comrades or friends, they don't get their own tour-de-force comic scenes, and they don't charm the audience by bumbling into situations they don't understand. Instead, they prowl around like trickster demons or mad prophets, cutting in and out of other people's plots, disrupting other people's conversations, always in the shadow of comic characters (Rosalind, Malvolio, Sir Toby) bigger than themselves. They are acid compounds, burning away the appearances and values that everyone around them would otherwise have been happy to accept.

Armin's arrival corresponds with a new emphasis, in Shakespeare's drama, on skepticism and bad faith, on identities that dissolve and interchange. In *Hamlet*, which Shakespeare wrote at about the same time he wrote *As You Like It* and *Twelfth Night*, the clown who represents the old regime is again conspicuously gone: alas, poor Yorick. And it's curious that in this play, there's no replacement in sight, no one for the company's resident comedian to enact beyond the gravedigger who digs up Yorick's skull. But if there's no sustained role for a clown here, Hamlet himself takes up the part of the elusive outsider-cynic, practicing the same antic insurgency that Armin was at that moment bringing to his performances as Touchstone and Feste. It's almost as if this play's manic hero (played by the company's other major star, the leading man Richard Burbage) has absorbed Armin's peculiar sort of folly into himself. More even than the comedies Shakespeare wrote to put his new fool on display, *Hamlet* suggests that Armin brought something consequential to this playwright's work. And the immense vitality of Prince Hamlet suggests that Shakespeare, likewise, could offer Armin something special, a grasp of the possibilities that his distinctive comic performances opened up.

Audiences and readers have long regarded *Hamlet* as a key moment in the emergence of modern culture, Shakespeare's articulation of a world governed by radical doubt, relentless inquiry, idiosyncratic selfhood, and a drive to break away from the histories and structures by which the self is defined. No accident that Robert Armin was there at the moment of that play's consequential begetting. The history of modern comedy depends in all sorts of ways on what he and Shakespeare were beginning to discover.

*

Armin published a few more texts in his Shakespearean years, including an edition of his earlier play *The Two Maids of Moreclacke*, a versified translation of an Italian tale, and his remarkable study of the "naturals" he so admired. But the best record of his development over the next decade is written in the characters he and Shakespeare created together. Everything Shakespeare wrote from 1601 to 1611 has a potential role for Armin, from Lavatch (*All's Well that Ends Well*) and Thersites (*Troilus and Cressida*) to Autolycus (*The Winter's Tale*) and Caliban (*The Tempest*). There's room for disagreement about exactly which roles Armin played, but even so, in all these characters, the patterns set down in Touchstone and Feste deepen and mature. Armin's fools always function as touchstones, foils against which the motives and actions of others are tested. He is always in the fray, but he somehow keeps himself always removed, always alone. He doesn't act so much as he *plays* at action, a mirror-image of others, never wholly real. His fools have a vocation to spoil things, which is why Feste, sometime jester to Lady Olivia, says, "I am indeed not her fool, but her corrupter of words."[10] This verbal troublemaker, like all Armin's creations, is a critic at heart.

Armin presents this critical instinct both as a prophetic gift and as a disease. His Shakespearean fools expose, clarify, and testify; but they also spew, blaspheme, and abuse. They are corrosive figures, and the characters around them tend to regard them not just as purveyors of truth or amusement but also as degradations of human life, to be beaten like bastards or dogs. When Armin's Thersites, the "bitch-wolf's son," meets Margareton, the bastard son of Priam, he lays it right out: "I am a bastard, too. I love bastards. I am a bastard begot, bastard instructed, bastard in mind, bastard in valour, in everything illegitimate. One bear will not bite another, and wherefore should one bastard?"[11]

This is Armin in his element: aggressive and evasive all at once, a practitioner both of scorched-earth insult and of an almost mystical empathy. In all his roles he orchestrates a paradoxical persona, a mingling of cruelty and delicacy. Many of the most affecting songs in Shakespeare's later plays are for him—Armin, unlike Kempe, was a gifted singer—but he also had an influence on the moral monsters Iago and Edmund, who joke their way into terrifying orgies of violence as the witty villains of *Othello* and *King Lear*. This duality reached its apex in what was probably the last character he and Shakespeare created together, the Caliban of *The Tempest*. As this enslaved man-monster, Armin made himself comically repulsive, a stinking, sniveling, lecherous, bilious thing. But he also hinted at deep currents of memory and longing, whispering of dreams so beautiful that, "when I waked / I cried to dream again."[12] Even as a monster, he evinced a tender and suffering humanity.

It's a striking fact, though, that Armin's most powerful elaboration of his comic art seems to have come in the context of a tragedy. King Lear, with its exquisite, angelic, unfathomable fool, bears this comedian's stamp all over. It isn't just that Lear's fool hones his jests into such penetrating, prophetic instruments. And it isn't just that Edgar, Kent, Gloucester, and Lear all become prophetic fools, trembling and riddling and slouching toward insanity. The play also mines, more intently than anything else Shakespeare wrote, the deep kinship between hilarity and suffering, between comic schtick and moral truth. Under the guidance of his fool, Lear looks at the naked body of Poor Tom and declares him "the thing itself."[13] *This*—this image of mutilated grandeur—this is the truth of the human. Not power but poverty, not strength but weakness. "Take physic, pomp," Lear says to himself, at one of his key moments of discovery: "Expose thyself to feel what wretches feel."[14] The Lear who makes this pronouncement has believed the gospel that his fool, embodied by Armin, came to preach. In the beginning, the proud king thundered, "Dost thou call me fool, boy?" Now he has come to believe the truth of the fool's reply: "All thy other titles thou hast given away. That thou wast born with."[15]

We've heard that gospel before. Snuff the clown speaks it when one of the voices of *Quips upon Questions* asks how anyone can be called a fool when "he's a more fool that accounts him so?" His message is that all of us, with our good moral sensibilities and our presentable public faces, are fools, grasping about in bewilderment and haunted by death. In *Lear,* more explicitly than anywhere else, this proclamation of folly gets a name. "I'll speak a prophecy ere I go," the Fool says in one scene, before chanting some apocalyptic nonsense-verse about the age to come.[16] And that's what Armin has come to speak: a prophecy. In his championing of the tainted and the despised, and in his erasure of the difference between his own afflicted self and the respectable people he confronts, this comedian contained within himself the many prophetic fools he would come to enact, including the one who guides the dying King Lear in the mysteries of human frailty.

*

There's nothing ethically simple about this prophetic art. We don't know the details of Armin's physiognomy, but it seems clear that he built his career around his own aura of disability and atypicality. Can we laugh, in good conscience, at this man's self-exposure? Can we laugh at the other images he conjures up for us: the amputated ears and flayed animals, the misshapen Caliban wailing in pain? He dares us to try. And he keeps finding ways of spiking our laughter with discomfort, of making sure that we, like Lear, expose ourselves to feel what wretches feel.

Robert Armin's contribution to modern comedy begins here, in the way he teases laughter out of his own vulnerable personhood. In his prophetic performances, he helped write the blueprints for a comic art that tries to say something true about suffering, and he tested the boundaries between cruelty and empathy, between a laughter that wounds and a laughter that heals. He made an early experiment in asking what happens when we laugh at others as a way of laughing at ourselves.

One of the most revealing records of Armin's comic imagination is *Fool upon Fool*, the little book in which he writes portraits of six "natural fools" and tells stories of their lives and misadventures. Armin in these portraits pays extensive attention to the atypical physical features of the fools he profiles: the lengths of their legs, the sizes of their heads, the shapes of their lips and hands, their many quirks of symmetry and proportion. He seems to find something of each fool's essence, something of his folly, in the idiosyncrasies of his body. No surprise, perhaps, that throughout these portraits he expresses his affinity with these uncommon men. He shares their profession—most of them are kept as entertainers in great houses—and he shares their birthright of bodily difference. Armin's first Shakespearean character, Touchstone, is called "Nature's natural" as he makes his first grand entrance. That label is his calling card.

It might be fitting, in a way, that the only surviving image of Armin depicts him in costume as John in the Hospital or "Blue John," a role he enacted in his own play *The Two Maids of Moreclacke*. "Blue John" seems to have been the sobriquet for John Smith, an actual London man, born with mental disabilities, who spent his whole adult life at the charity institution Christ's Hospital.[17] Armin, who would have been in his mid-twenties when John died, called him "my old acquaintance, Jack, whose life I knew." He wrote about John not only in *Two Maids* but also in the last portrait of *Fool upon Fool*, where he tells John's story with warm affection, insisting that the overseers of Christ's Hospital "did well" to make a place for this man, "seeing he was one of God's creatures, though some difference in persons."

Two Maids, which probably dates from Armin's pre-Shakespearean days, seems to have owed its success to Armin's portrayal of John. The jesting fool appears in only a couple of scenes, but Armin clearly regarded those scenes as something special, both a song in praise of a departed hero and a flagship vehicle for his own talents. The John he presents in these scenes and in *Fool upon Fool* is a natural-born comedian. In the demented innocence of his antics—the time he rang the church bells in memory of a chicken, or the time he preached at St. Paul's using his dirty handkerchief as a text—Armin finds something essentially human, something that speaks to his own tender core of suffering hilarity and wounded love.

All the while, he verges on mockery: it's hard to forget that this "innocent" is being written and acted by a performer who is no innocent at all. But Armin tries—and he will keep trying, down to his last role—to discover and know himself as a natural fool. And he keeps inviting us, his audience, to discover that we are all fools, however powerful or intelligent or respectable we may seem. "Where learned you this, Fool?" the Kent of *King Lear* demands, from the stocks. "Not in the stocks, fool," Lear's fool replies.[18]

Who's the gentleman, and who's the fool? Armin's character suggests that it might not be easy to tell.

In the final lines of *Fool upon Fool*, Armin reports that Blue John was buried without an epitaph. As a last gift to his departed hero, he offers one himself:

> Here under sleeps Blue John, that gives
> Food to feed worms, yet he not lives.
> You that pass by, look at his grave
> And say yourselves the like must have.
> Wise men and fools, all one end makes,
> God's will be done, who gives and takes.[19]

There are plenty of graveyard commonplaces here. But there's also the hint of something distinctively personal in these lines. The epitaph could almost be his own, Robert Armin's prophetic witness to a fellowship rooted in strangeness. Want to know, he says, who you really are? Here's how. Go to an asylum. Find a freak, moldering in an unmarked grave. And discover there your own true self, and your one sure destiny.

Is that the joke you came to hear from Snuff the Clown? Laugh if you dare. The folly you deride may be your own.

4

THE PROPHET CONFESSES

RICHARD PRYOR

In 1978, Richard Pryor invented the postlapsarian stand-up set. This is the kind of set you perform onstage after you've done something very bad indeed. If you're Pryor in 1978, it's the kind of set you perform after you've married a woman you barely know, collapsed with a heart attack a few coked-out weeks later, and then shot your new wife's car up with a .357 magnum a few coked-out weeks after that. You go to the hospital, you go to jail, you go to divorce court, and then you go back onstage. What do you say?

Plenty of American comedians had faced this problem before. For a long time, they dealt with the problem as American celebrities traditionally do: by going on "vacations" to unspecified places, bribing doctors and underage women to lie, staying out of sight for a while, telling jokes about other things. That's how Chaplin dealt with his pregnant lovers, Lucille Ball with her disintegrating marriage, Jerry Lewis with his painkillers and serial infidelities. Lenny Bruce rewrote the script by getting onstage, right after his various narcotics and obscenity busts, and talking about what just happened. But he always talked about the same thing: the cops. Even when he shocked a nightclub crowd in Philadelphia by rolling his sleeve up and showing them his track-marked forearm, what he commented on was not his disfigured flesh but, rather, the cops.

They had drawn little circles around his needle punctures, and he wanted to talk about those circles. Never mind me: look at what the cops drew!

At its best, in Lenny's hands, this sort of disclosure rose to the level of social critique, a revelation that the prosecutors are complicit in the crime. Lenny's postlapsarian monologues also had a tendency, though, to become just another form of obfuscation, another way of telling jokes about other things. Those who knew Lenny were pretty sure there was more to say about that arm.

But then came Richard Pryor, who in 1978 was trying to recover from a run of events that were egregious even by his standards. It was New Year's Day when he rammed his wife Deboragh's Buick with his Mercedes and then shot it up after she and two of her friends got out and ran.[1] On January 17, one of those two friends sued him for seventeen million dollars; on February 3, Deboragh sued for divorce. As all this went down, the January issue of *Ebony* featured Richard and Deboragh on its cover, smiling and showing off her wedding ring.[2] But the newspapers were telling a different story, and when Richard got back on stage later that year, that other story was the one he wanted to talk about. He talked about that story without talking about the cops or his ex-wife or the NBC executives who had (he felt) undermined his TV show just before everything blew up. He talked about it without relying on the teeming world of characters and voices he had created in his 1970s stand-up work. He told the story, instead, by talking about himself. He talked about his "Mama," the grandmother who had raised him and who would die in December 1978 as Richard clung to her and called her name like a child.[3] He talked about his cocaine addiction, his father, his sexual fantasies and fears. And as he wound through these topics, he returned again and again to intimate ruminations about birth and death, human bodies and animal bodies, failure and survival, need and desire.

He worked out this material at the Comedy Store in Los Angeles for much of the year and took it on the road that fall, though his tour was truncated by his grandmother's stroke and subsequent decline. And then on December 28, within a couple weeks of her death, he laid it all out in a concert in Long Beach that was filmed and released theatrically as *Richard Pryor: Live In Concert*. The film remains a touchstone for the history of stand-up comedy. It's the first fully fledged stand-up concert film, the model for a thousand similar productions to follow, a work that many contemporary comedians imitate even when they don't know they are doing so.

Pryor in this concert is as outrageous and obscene as he was throughout his 1970s stand-up work, and perhaps in ways he is still doing what observers throughout that decade had understood him to be doing: gathering up a whole world of African American folklore, speaking with the compound voice of a culture, disappearing into the identities and idioms of people whose voices had not been heard on stages like these before. But in this concert, after his fall, he also delves deeper than ever into his own layers of personhood, and he drags to the surface something that hadn't been visible before. "I am really personally happy to see *anybody* come out and see *me*, right," he confesses, near the start of the show. And then he lays it right out: "I don't want to never see no more police in *my* life, at *my* house, taking *my* ass to jail, for killing *my* car. And it seemed fair to kill my car to me, right, 'cause my wife was gonna *leave* my ass!"

There it is, in about forty seconds: the car-killing, the trip to jail, the flimsy self-justifications, and an admission that his fans aren't the only people Richard Pryor is worried about losing. From there, he takes off at full speed, conjuring his way back to the scene of the crime. He plays Richard Pryor in that scene—"Nah, unhh-unhh, if you leave, you be driving them Hush Puppies you got on," he taunts Deboragh—but he also enacts the world around Richard Pryor, a world that responds to and participates in his rage. "I shot at the car, it said *phooommm!* The tires said *aawwhhaawwhhaawwhhah.* It got good to me, I shot another one: *Phooommm! Aawwhhaawwhhaawwhh.* And that vodka I was drinking said, *Go ahead, shoot something else.*" As he narrates, he embodies the story and everything in it, exploding and whinnying, menacing and murmuring, whirling from shape to shape as a car, a gun, a vodka-demon, a man losing control.

From this first confession, he rolls on into a series of bizarre reflections about violation and loss—how his pets try to molest him, how he grieved for his pet monkeys when they died, how he wishes women were equipped with rape-proof bodies—and just as he finishes that last bit he suddenly twitches his mouth and puts his hand on his chest. "Had a little pain in my heart there," he says, cutting his eyes to the crowd: "I thought I was having another heart attack." And then he takes off again, this time into an enactment of the heart attack, complete with falsetto whimpering and writhing on the floor. Like the vodka before, Richard's heart is an interior demon with a voice:

Richard: Okay, I'll shut up, don't kill me don't kill me don't kill me!

Heart: Get on one knee and prove it!

Richard: I'm on one knee I'm on one knee. Don't kill me don't—

Heart: Thinking about dying now, ain't you?

Richard: Yeah, I'm thinking about dying I'm thinking about dying.

Heart: You didn't think about it when you was eating all that PORK!

With that shout, he collapses onto his back, half-fetal on the stage floor, where he convulses and silent-screams for twelve wordless seconds. He finally props himself up on an elbow and keeps telling the story, and by the time he gets to the end of it, he's talking about dying in the hospital and nobody caring. People only care, he says, about guys like John Wayne. And Richard Pryor knows perfectly well that he's no John Wayne.

It's brutal. His red silk shirt is open to the bottom of his sternum and soaked with sweat. He looks like an open wound as he carries breathlessly on from his heart attack to a whirl of stories from his family history: how his "Mama" found him snorting cocaine and wailed until he promised to quit, how she used to beat him with the hose from an old-fashioned douche bag, how his father died while having sex with a woman (a scene Richard interprets as a return to the place of birth at the moment of death: "We call that recycling"). Like much of this concert, these bits are crude and transgressive, but they are also an expedition along the back passages of this man's haunted id, teeming with images of mothers and children, of small creatures in pain, of birth and copulation and death. In response to the ordeals of legal trouble and public shame, the fallen comedian gets onstage and shows us his wounds, invites us to touch his hands and side. Did you hear the rumor about the great man's heart attack? Here, in his theater of comic pain, you can watch it happen. And you can watch and hear not just the drama of that New Year's Day shooting but also the subterranean forces that didn't make it into the police report: the fear of abandonment, the preoccupation with sexual fertility and failure, the screaming presences of furious, libidinous, hose-wielding grown-ups. The concert is a confession, and Pryor's enactments of every object and event in the scenes of his fall erases any distance between himself and those scenes. Richard is the gun, and the gun is Richard. The event isn't something he remembers. It's who he is, here and now. By entering bodily into these scenes, he goes full-immersion into his history of shame and dares us to follow him there. Will we do it? Our laughter will be our answer. And Richard Pryor, on this particular night, bids for our laughter with desperate need, because this confession, like all confessions, is also a plea for forgiveness.

*

That's the pattern that Pryor's genre-defining performance laid down: the scandal-stained comedian confesses, looking for absolution in the laughter of the crowd. Pryor himself returned to the form after the sensationally publicized day in 1980 when he freebased his way to total insanity and set himself on fire. In the 1981 concert captured in the film *Live from the Sunset Strip*, even the freebase pipe talks: "Come on in the room with me, I got you covered; I know how you feel, Rich; I understand, just light me up." And a good many others have adapted his postlapsarian comedy to their own scandals and purposes. Stand-up performers of all sorts—Ali Wong, Kevin Hart, Aziz Ansari, Dave Chappelle—have taken up the form to respond to all sorts of shames: failing marriages, drug addictions, sexual misconduct charges, controversial tweets. Other comics, such as Ellen DeGeneres and Louis C. K., have provoked controversy by apparently refusing to take up the form, with its mechanisms of confession and absolution, after their own falls from grace. It's as if there's something in us and our culture that *needs* these confessions from fallen comedians. It might be that we need the morality tales of success and failure that prompted these confessions in the first place.

At the outset of his 2023 post-cocaine-rehab special *Baby J*, John Mulaney more or less names the stakes of the thing. He begins by admitting that as a boy he actually *hoped*—he even *prayed*—that God would kill one of his grandparents so that he could be the center of attention for a day at school. "I did, I did do that," he admits, three and a half minutes into the show: "and *some of you did too*! And I *know* you did, because you started laughing from the very beginning of the joke!" And then, having made this accusation, he offers reassurance: "If you did, don't feel too bad, okay? Yes, it's a super dark memory—but you were a little kid. Also, you were a little kid, so you probably still had, like, four grandparents. This is a lot of grandparents."

So we're forgiven, right? I'm okay, and you're okay. Now, about that cocaine.

There is a promise of kinship in these self-abasing performances, as there is in the performances of the shabby comedians we met earlier. The fallen comedian enacts again her failures and transgressions, and by her enactment, if Mulaney's promise is any indication, more sinners than just this one performer find forgiveness. *Some of you did too*, he pronounces, because we too have sins to confess, charges to answer, a stain that needs cleansing. The comedian is here for us in our shame.

But it isn't as easy as that. Pryor knows, in 1978, that there's something else, a grievance or distance, between him and his audience. He acknowledges that distance when he says up front that he's glad his audience hasn't left him. In the closing seconds of his 1981 post-immolation concert, he names the distance even more pointedly when he tells the crowd that he knows they've been talking about him behind his back, "since you *luvvvv* me so much," and then tells them one of their own jokes: "I remember this one—just strike the match like this—and say, *What's that? Richard Pryor, running down the street!*"

Ouch. Did we really say that? And did this junkie just pivot from confessing his own sins to naming ours? Yes we did, and yes he did, and in telling that joke, Richard says out loud something that needs to be said out loud. Be honest, people, he says. You didn't just come here to show love, did you? You came to be entertained by the Crazy Junkie. You came for some more of those *Richard Pryor* jokes.

It's a strange sort of self-abasement, then. This disgraced sinner has come to tell us about his shame. And he has also come to tell us about what happens to us when we look at his shame and laugh. He remembers the image, of himself tied to a stake, that he had dreamed up a few years before for the cover of *Is It Something I Said?*—and he remembers the many images of American violence that inspired that one. He wants to ask us what it is that we intend to do with all these torches.

*

Pryor's emergence as a mature stand-up comedian began at a moment when he refused to let his audience keep laughing. In September 1967, he went onstage for his opening night at the Aladdin Hotel and Casino in Las Vegas, looked at the mainly white crowd, and then walked right back off, abandoning a career he had spent years trying to build. He had been coming to see with increasing clarity that he needed to address the distance that was there, unacknowledged, between him and his audiences. He didn't want to be a reassuring colored entertainer for white tourists in Vegas. So he quit. And then, for the next three or so years, he floundered, casting about for a sense of artistic purpose and struggling to keep his personal life under control. He felt that none of the silly antics of his still-young comic career had expressed anything true: he was just making faces and begging for approval. Even Groucho Marx, at a party in Los Angeles, took him to task for the stupidity of a *Merv Griffin Show* appearance in which Pryor and Jerry Lewis had gotten laughs by spitting at each other. "Do you want," Groucho asked, "to end up a spitting wad like Jerry Lewis?"[4]

All the while, Richard carried the weight of a profoundly violent and vulnerable early life. In the brothel where he spent his childhood in Peoria, Illinois, he had watched his father shoot a man, had seen his mother service a client, had cowered as his parents beat each other. He had been forcibly molested by an older boy in the alley behind the house. He had seen a dead baby in a shoebox.[5] What did any of this have to do with the tourists and their cocktails at his Vegas shows? What did the world of Ed Sullivan and Merv Griffin have to do with the world of his grandmother, who ran the family brothel and loved her Baptist church, or with the many-layered community of his childhood? He couldn't figure out how to connect the dots, and he was a man in trouble when his friend Paul Mooney finally told him he needed to get out of LA and took him up to Berkeley.

It was there, in the early seventies, that Richard had his breakthrough. He himself dated his transformation to a performance in which he went on stage and said the N-word, and then said it again, and then said it again, and again, and again, as he later remembered, "like a preacher singing hallelujah."[6] In performances like this one, he began to discover what happened when he reached out and touched the things in this world he most hated and feared. This discovery was, for him, a portal to the comic idiom he'd been looking for.

As he developed that comic idiom over the next few years, Pryor fashioned himself into something strange. He became, on the one hand, a teller of truths, with all the fury of politically attuned comedians like Dick Gregory, Godfrey Cambridge, Mort Sahl, and Lenny Bruce. But he projected little of the moral righteousness that gave those performers their fire. When Richard came on stage, he came naked, without critical distance, smoldering with undigested shame and rage. And he alchemized all this energy into a one-man theatrical universe, creating and enacting characters who embodied their own histories of suffering and survival. In his stand-up act, he played hustlers, preachers, bar-maids, grandmothers, old men and children, addicts and slaves. He had a preternatural way of disappearing into the identity of whatever character he was enacting, and it became hard to separate some of them—Junkie, Wino, Mudbone—from Richard Pryor himself. They seemed to be the makers of his comic performances, their lives and voices the stuff that he himself was made of. From the time of his breakthrough in Berkeley, Pryor more or less stopped doing gags and jokes. There were no punchlines in his act. His comedy was simply an acting out of the many selves in his imaginary world.

There was always an element of celebration in Pryor's shape-shifting performances. Characters like Mudbone are brilliantly alive, poetic and shrewd, blazing with imaginative energy. By disappearing into those characters, Pryor offered his comic art as a kind of love letter to the communities and folk traditions these characters represent. He found ways of talking about Blackness without talking about Jim Crow or lynching or civil rights or Black Power, and it's easy to believe him when he says that his use of racist slurs, which became a trademark of his act, was like a song of praise, a shouted hallelujah. These slurs became part of his refusal to reduce Black lives to the meanings assigned to them by the history of American racism.

And then again. The literary scholar Glenda Carpio, in her book *Laughing Fit to Kill*, argues that the power of "conjure"—what she describes as "the ability to transform people into things and objects"—plays a complicated role in African American culture.[7] This power is rooted in long traditions of folk practice and ritual, but it is also hard to separate from the cultural legacy of chattel slavery, which also attempts to transform Black people into things and objects, commodities on a market. Carpio links Pryor's metamorphic art to the history of conjure, and she makes the case that his performances, too, are haunted by the danger of dehumanization, the possibility that when Pryor calls himself by racist slurs, he's simply using the brand name that the market has assigned to him. She observes that Pryor's Wino and Mudbone bits weren't just enactments of Black lives: they were enactments of Black stereotypes, offered to boys like the young Richard Pryor as the only lives available.[8] When Pryor disappeared into these stereotypes, he willed himself to become the thing that American racism had told him he was. It was like putting on a voodoo mask, submitting to and confronting its soul-stealing power.

When Paul Mooney warned Richard in the early 1970s that if he worked out his material at the Comedy Store, other comedians (especially white comedians) would steal it, Richard shot right back that *no one* could ever steal his material. He was right. His material, he knew, was himself, rendered into all the forms the world offered to him. Every performance he gave in the middle years of the 1970s was a tearing down of the walls between himself and the stereotypes he wanted to confront, and it can be hard to tell, listening to him, whose voice we're hearing. The obscene language and bawdy humor of his mature stand-up wasn't just an unleashing of some authentic Pryorian idiom, or the bringing to light of an authentic African American tradition. Like the racist slurs, Pryor's rampant obscenities, his shrewd lies and wily tall tales, and his exaggerated voice-impressions of addicts, hustlers, and preachers all enacted racist stereotypes. He played exactly the parts that white people—and not only white people—expected a man like him to play.

In his journeys into these stereotypes, Pryor explored the labyrinths not just of his own id but also of the vast myth-systems of American culture. And he intimated the dangerous truth that those two imaginative worlds are impossible to disentangle, that they have fed on and formed each other for a long time. He knew as well as anyone that his forays into these imaginative worlds were perilous, as much a lament as a celebration. If Lenny Bruce and George Carlin tried to maintain that their obscenities were weapons in a liberal crusade for free expression, Pryor himself entertained no such fantasies. There's not a whole lot of time for free expression, he knew, when you've been tied to a stake since the day you were born.

*

Which is to say that Pryor, throughout his mature career, was looking for ways to fashion himself as a prophet. From the moment of that breakthrough moment in 1971, he offered his audiences something other than kinship. That image from the cover of *Is It Something I Said?*—of Richard tied to a stake, with torches all around—is an image not of kinship but of confrontation, of something terrible between the comedian and the people who have come to laugh at him. But he doesn't look very righteous up on that stake. He looks bewildered, scared, and a little ashamed, because he knows he can't fully distinguish himself from the thing he has come to denounce.

Comedians long before Pryor have played out stereotypes and made comedy out of their own abasement. But Pryor pushed that spectacle of abasement to its extremes, to the point at which it converges with the comedian's own personal sins and makes him nearly impossible to stomach. After him, many comedians have tested the boundaries of social transgression in similar ways, pushing us to the point at which we boo, or take to social media, or revoke Oscar-hosting invitations. It's a dangerous game. At its stupidest and worst, the comedy of extremes that Pryor helped to unleash can be pointlessly abusive and gratuitous, a degradation of both the comedian and the audience. But that danger is the place where these comedians have to do their work. "You have a responsibility to speak recklessly," Dave Chappelle says to the comedians in his crowd in his special *The Bird Revelation*. Because if comedians don't speak recklessly, there are things that might never be spoken at all—and that, too, is dangerous.

Chappelle has been among the most incendiary practitioners of this recklessness. In his post–*Chappelle's Show* stand-up work, he's persistently tested the limits of what we are willing to say or contemplate, of what is forgivable and survivable. He's prodded and experimented, transgressed at this point and that point, as if he's testing the defenses around a perimeter. In the 2016 concert released on Netflix as *The Age of Spin*, Chappelle reckoned not just with his own capacity for transgression but with the transgressions of two other performers,

O. J. Simpson and Bill Cosby, and with the things these figures might or might not reveal about the lives of Black men in this celebrity culture. He structured the set partly around his tales of the four times he met O. J. Simpson, and he wound his way from his own hideous idea for a movie about a tragic superhero—this superhero has to rape people to keep his superpowers—to an earnest reflection about how we understand the heroic role that Bill Cosby, the man we now know as a rapist, really did play for many people. All the while, "Dave Chappelle"—with his mischief-making persona, his shocking fantasies, his own abusive sexual jokes—makes a sort of live contact with these disgraced sinners, arcing and buzzing with an energy that's partly theirs. The concert is all sorts of things: an accusation, a repudiation, a love letter, a farewell, a gross caricature, a tender humanization, an attempt to understand, and an acknowledgment that certain things can't be understood. It isn't a moralizing response, because Chappelle doesn't allow himself enough distance for moralization. But could it be a moral response, a response that begins in revulsion and then asks where we go from there?

Maybe. Even so, Chappelle doesn't make it easy to watch. How could it be easy to watch? A celebrity naming his sins in sanitized language and then apologizing would be easy enough to watch. We could watch, after all, from a safe and studied distance. But Pryor and his cultural heirs enact their bad selves right before our eyes. They take upon themselves their own sins, and the sins of others. Revulsion isn't the point. But it's the path.

*

The image of Pryor at the stake suggests winkingly that he didn't exactly choose to be our flammable messiah, and there's a running joke in his comedy that he stumbled into this whole business by accident. At times he joked that even his Blackness itself was a hilarious mistake. "You mean I'm not white?!? This is a scandal!" his blind character shouts, as if he didn't know before now, in his

1988 movie *See No Evil, Hear No Evil*: "Does Dad know?" Chappelle developed this joke further in his *Chappelle's Show* sketch about Clayton Bigsby, the Black white supremacist, who's blind and doesn't know this one inconvenient fact about himself. And Chappelle, too, has riffed in his stand-up on the idea that as a Black man in America he's a kind of reluctant prophet, an unlucky winner who didn't sign up for this gig. "'Cause I can tell you right now," he said in his 2016 *Saturday Night Live* monologue, "if I could quit being Black right now, I'd be out of the game." Issa Rae riffs on this joke when she puts "Awkward" and then "Black" at the very bottom of her "WORST THINGS ANYONE COULD BE" list and expresses surprise that *these* are the numbers she pulled in life. There's a wry irony in all these bits, of course, an accusation leveled against a social order that makes it possible to associate the racial or cultural identities of these comedians with bad luck. But there's also a more complicated reflection on the roles others want them to play and the roles they themselves have chosen to play. Here they are, in full costume for their performances as Junkie and Wino and Awkward Black Girl. Who's responsible for that?

The answers to that question aren't easy, and so it's no surprise that these unwilling prophets periodically renounce their own performances. The shames and sins they act out are too degrading, the lines between comic pain and real pain too hard to define. So they walk away, as Chappelle did from his TV show, or they renounce the whole thing, as Hannah Gadsby did in *Nanette*, or they hang up their jester's cap and rebrand as free speech attorneys or political commentators, as Lenny Bruce and Mort Sahl increasingly did in their later careers. Pryor made his own renunciations in the final years of his stand-up career, as he moved toward taking more responsibility for the addictions and excesses that had fueled his circus of self-destruction.[9] Starting with his 1978 postlapsarian shows, he abandoned the characters and alter egos that had been the mainstay of his work in the years preceding. After a trip to Nairobi in 1979, he renounced his use of the N-word: this, too, was a mantle he would no longer consent to wear. And in the concerts he gave after his 1980 freebasing incident, he began groping his way toward a new language for talking about his addiction, refusing to reduce it to merely another Junkie bit in his dramatic repertoire. You can almost see him beginning to let go in these late stand-up shows, acknowledging what it has cost him to play the role of everyone else's truth-telling prodigal. Unlike Chappelle and Gadsby, who have come back from their renunciations bearing a new kind of authority and charisma, Pryor more or less lapsed into silence after making these last confessions. It's hard to blame him. The warfare he had practiced in the comic arena required a nearly superhuman strength.

In 1974, Pryor told the journalist David Felton that he was working on a screenplay for an autobiographical movie called *This Can't Be Happening to Me*. In one scene, the character Richard Pryor is in a church, and Jesus on the crucifix asks Richard to help take him down. "I've been hanging around here two thousand years," he says, "and they ain't buried me yet, and I'm tired," and so Richard removes the nails from Jesus's hands and feet and helps him hobble out of the church.[10] It's a bizarre and heterodox fantasy—when the two of them get outside, they are attacked by a bunch of monks, who beat them up and drag Jesus back to the cross—but it might say something about Richard's sense of himself. The man with whom he suffers, in this story, is himself an incongruous figure, a walking paradox. He is a blameless criminal, a priest and a sacrifice, a son both of a common girl and of the Most High. In his crucifixion, he enters into an abasement that is also a proclamation, and a willing death that also turns to life.

More comedians than Richard Pryor have seen something in themselves of this man on the cross, and it's no accident, perhaps, that Richard dreams of a story in which their plots converge. In the spectacle of the battered comedian showing us his wounds, there is an element of self-giving. As he confronts a bad world with the truth of his own badness, Pryor comes close to the company of other reluctant and stumbling prophets: of Hosea with his prostitute bride, of Jeremiah with a yoke on his neck, of Isaiah walking around naked. He perhaps bears some memory of Robert Armin, putting his atypical self on display and asking us what it is we see here. Is it a sinner? A fool? A crazy junkie? Is it a creature of our own making? Or could it be, just possibly, a mirror? We are never entirely sure. The flames make the face hard to see.

INTERLUDE
COMEDY IS A CARNIVAL

The ancient Greek festivals in honor of the god Dionysos began with a ritual procession. The devotees of the god marched through whatever city or village they were in, carrying baskets of offerings, singing hymns, and hurling insults (this was part of the ritual) at spectators gathered along the way. When they arrived at the place appointed for the festive celebration, the worshippers made the first animal sacrifices, and a priest cried, "Call the god!" At that moment, the crowd shouted the terrible name, and Dionysos came.[1]

We tend to think of Dionysos as a god of wine, and ancient Greeks thought the same thing. But for his ancient devotees, he was, even more, a god of the powers most strongly associated with wine. He was, for one thing, a god of what the Greeks called *mania*: ecstasy, madness, divine frenzy. He had a connection both with frenzied violence and with inspiration, with the human capacity for artistic creativity and prophetic insight. And he was also a god of the vine, of green and growing things, of sexual potency and springtime fertility. When he descended upon his followers, he unleashed something vital and ferocious.

The worship of Dionysos always involved singing and dancing, and as his devotees performed their songs and dances, they channeled the god's maniacal life. They stomped, chanted, circled, whirled, and hymned the world-shattering acts of Zeus's most prodigal son. Sober people who saw these performances found them terrifying. But the uncanny music of Dionysos also became central to Greek civic life, and in the early years of the fifth century BCE, performers at his feasts—most notably at the Greater Dionysia, a massive springtime festival in Athens—adapted this music into a new kind of ritual art. It began, some ancient writers say, when a chorus-leader named Thespis donned a mask: instead of singing about the god, he came into the theater and sang *as* the god, and the art form that the Greeks called *drama* was born. The Greater Dionysia soon came to revolve around tragic plays, which acted out the god's energies of lust and destruction. The core purpose of these plays was to venture into dangerous territory. They dared to represent the worst extremes of violence, and they invited the ritual community (which, at the Greater Dionysia, was more or less the whole city of Athens) to pass through that enacted violence to a renewed experience of unity. As Rowan Williams has said in his book *The Tragic Imagination*, tragedies in Greece tested the boundaries of what sort of speech a human community could survive, daring to express things that are dangerous to name but even more dangerous to leave unspoken.

In the shadow of these first tragedies, another kind of drama was born. The Greeks called it "comedy," after the wild country revelry known as the *kōmos*, and it answered the catastrophic violence of tragedy with a mocking, mischief-making, life-renewing festivity. The festival audiences who watched the first comic plays must have found them a relief from the tragic spectacles that dominated the Greater Dionysia. But the comedies, too, made it their business to play with danger. They, too, tested the limits of what a community could say and do without destroying itself. Their performers wore big phalluses, mocked eminent audience members, and shouted obscenities with reckless abandon, and their playful misrule was always right on the verge of actual harm. Aristophanes, the preeminent comedic writer and producer of fifth-century Athens, crossed the line at least once. The surviving evidence suggests that he got himself in real legal trouble for some jokes he included in his play *The Babylonians*, and readers for millennia have argued about whether his mockery of Socrates, in *Clouds*, helped to fuel the rumors of "corrupting the youth" that ultimately led to the philosopher's death. It seems like awfully high stakes, for a lighthearted comic play. But this is the festival of Dionysos. It was never going to be safe.

This fact is worth emphasizing: comedy, as a developed art form, was born at a festival. It has always retained a festive quality. Historians of drama have long noticed that there are especially strong resemblances between comic theater and the later Roman Saturnalia, a winter festival that (at least in Rome's imperial era) occupied the seven days from December 17 to 23. During this feast, everything went topsy-turvy. No one conducted public business, waged war, or went to court. People of all social classes stopped buying and selling and instead exchanged gifts. Slaves insulted their masters; women took up weapons and engaged in mock combat; respectable citizens gambled, guzzled, fornicated, and generally made mayhem.[2] The commotion was wild enough that the Roman poet Horace, in one of his *Satires*, depicted himself as having fled to his country villa to get away from it all."[3]

The celebrants of the Saturnalia believed that all this madness brought something to life on the earth. The god Saturn, bound in captivity for the rest of the year, was released. For this moment, in this festival, the god's ancient reign was established once again, and the renewal of that reign, everyone knew, meant that the world returned to what many writers described as a golden age. In his great poem *Metamorphoses*, the Latin poet Ovid described this age as a time of innocence in which there was no law, no war, no property, no agriculture, no hierarchy, no human restlessness, no scarcity or strife of any sort, because "spring was never-ending," "streams of milk and streams of nectar flowed," and no one needed to seize, demand, protect, or worry about anything.[4] The festival, with its reversals of social order and its tables piled high with food, made this golden age seem real again, and it brought to the center of Roman civic life the memory of another, better life. The revelry was, in this way, utopian. It was provocative, an acknowledgment of the limits of the present social order. But it wasn't utopian in a revolutionary sense; it didn't try to overthrow that order and build something new. The revelers knew perfectly well that the age of gold wasn't coming back, and that at the end of the seven days everyone would strap on their swords and aprons and get back to work. The Saturnalia was utopian, rather, in an apocalyptic sense. It offered a glimpse of something else, a real and vital order of things that challenges and renews our own. It was not a revolution but a celebration.

In the Jewish and Christian festivities that developed elsewhere, this apocalyptic longing came to the center of the community's ritual activity. Hebrew writers, too, had a golden age to contemplate: they looked both backward to an Edenic age, when the earth brought forth fruit in abundance and "the man and his wife were both naked, and were not ashamed," and forward to a coming *shalom*, a new earth, in which "the wolf and the lamb shall feed together, the lion shall eat straw like the ox."[5] Jewish worshippers learned to enter into these times of gold in the weekly festival of the Sabbath, a ritual in which the community participates in God's seventh-day rest and renews the Creator's primal affirmation that the creation is good.

The festivals of the Christian tradition are rooted partly in these same remembrances of a creation that was good: the writer of the epistle to the Hebrews says that "there remains a sabbath rest for the people of God; for whoever enters God's rest also ceases from his labors as God did from his."[6] And the festive practices of Easter and Eucharist involve the idea of Christ as a second Adam, the beginning of a new creation story in which the golden age of Eden is restored. But the emphasis of Christian festivals is less on the memory of the primal moment of creation and more on the anticipation of a moment to come, a consummate feast-day when, as Christ prophesies over the wine at the last supper, "I drink it new with you in my Father's kingdom."[7] In the riotous inversions of the Christmas and Carnival festivities that flourished in medieval Europe, that kingdom, the *eschaton*, came crashing dramatically into the ordinary world. Boys dressed up as bishops and preached in church. Women arrested men in the streets and held them for ransom. Gifts, ale, and pancakes proliferated all around. The last became first, and the wolves and lambs of human life fed together, and there was no bondage or poverty known among the people of God. The kingdom, though far off, was also at hand.

Are these festivities likewise relevant to comedy? They are very relevant. They are, after all, irruptions into this ordinary world of something other, something that makes life go haywire. They dramatize realities deeper, and harder to see, than the reality of the everyday, and their upside-down misrule is a promise of a coming age in which, as the God of John's Apocalypse says, "Behold, I make all things new."[8] They are, all at once, festivals of hilarity and festivals of renewal, and they help to explain how it is that comedy can make us laugh even in the context of suffering and corruption. They raise the possibility that the laughter of comedy is a kind of defiance or hope, an assertion that the forces of injustice and misery are not ultimate. And they help explain why it is that when we feel the encroaching power of those forces, the laughter of comedy often grows louder still.

III

MARTYRS

5

HILARIOUS MARTYRS

FROM PERPETUA OF CARTHAGE TO LAWRENCE OF ROME

Picture this. You're in Rome, in the year 258, and a man is being burned to death by agents of your government, who have orders to make the execution as painful as possible. Or you're in Carthage, in 203, and a new mother, barely out of her teens, is about to be butchered by a Roman soldier. You're watching this happen in an arena. Their deaths are being staged for your entertainment.

His name is Lawrence; hers is Perpetua; it's hard to imagine watching their deaths take place. It's even harder, of course, to imagine enduring them. And here's something that makes contemplating them harder still. After he has burned and blistered for a while, Lawrence calls out cheerfully, "I'm done on this side. Flip me over and see how I taste!"[1] In a similar surprising turn, when the Roman soldier shies back from killing Perpetua, she grabs his sword hand, says, "Let's get on with it," and does the job herself. Perhaps your jaw drops at this moment—or perhaps you saw it coming. When you went the night before to gawk with the crowds at this young mother in prison, she took a big bite of her final meal, looked you right in the eyes, and laughed.

Here's the question: are martyrs funny? The ancient texts that tell the stories of these Christian martyrs tend to think they are. They treat these martyrs as comedians, stepping onstage in arenas and theaters and getting big laughs from their crowds. And the idea of the martyr as comedian might not be as strange as it seems. Martyrs, after all, have always been performers. The Greek word *martys* means "witness," as in a witness at a trial. A martyr in the ancient Greek world was a person who stands to testify, facing off with judges and orators in public spectacles of legal dispute. The Socrates of Plato's *Gorgias* talks about law-court rhetoricians who rely on many "witnesses" [*martyras*] to make a case.² Aristotle in his *Rhetoric* says that an orator can quote famous writers as a way of calling them "as a witness" [*martyri*]).³ In all these texts and plenty of others, the *martys* is called to take a speaking part in a drama of trial and judgment. Her work of bearing witness is a performance, and an effective *martys* has to be good on stage, keeping control of the narrative, maneuvering under cross-examination, and wearing the face the audience needs to see.

These senses of the word "martyr" are still in play in the Greek New Testament (Jesus tells his apostles that "you shall be my witnesses" [*martyres*]), but the word also begins to indicate a particular sort of witness-bearing: the "cloud of witnesses" [*martyrōn*] in Hebrews 11 includes quite a few witnesses who did not just speak the truth but suffered and died for it.⁴ In the second century C. E., all over the Roman Empire, texts began to appear that told the stories of these dying witnesses. The "legends" (as these texts are often called) recounted dramatic spectacles of trial, judgment, and punishment. But they made the witnesses the protagonists of the drama, and they called the gruesome ordeals and deaths of these witnesses *martyrdom*.

The heroes of the legends come from all sorts of places: there's the ex-priest-of-Zeus Sharbil (martyred in Edessa, around the year 113), the old bishop Polycarp (Smyrna, 155), the philosopher Justin (Rome, 165), the disabled slave Blandina (Lyons, 177), the young aristocrat Perpetua (Carthage, 203), the deacon Lawrence (Rome,

258).⁵ But their stories are all, in essential ways, the same. They all get arrested for their allegiance to Jesus of Nazareth and their refusal to bow before the cult of Roman imperial religion. They all give testimony in the theaters of Roman law, confounding their inquisitors with exhibitions of upside-down logic and incomprehensible defiance. And they all offer the final testimony of their own bodies, in blood-bathed pageants of torture and death. They are also all funny.

If the traditional dating is correct, the first surviving post-biblical text that used the word *martys* as a label for this new kind of witness was *The Martyrdom of Polycarp*, which claims to have been written by Polycarp's fellow believers in Smyrna soon after the deed was done, around the year 155. This legend promises to tell the story of "a martyrdom becoming the Gospel," and it narrates the escapades of a mayhem-making bishop who vaults through the stages of his ordeal with miraculous agility.⁶ Polycarp in this narrative glows with a kind of comic energy. When the soldiers come to arrest him, he is lounging serenely, and he offers them food and drink to keep themselves busy while he takes a couple hours to pray. They are amazed by his audacity, and by his aura. An unforgettable performance has begun.

It only gets better. The officials in Smyrna parade him on an ass and display him in the stadium, "where the tumult was so great, that there was no possibility of being heard," and then, as an unruly crowd looks on, he stands to testify before a Roman proconsul, responding to the questions of his examiner with provocative silences and slashing denunciations. Depending on your perspective, the whole spectacle is either utterly maddening or oddly hilarious. When the proconsul pleads with Polycarp to proclaim, "Away with the Atheists" (that is, with his fellow pantheon-denying Christians) aloud, the bishop waves his hand to indicate the crowd and thunders, "Away with the Atheists!" When the proconsul boasts that he can bring wild beasts in to devour him, Polycarp replies,

"Call them then… it is well for me to be changed from what is evil to what is righteous." When the proconsul threatens that he'll be burned with fire, Polycarp replies, in so many words, "That's not the fire I'd be worried about."[7] The agents of Roman power throw everything they've got at this eighty-six-year-old man, and nothing sticks. A holy gymnast, he eludes touch and defies gravity, as if he lives already in some other universe to which the laws of this one don't apply. It's no surprise that when the soldiers at last prepare to nail him down to his funeral pile, he says, "No need for that," gets himself settled, and then begins thanking God loudly for all the good things happening today.

Was anyone laughing at the marvelous bishop as he gave his performance on Smyrna's biggest stage? His repurposing of "Away with the Atheists" turned the phrase into a pretty good one-liner, and his jaunty defiance turned the whole event, which was supposed to be a pageant of Roman justice, into something completely different, a three-ring circus featuring his own astounding acrobatics.

If the legends are to be believed, the early Christian martyrs performed these sorts of acrobatic feats again and again. They played in huge venues, in theatrical spectacles carefully stage-managed by the Roman authorities. Ignatius of Antioch, an old friend of Polycarp martyred in Rome sometime before 117, endured his trial at the festival of the Saturnalia, in front of the biggest and rowdiest crowds of the season. The slave Blandina took her stand in the amphitheater at Lyons, the aristocrat Perpetua in the amphitheater at Carthage, the Syrian priest Sharbil in front of a huge crowd that ran alongside him, as he was paraded out of Edessa, to see what he would do next. Like Polycarp, led into town on a donkey and harangued by a director-proconsul who practically waved the script in his face, all these martyrs were put into costumes and pushed into their places in the arena. In the texts that tell their stories, their Roman handlers try awfully hard, and the sweaty anxiety of, say, the soldiers trying to get Ignatius to Rome before the season for public spectacles ends, or the officials trying to persuade Perpetua and her friends to get into their state-provided martyr outfits, is part of the setup for what inevitably happens when the martyr finally takes the stage.

What happens, in one legend after the next, is that the martyr steals the show. Polycarp does it when he takes the line foisted upon him—"Away with the Atheists!"—and turns its meaning inside out, so that it becomes a pie hurled right back in the faces of his inquisitors. Things get even worse when he shrugs at the horrors the proconsul parades before him, and worse still when he stands untouched among the flames, so that a soldier finally has to come and dispatch him unceremoniously with a dagger. His retorts and bored sighs have the effect of turning the whole production on its head, so that the values on which the drama is predicated (suffering is scary; death is defeat) go upside down. Polycarp's friend Ignatius works this inversion before he even arrives at the arena, when the soldiers tell him to hurry it up because they're worried about arriving too late for the public exhibitions, and he tells them he's in more of a hurry than they are. From this moment on, he owns the initiative. So does Perpetua, when she refuses to put on her costume, goes into the arena singing, and finally grabs the executioner's hand and slashes his sword across her own throat. The officials who were supposed to make spectacles of these martyrs have nothing left to do but panic, shrieking pointless stage directions and groping for the curtain-ropes as the martyr takes her delirious stand among the burning scenery.

These legends of martyrdom seem funny, to me, in the way that farces of theatrical floppery are always funny. Their heroes are like Bugs Bunny stage-crashing a pompous magician or the Little Rascals pea-shooting Spanky as he tries to declaim some Shakespeare at a talent show. In their disruptions of official political spectacles, their heroes are like Groucho Marx wrecking a meeting of state or

Joe Pesci's Vinny Gambini turning a Southern courtroom into a carnival side-show. These martyrs are judo artists of mischief-making, getting underneath the big men of this world and flipping them onto the mat. It's quite a thing to watch, if you're a secret believer or a ravening mob, and the whole production becomes even more deliciously absurd, within the social order of the Roman empire, when the person doing the flipping is a disabled slave or a woman barely out of her teens. If there's a thread of comic laughter in the lives of the martyrs, their exhibitions of emperor-throwing might not be a bad place to start looking for it.

But these scene-stealing antics aren't the whole story, either. The comic inversions of the martyrs take more forms than scene-stealing misbehavior. Polycarp, in the text that tells his story, takes witty jabs at the raging crowd, but he also, at the moment of death, has a dove come flapping miraculously from his stab wound. Does *that* have anything to do with comedy? And what about the plain fact that legends of martyrdom invite more responses than just laughter? The stories of these martyrs are not just hilarious, after all, but also horrific, shockingly raw in their remembrances of anguish and loss. Does this entanglement with suffering make the acts of the martyrs more like or less like the performances of comedians? Is it possible that the agonies of martyrdom—or the miracles of martyrdom—are still a part of what we laugh at when we laugh at comedians?

I suspect so. The laughter of the martyrs tends, after all, to mean something very particular. Its significance is especially clear in the story of Lawrence, one of the funniest martyrs of them all.

*

Lawrence was a deacon of the Roman church when the emperor Valerian carried out his purges of the Christian clergy in 258. On a single day in August of that year, the Roman authorities executed the bishop of Rome and most of the city's deacons. According to the Latin poet Prudentius, who wrote Lawrence's story about a century and a half later, the Roman prefect in charge of the executions spared Lawrence at first, because he wanted to ask this particular deacon about his area of oversight: the church's treasury.[8] Lawrence cheerfully affirmed that the church was very rich indeed, and he promised to hand all that wealth over to the prefect. All I need, he said, is three days to gather everything together.

The prefect agreed, and Lawrence got to work. For three days, he recruited a little army of street people, destitute and disfigured. Prudentius describes some of them: a man with two eyeless sockets, a man with festering sores, a man with a withered hand, a man with a chopped-off leg. Lawrence got this grubby company assembled in one of the church's basilicas, and when the appointed time came, he reported back to the prefect as promised. Come with me, he said, and "you will see the great nave gleaming with vessels of gold, and along the open colonnades course on course of precious metal."[9] The prefect could hardly contain himself; he followed Lawrence like a hungry puppy. Then Lawrence threw open the doors, and the prefect saw them, gathered into a single, mouth-breathing horde: the treasures of the church.

The blast of this surprise must have lingered in the air for at least a few moments. But Lawrence wasn't finished. Before the prefect could say a thing, the deacon took off into a flame-throwing tirade that named out loud, in case anyone had missed it, the prophetic meaning of his stunt. Do you think you see here a crowd of lepers and beggars? Well, I'm here to tell you, he cried, that the beautiful people of Rome are lepers and beggars at their core, bleeding and stinking and *mucculentis naribus*—snotting at the nose—whereas this company of unfortunates will soon enter into "their Father's house on high, no longer dirty or feeble as for the present they appear, but bright with gleaming robes and golden crowns."[10] The performance you've just witnessed was not just a prank but also a vision, the revelation of a kingdom that your pretty Roman citizens don't have the eyes to see. Put *that* in your treasury, he dared the prefect, and see what happens.

There's a spectacular comic artistry in Lawrence's little production. When, in Prudentius's account, the prefect finally responds, he fumes that he has been mocked by all this "comedian's quibbling and theatrical buffoonery," and that a serious matter of state has been turned into a "piece of entertainment."[11] At a certain level, it might be an uncomprehending answer to Lawrence's thunderous disclosures. A piece of entertainment? Really? Is this all the idiot-villain has seen here? But the prefect also names exactly what has just happened. Lawrence has mounted a pop-up theatrical production in the midst of a fatal cultural and legal conflict. The transaction wasn't supposed to be a public spectacle, and it wasn't supposed to be funny, but Lawrence has made it both spectacular and hilarious. In a way, his act is more audaciously theatrical than anything in the earlier narratives of martyrs. He doesn't just spoil a Roman spectacle of judgment, as Polycarp and Perpetua do. He mounts his own spectacle of judgment, and he dares his persecutors to come and watch. When the prefect calls the stunt a "piece of entertainment," the Latin word he uses for "entertainment"—*festivum*—captures well the flavor of the deacon-jester's performance. Lawrence has turned a financial exchange into a festive one, a carnival enactment of a golden age to come. In this turn, he confounds the logic of fiscal calculation and Roman power with another logic, the upside-down calculus of the powerless ones who fight with tears and overcome the world.

Where is there to go from here? Might Lawrence, as a reward for his brave stand, have had his mortal life spared and his material treasures preserved? Hardly. Prudentius keeps hinting, after all, that this prophesying deacon already lives somewhere else, in a world of hilarious inversions beyond the horizon of mortal life.

The second act of Lawrence's drama confirms his citizenship in this other kingdom. It's a brief second act; there isn't much left to say or do. But what happens is unforgettable. The prefect, now furious, orders that Lawrence be roasted on a gridiron as slowly as possible, to prolong his suffering. Lawrence, in the scene I mentioned at the beginning of this chapter, reclines on the gridiron for a while and then cracks his final joke: Flip me over! And with that last flourish, he completes the course of his martyrdom, on fire in more ways than one.

Some Christians have regarded Lawrence as a patron saint of clowns and buffoons. No surprise there. But if Lawrence presides over the history of comic laughter, he might do so not just because he once out-heckled a Roman prefect. The power of his laughter, its authority to tear down empires, comes from an eschatological order that translates weakness into strength and death into defiant life. For those who had eyes to see, Prudentius reports, Lawrence's face blazed with brightness and his flesh smelled of nectar, while to his persecutors he just looked and stank like a body on fire. When he invited the prefect to turn him over, it was an explicit challenge: "Let's see what your blazing Vulcan has done."[12] It's as if two divinities were battling to consume the man on the altar, and the fire of the Christian God prevailed so powerfully that Lawrence couldn't feel the heat of Vulcan at all. "For Christ," as Prudentius says, "is the true fire."[13]

His comic bit about beggars and treasures has this same apocalyptic disclosure at its core. At the outset of the story, Lawrence could have replied to the prefect's offer with a simple and defiant *no*—but instead he chose another kind of witness-bearing, a martyrdom that prophetically and festively enacts a kingdom to come. I sometimes wonder what was it like for those hundreds of indigent extras. Perhaps it was terrifying. Perhaps it was life-changing, world-making. Perhaps it was good fun. If, as Prudentius's contemporary Ambrose of Milan claimed, Lawrence gave the church's treasures to those gathered beggars, it might have been *really* good fun, at least for a while.[14]

In any case, Lawrence's laughter has resonated powerfully in so many Christian traditions because it was also a promise, made in the midst of the worst atrocities the Romans could inflict upon him. He reminds me of the first- and second-century Rabbi Akiva, who, according to the Talmud, likewise astonished his Roman persecutors by smiling merrily as they tortured him to death. In an episode earlier in his life, Akiva sees a fox coming out of the ruined temple in Jerusalem and responds with buoyant good cheer. How can you be so cheerful, his companions ask, when we all weep at the desolation of our people? The Rabbi's answer, like Lawrence's, is apocalyptic: if the prophecy that *therefore shall Zion for your sake be plowed as a field* has come true, he says, so likewise will the prophecy that *there shall yet old men and old women sit in the broad places of Jerusalem*. And so I laugh, he says, and my laughter is the promise of a *shalom* that the Roman oppressors cannot plow down.[15]

*

Martyrdom isn't the only way to die, of course. It isn't even the only way to die for your faith. Jewish writers don't typically call Akiva a martyr, though he's executed by the Romans, and they don't typically call others like him martyrs either because, as I've said already, the deaths of these figures are less about bearing witness in the face of Roman opponents and more about confronting the decrees of a holy, inscrutable God. Martyrdom is a specific cultural idea and experience. It tends to produce a specific kind of laughter, triumphant and defiant.

It also raises some specific ethical problems. Think about it. The laughter of a comic prophet such as Lawrence depends on his promises of a kingdom to come—but it also depends on his suffering, and on the people and systems that cause his suffering. His hilarious performance might be a triumph of witness-bearing in the theaters of imperial power, but his story is also hard to stomach. How could it not be, when it represents so graphically his experience of violence and death?

The legends of the early martyrs know perfectly well that the stories they tell are absurd. They know that no sane person would respond to her own torture and murder by laughing. When Perpetua and her friends laughed at the curious onlookers who came to see them the night before their martyrdom, the legend recounts, those onlookers "departed thence astonished."[16] Of course they did. The apostle Andrew smiled as he hung on his cross, and the apocryphal account of his martyrdom reports that one of the believers watching asked, "Why art thou smiling, Andrew, servant of God? Thy laughter makes us mourn and weep, because we are deprived of thee."[17] I'd ask the same question, I expect. All this laughing and merriment depends, after all, on a certain denial. The ordeals of these martyrs are atrocious. How easy is it to accept that Lawrence went down cracking jokes and smelling great? Or that Perpetua didn't even know she was injured in the arena because her joyful ecstasy removed her so completely from the violence at hand? These joyful martyrs seem oddly different from the martyrs who, in the biblical book of Revelation, cry out in agony and are told to wait a little longer. The Perpetua who laughs on the eve of her passion is strikingly different from the Christ who weeps blood on the eve of his. Does the laughter of these martyrs evade something that even Christ himself found inescapable?

This problem is even more difficult in a culture that understands martyrdom as performance. To bear witness is to exercise agency, to take initiative. The martyrs can't be mere passive victims, or they wouldn't be witness-bearers at all. That's one reason why the legends of ancient martyrs insist so loudly that the martyr really *wants* this death. Ignatius forecloses all sorts of possibilities—grief, anger, his own victimhood—when he insists that he's more eager than anyone to get to the arena and make this thing happen. The many martyrs who announce that their persecutors are doing them a favor foreclose those possibilities too. The Syrian martyr Habib is so hot for a martyr's death that he approaches one of the Roman governor's attendants and asks to be arrested. The attendant begs him to go home, and Habib refuses. In which case, who's the real perpetrator of this martyrdom? Habib leaves no room for doubt that it was all his idea.[18]

Like their laughter and pranks, the two-thumbs-up enthusiasm of these martyrs relegates their pain to a kind of unreality. Even in some of the most gruesome passages of the legends, there's a quality of leering or fist-pumping triumph: *and guess what she endured next!* In a text such as the legend of Sharbil, the unflappable gusto of the martyr becomes almost a farce, as the litany of tortures goes on and on and the hero, who would in any ordinary story be dead, just keeps begging for more. They scorch his face, flay his skin, pound nails into his eyes, stick hot lead in his armpits, and hang him upside down in various positions, and Sharbil's miraculous motor-mouth never stops running. An Energizer Bunny or Monty Python Black Knight, he keeps preaching, taunting, and trash-talking all the way through, as if he feels no pain. It's funny, in a way, a joke on a perspiring Roman judge who can't believe this is happening.

My point here is that these scenes of miraculous good cheer have the potential to obscure the reality of the sufferer's pain. When the legends acknowledge that pain, a real tension develops, and the martyr's capacity for laughter comes under threat. Perpetua's legend often comes perilously close to that point, especially in the portions she composed in her own voice, and most of all, perhaps, when she describes her father's grief and her own anguished dreams about the seven-year-old brother she lost to illness many years before. The epistle that narrates the ordeals of Blandina and the martyrs at Lyons, too, is a heartbreaking thing to read, very sensitive to the trembling anguish of these world-defying heroes. To turn around and set the martyr laughing, or to insist that she didn't feel a thing, is to engage in a high-wire act, miraculous or foolish, with the dangers of falsehood and cruelty all around.

That tension is closely related to the inconvenient truth that often troubles comedy. It's harder to laugh, in the context of suffering, when we actually draw close to the pain of the sufferer. If laughter depends on our distance from the pain of those who suffer, is it predicated on a certain kind of denial or dehumanization? We've encountered this question before. Lawrence dies on a gridiron and turns it into a barbecue joke. Richard Pryor lands in a burn unit and comes back doing Pryor-on-fire bits for his audiences, complete with a flaming match. Hannah Gadsby tells a bunch of Gadsby-gets-beaten-up jokes and then turns around and thunders that this pain is *real*. Good luck figuring out when we're supposed to laugh. These performers play by the rules of a game in which the charism of laughter is, paradoxically, granted only to those who step into the arena, ready to give it and take it where it hurts.

*

Even so: the miracle of comedy happens right at the center of this paradox. Comedians invite us to stay within the tension raised by their pain, and to find our way to the possibility of laughter. And the culture that grew up around those early martyrs paid attention both to the reality of their suffering and to their incongruous, inexplicable joy. The legends of the martyrs emphasize their jaunty pranks and laughter partly because they are trying to get at a mystery. How do we explain the miracle of the martyr's gladness? In the centuries since the early legends were written, Christian depictions of martyrs have lived with this question, developing an intricate language for talking about suffering even as the feasts and stories of the martyrs became the basis for holy folly, ritual misbehavior, and carnival mayhem. The pain and the laughter, in those observances, are always intertwined.

The laughter of the dying Lawrence might help to explain why. In his hands, laughter has other powers. It can deny the weight of suffering, yes. But Lawrence's joke about the beggars of Rome and the treasures of the church also asserts the weight of suffering. By naming these beggars for what they are and what they will be—by speaking apocalyptically—Lawrence confronts the present age both with the inconvenient truth of its own sins and with the visionary truth of an eschatological future. His laughter in the face of the Roman prefect is not so much a way of ignoring atrocity as a promise spoken in the midst of atrocity, in defiance of the systems of power on which atrocity depends. As he speaks this promise, the comedian-saint goes out of his way to bait, antagonize, and insult his Roman audience, to arouse maximum discomfort among the comfortable. Like Perpetua, who has prophetic visions of herself overcoming warriors in battle and climbing a ladder to the company of the dead in heaven, he refuses the identity assigned to him within the economy of Roman power, and like many of the martyrs he leaves us with a revelation. Didn't you know? This martyr wasn't a criminal, or a slave, or a woman fresh out of childbirth. He was a prince. She was a warrior. And the death you just watched was also the beginning of a victory.

Lawrence's laughter looks like a denial of suffering, in other words, partly because it feeds on a vitality more powerful than suffering. His hilarity is connected to his citizenship in another kingdom, and in a certain way the hilarity of his ordeal is like the story of the three hermits with which this book began, or like comic stories of a North Pole elf coming to live in contemporary New York or a twelve-year-old kid getting stuck in a grown-up's body. We've all seen the movie in one form or another and so know what happens: this ordinary-seeming body turns out to possess strange powers because it belongs to a whole other world. Around that super-charged body, miracles happen. There are walks on water, doves ascending out of wounds, a guy in a pointy hat throwing snowballs with machine-gun speed. The narrator of Blandina's story says it out loud: "Though she was an insignificant, weak, and despised woman"—that's the body we see—"yet she was clothed with the great and invincible body of Christ."[19] That's the body we don't see—not, at least, until the martyr, in a flash of laughter, lays it bare.

So much for laughter as a waving away of pain. When figures like Lawrence and Perpetua bring laughter as a holy fire, they know full well that they themselves are going to get burned in the bargain. They align themselves with the people who suffer the most in this world—cripples, lepers, beggars, dying children—and they proclaim, against all odds and opposition, that these outcasts will inherit the earth. In that proclamation, they point ahead to a kind of comedy, perilous and strange, that derives its authority from the performer's defiance in the face of corruption and wrong. They suggest that if we learn that defiance, it just might be that our laughter can become something holy, the special possession of those who live in pain but speak in hope.

6

HOLY FOOLS

FROM THECLA IN THE DESERT TO SYMEON IN THE CITY

Sometime in the second half of the sixth century, on a Sunday morning, a man burst into a church service in western Syria. No one in the city of Emesa—modern-day Homs—had seen this man before. He had first appeared in the city just a day earlier, stinking of excrement and dragging a dead dog behind him with a rope. Now he was back, and he came rampaging into the Sunday morning service like the devil himself, blowing out candles and throwing nuts as everyone jumped up in surprise. When a group of parishioners tried to chase him, he leapt up into the pulpit, hurled a few more nuts, and then took off for the door. He slowed down enough on his way out to overturn the tables of some pastry sellers, and they got their hands on him and beat him half to death, as he shouted to himself, "Poor Symeon, if things like this keep happening, you won't live for a week in these people's hands."

For that was his name: Symeon. Soon enough, everyone would know it. He went on to spend the rest of his life in Emesa, building a brand as the city's craziest man. Along the way, the stories of his antics became the stuff of legend. He got a job at a baked-bean shop, where he ate huge piles of the merchandise and gave even more of it away to lucky customers. He got another job carrying hot water at a tavern and became such a popular attraction that the tavern-keeper kept him on, even when he smashed wine-jugs and habitually stopped working to dance in the street. He flirted with prostitutes, pooped in the middle of the marketplace, pranced into churches with big strings of sausage around his neck. In one particularly notorious incident, he stripped his clothes off and burst naked into the women's public bathhouse, where the women beat him and threw him out. And then, after he died, the people who remembered his antics did something that might seem just about as crazy. They canonized him—for real, and without irony—as a saint.

Saint Symeon Salos was in fact the first figure of his kind to be recognized as a saint in the Christian church. He still is a saint (you can buy his icons online or pray to him on his feast day in July), and that fact has never seemed anything other than bizarre. The people of Emesa never really knew what to make of him. It's hard to know what to make of him now. But he represents a way of life that began to take shape in the earliest days of the church and that still haunts our cultural imagination. He also represents a significant chapter in the history of comedy. You can't tell the story of comedy, after all, without telling the story of the holy fool.

*

Christian believers were already talking about the link between holiness and folly when the apostle Paul wrote his biblical letter to the church at Corinth. "For I think that God has exhibited us apostles," he wrote in that letter, "like men sentenced to death; because we have become a spectacle to the world, to angels and to men."[1] Paul thinks of himself and his fellow apostles here as "men sentenced to death"—as martyrs. So it makes sense, given what we know about martyrs, that he also thinks of the apostles as "a spectacle to the world"—in other words, as theatrical performers. The Greek word that many English translations render here as "spectacle" is *theatron*. The apostle is a *theater*, a site for the display of something, and the word translated "has exhibited" comes from the verb *apodeiknynai* (to put on a show), a word that often, in the ancient Greek-speaking world, indicated what actors do on a stage.[2] In using this language, Paul seems to say that the apostles are holy players on the stage of this world, acting out spectacles of death like convicts in the Roman arena. As their chief performer, he knows very well that to bear witness is to act something out, to be made a theater. And from this profession of a theatrical calling, he goes right on to make a declaration that will resonate seismically through the history of holy folly: "We are fools," he says, "for Christ's sake."[3]

Commentators have sometimes read this statement as a sarcastic retort to skeptics who fancy themselves wise: *If that's what wisdom means, then I must be a fool.* So it is. But Paul's language also suggests something more. The word translated "fools" here is, in the Greek, *mōros*.[4] That Greek word often referred to the social type of the low-born buffoon (it's the parent of the English word "moron"), and some scholars have proposed that in the context of the theatrical language Paul has just used, *mōros* might suggest a particular kind of performer, the "fool" who specialized in playing buffoons in the ancient theatrical art known as "mime."[5] Paul must at least have been aware of that possibility. Mime plays were immensely popular in the regions where he worked. Everyone from aristocrats and philosophers to slaves and laborers loved them. In cities such as Corinth, these shows were everywhere to be found, both in the streets and in the established theaters where much of civic life took place.

"Mime" in the ancient world doesn't mean what it means to us: silent clowns with stripey shirts stuck in invisible boxes. The mime plays of the ancient world were full of talking and noise. And by all accounts, they were just ridiculous: dirty, farcical, romping, rude, sometimes brilliant in their verbal wit, often scandalous in their theater of sex and violence. The performers of mime plays, unlike the performers of theatrical comedy, appeared on stage unmasked (sometimes unclothed), and their plots and performances tended to evoke the ground-level textures of contemporary life. In the context of these plays, the *mōros* was a secondary performer, a foil to the arch-mime. He presented himself as a ragged figure, a vagrant trickster on the fringes of society, and in the course of the show he provoked, parodied, and took abuse from the main performers. Sometimes he was visibly atypical or disabled. Sometimes he carried a stick while he performed, and part of the drama depended on everyone's knowledge that eventually he'd get beaten with it. Sometimes—including in some of the most popular mime plays of the first century—he got himself crucified in the end, his fake blood gushing in ludicrous profusion all over the stage.[6]

There must have been a strange *frisson*, and perhaps a shadow of reality, in these farces of crucifixion. Roman crucifixion was, after all, already a kind of theater. Public executions happened on the same playbills as theatrical games and entertainments. And the distinctions between criminals and theatrical performers in imperial Rome were never absolute, because actors (like gladiators and prostitutes) had sold their bodies for public use and so, in the eyes of the law, had a legal status similar to slaves. They were beaten and punished so often by irate Roman officials that the emperor Augustus had to institute measures to protect them. The indignities they endured might help to explain the litany of confessions Paul goes on to make just after he has identified himself as a fool for Christ: "we are weak"; "we are hungry and thirsty"; "we are ill-clad and buffeted and homeless"; "we have become, and now are, as the refuse of the world, the offscouring of all things."[7] The fools of the theater were all those things too: ragged and beaten and hung up on crosses for everyone to howl at. If Paul really does mean to include himself in their company, it might make sense that he goes on to call himself the scum of the world. It might well be that for Paul, devotee of the cross, the pain suffered by the fools put them in touch with something powerful and real.

Paul, in other words, might mean to express a genuine sense of calling when he takes up the title of fool. And he might be expressing more than just sarcasm when he beckons his disciples in Corinth, too, to fashion themselves as fools, nailed to crosses and dead to the world. "The word of the cross is folly," as he says here, not just because the clever people don't get it, but because crosses are for fools, and only a fool would identify with a man who hung on one.[8] Paul is willing to name himself as a fool because he has seen in the spectacle of the crucified messiah the world-inverting revelation that "God chose what is low and despised in the world, even things that are not, to bring to nothing things that are."[9] So he commits himself to being a thing that is not, in imitation of the total emptying (theologians, following Paul's Greek term, call this emptying *kenōsis*) of the God who submitted to become the refuse of the world. To practice folly, for this apostle of the cross, is to follow Christ's descent into abasement, emboldened by the hope that the "the foolishness of God is wiser than men, and the weakness of God is stronger than men." He urges his Corinthian readers to believe that the paradoxes of the cross—of power in weakness and wisdom in folly—are the only hope of bearing witness against the false power and deceptive wisdom of the present age. "If any one of you thinks he is wise in this age," then it's time, Paul says, to remember the calling: "Let him become a fool that he may become wise."[10]

From the beginning, sober-minded interpreters of Paul have been wary of taking his praise of folly too literally. But not all interpreters are sober-minded. Already in the legends of the early martyrs, there are hints at a notion of witness-bearing as a wild and wonderful sort of antic performance. It's hard not to see elements of mime-show folly in the spectacles of Polycarp paraded through

Smyrna on a donkey, of quick-witted prisoners in verbal contests with pompous officials, and of women, slaves, and disabled beggars stealing the thunder of powerful men. Some of these images of folly, such as the donkey-riding, might have been attempts by the Roman stage managers themselves to paint the martyrs as theatrical fools. When the prefect in Lawrence's story realizes that he's been pranked and pronounces his judgment, he assures the laughing deacon that he's going to face the consequences of this *strophas cavillo mimico*, this "mime-jester's trick."[11]

Those words are supposed to be an insult, but some of the first Christians who read the legend might have regarded the prefect as speaking more truth than he knows. Lawrence is a mime or jester of holiness, a prankster of the cross. At about the time the poet Prudentius wrote Lawrence's story, near the turn of the fifth century, small armies of spiritual pilgrims were retreating into the deserts of Egypt, Turkey, and Syria, and these pilgrims increasingly referred to their practices of holiness as expressions of *mōria*, of folly. The *Sayings of the Desert Fathers*, which gathers various pieces of fourth- and fifth-century lore from the desert communities of Egypt, recounts the story of a good elder who instructed a young child in the ways of holiness. "When somebody reviles you, bless him," the elder said, "and if you are sitting at a table, eat what is decaying and leave what is good, and if you are to choose a garment, leave the good one and take the one that is worn out." The child was taken aback and retorted, "Am I a fool, that you tell me to behave like that?" And the elder replied, "I am telling you to do those things for this reason: that you may become a fool for the Lord's sake."[12]

Stories of fools for the Lord's sake circulated throughout the fifth century, not just in Egypt but also in Turkey and in Syria, where the holy figures who went into the hills and mountains were famously solitary and strange.[13] Those who traveled to see them found a special charisma in figures such as the mad nun Isidora, who never ate anything but the crumbs dropped by others at the table; the holy vagrant Sarapion Sindonites, who once strolled around Rome completely naked; and the famous Syrian ascetic Symeon Stylites (no relation to the other Symeon we've met), who climbed up onto a fifty-foot column and stayed there for over thirty years. In the presence of these holy weirdos, the stories say, those with eyes to see were struck with wonder. The power in Isadora's folly was revealed when a visiting holy man fell at her feet and cried out in the presence of her fellow nuns, "She is your mother and mine."[14]

These figures don't quite get us to the practice of holy folly as a form of theater, but they get us pretty close. Symeon Stylites, especially, was a fantastic showman, one of the biggest attractions in Syria. For decades in the early fifth century, pilgrims flocked from all over to watch as he preached twice a day, worked miracles, heard petitions, handed down judgments, and did toe-touches by the millions at the top of his column. Queens and kings sent envoys to ask Symeon's blessing and bring reports of his antics. The bishop Theodoret, who journeyed to Symeon's column and wrote about what he saw, tells of a man standing next to him in the crowd who tried to count the great saint's toe-touches one day but gave up when he reached 1,244.[15] The holy acrobat's circus in the sky was a vivid realization of Paul's claim about the apostle as a *theatron* of suffering, and the success of his performances spurred a whole movement of *stylites* (from the Greek word *stylos*, pillar), saints who mounted years-long productions from the tops of their very tall stages. In the miracles and jackass shows of these holy performers, the boundaries between the fool for Christ and the fool of the theater seemed to dissolve. And it wasn't just the stylites who made it hard to tell where the holiness ended and the jackassery began. Sarapion Sindonites had blurred the boundary in his own way a few years earlier, when he kicked off his ministry by selling himself to a troupe of actors. The holy duo Theophilus and Maria would do it again a few decades later, disguising themselves as a mime and a prostitute and performing what their biographer John of Amida called "drolleries and buffooneries" in every city they visited.[16] What to make of that? Was Sarapion really an actor while he was with that troupe? Or was he just acting?

In the decades after the death of Symeon Stylites in 459, fools for Christ would come to establish a whole way of life at the heart of that ambiguity. These figures were seized by folly, crazy with the madness of the cross; and at the same time, they were faking it, shrewd performers playing at a mime-jester's art. By the end of the fifth century, a new Greek word—*salos* or *sala*—had come into widespread use to name a person called to this paradoxical folly. The word comes pretty much out of nowhere and probably originated, many scholars think, in a bit of derogatory slang, a slur meaning something like "wacko" or "nut job."[17] Even as *salos* came to mean "holy fool," the word retained its derogatory force, and the fools for Christ embraced it with all the more gusto for that, taking it upon themselves like a mantle, or a cross.

*

So they are performers, and they are weird, and they want to align their weirdness with the surprising fact of the crucified messiah. That's more or less what I've said. But there's more to say about the holy fools. If we pay real attention to the content of their performances, we might begin to understand better why it is that a whole culture came to regard folly as a spiritual path. There are two figures who express the meaning of holy folly with particular clarity. One of these figures, Symeon of Emesa, represents the end of this early tradition, the moment when holy fools matured into real live saints. (I'll come back to him.) The other represents its beginning.

We don't know whether Thecla of Iconium actually existed. She's a strange phenomenon, a person who might be a fiction and who was nevertheless one of the most prominent heroes of the early

Christian church. When her spiritual journey began—so the story goes—she was eighteen years old, good-looking and naïve, soon to be married to a man who was very pleased indeed about the match. She probably didn't strike anyone in her first-century community as a fool in the making. But in a turn of events that would change her life, her home city of Iconium (the modern-day Konya, in southwest Turkey) was paid a visit by the apostle Paul.

According to the earliest written version of the story, a second-century text called *The Acts of Paul and Thecla*, Paul set up shop in the house of a guy named Onesiphorus, where he proclaimed to everyone who would listen the blessings of an uncommon form of life: "blessed are they that have kept aloof from this world, for they shall be called upright"; "blessed are they that have wives as not having them, for they shall have God as their portion"; "blessed are the bodies of the virgins, for they shall be well pleasing to God, and shall not lose the reward of their chastity."[18] In these apocalyptic beatitudes, the apostle (or an apocryphal version of him) preached a gospel of renunciation, a gospel against the values of the ordinary world. He called his listeners to enact the coming kingdom in the theater of the everyday, in their marriages and social lives and bodies. And he issued a radical call—arguably very different from the call of Jesus's beatitudes—to become aloof: free of attachments, resolute in sexlessness, living already like the resurrected saints who, as Jesus had prophesied, "neither marry nor are given in marriage, but are like angels in heaven."[19]

Thecla, as the *Acts* tells it, wasn't invited into the house, but she found a spot outside a window and sat there listening, first for hours and then for days. For three days and nights, she didn't eat or drink; she wouldn't move or speak. She was utterly rapt. Her mother saw what was happening and sent for Thecla's fiancée, a prominent man of the city named Thamyris. Together they went to Thecla where she sat entranced, and there they implored her, kissed her, wept for her, shuddered with a newfound fear of her.[20] But she did not move a muscle. She was, her mother said to her, "like a mad woman," caught up in the spell of some enchantment or insanity.[21] So Thamyris, the fiancée, raised up a mob, and a classic spectacle of early Christian martyrdom began to unfold. Paul was hauled before a proconsul and thrown into prison. Thecla bribed her way into the prison and sat at Paul's feet, "enchained by affection."[22] Both were brought before a tribunal as a crowd heckled and clamored, and both had to bear witness in a spectacle of public examination. Paul engaged with the officials and got himself ejected from the city. But some sort of strangeness was stirring in Thecla. Still entranced, she refused to speak, and her own mother made the fatal pronouncement: "Burn the wretch; burn in the midst of the theatre her that will not marry, in order that all the women that have been taught by this man might be afraid."[23]

And so Thecla's great performance began. The gathered crowd "went forth to the spectacle of Thecla," the *Acts* says, and the virgin was brought into the theater fully naked, her body so powerful in its effect—the text doesn't clarify whether its power was erotic or heavenly—that even the Roman governor wept to see it. The virgins of the city brought smoldering embers to light a fire under her. She made the sign of the cross and climbed up onto the pyre. And then, just as the flames began to engulf her, God sent a miracle. Specifically, he sent rain, in the form of a sudden cloudburst that doused the fire and saved Thecla from harm.

It wouldn't be her last miracle. Freed by the authorities in Iconium, she found her way to Paul out on the road, and together they went to Antioch, where she aggressively rebuffed the sexual assault of a high official (she yanked his crown off and tore his cloak) and got herself hauled before a Roman governor yet again. This time she was sentenced to death by wild beasts. And this time, more even than the last, a whole world of miracles sprang into being around her. When Thecla went into the arena the first time, the lioness appointed to destroy her became docile and licked her feet. When she went into the arena for the second time (naked again, save for a loincloth), everything went topsy-turvy. A lioness killed the other lions unleashed upon her. A bolt of lightning killed a pack of woman-eating seals (yes, seals) that was about to devour her. A cloud of fire enveloped her naked body. And as these miracles unfolded, the women in the crowd came around to Thecla's side, throwing herbs and perfumes into the arena and cheering so loudly for her "that the foundations of the theatre were shaken by their voice."[24] It was all so excruciating for the officials presiding that the libidinous Roman who had started the whole ordeal begged the governor to "have mercy both on me and the city" and let this woman go.[25]

The whole spectacle of Thecla in the theater is funny in the way that the show-stealing mayhem of the martyrs is often funny. She belongs to the same history of comic laughter as Perpetua, Lawrence, and the other topsy-turvy performance artists of the early Christian martyrdom legends. But this martyr is also different, because she walked away from her ordeal. The officials did indeed let her go, and she began the work of figuring out what it means to sustain martyrdom into a way of life.

Where does one start? Thecla started by putting on the clothes of a man, giving her possessions to the poor, letting Paul know that she had no need of baptism (because, she said, I was baptized in the arena when I plunged into the water with the woman-eating seals), and heading out to the desert. In the wilderness outside her native city of Iconium, she crafted a form of life beyond the laws and necessities of the secular world. She didn't need food: she subsisted for seventy-two years on water and herbs. She didn't need shelter: she lived in a hole in a rock. Perhaps, if her man's clothes are any indication, she didn't need gender: she inhabited the kingdom Paul had preached, in which marriage becomes obsolete and "there is neither male nor female."[26] And she didn't even need baptism, because she lived beyond the sacramental economy that sustains the church in this present age. Freed from all these laws of mortal life, she became strange, and the miracles of her martyrdom became the anti-gravitational field in which she lived every day.

Martyrdom doesn't necessarily lend itself to a sustainable practice of holiness, or of comic theater, or of anything else. The performances of the early martyrs were necessarily one-night-only sorts of events. Thecla's story represents something different, an early stage in the development of martyrdom as a code to live by. Where she went, people followed. The *Acts* says that many people went with her out of Antioch, and throughout the seventy-two years of her sojourn in the desert, pilgrims flocked to her little cave to hear her teaching. The daily ordeal of her desert life invested her with such charisma that when, at the end of her career, others again tried to exert force against her, they found that they could hardly touch her at all. Offended that she was stealing their business, a group of physicians from the city came out to the ninety-year-old Thecla's cave with the intention of sexually violating her and so destroying the source of her sacred power. It was a buffoonishly bad plan. When they seized her, she spoke to them with thunderous serenity—"You cannot"—addressed a final prayer to God, stepped into a cleft that opened miraculously in the rock, and was gone. "Thus, then, suffered," says the *Acts*, "the first martyr of God, and apostle, and virgin, Thecla."[27] She had performed to the utmost in her theater of living martyrdom, a spectacular witness to the end.

*

Or so the story goes. Plenty of scholars have assumed that Thecla didn't really exist. Some have thought there might be a kernel of truth in the stories ancient Christians told about the long-haul martyr of Iconium.[28] Either way, these stories traveled far and fast. Way over in Carthage, at the end of the second century, the theologian Tertullian commented on the influence of Thecla's legend, and it's likely that the text of the *Acts* was already circulating by that point, seventy-five years or so after the purported time of her death.[29] Some scholars think the written account in the *Acts* shows signs of having origins in oral tradition, in stories passed around at least partly among communities of women.[30] By the middle of the third century, Thecla's little cave in southern Turkey had become a shrine, the Hagia Thekla, that attracted both a permanent community of monastics and a steady traffic of international pilgrims. It might be a stretch to say, as one scholar has, that Thecla's popularity "rivalled that of Mary in the early church," but her story clearly exerted tremendous magnetic force.[31] Thecla drew women, especially—women such as the second-century fire-breathers Maximilla and Priscilla, who left their husbands to become wandering prophets, and the fifth-century Syrian ascetics Marana and Cyra, who journeyed from Beroea to the Hagia Thekla without eating a thing—out from the structures of ordinary life.

Thecla's story offers a clue about the meaning of holy folly. Her peculiar form of living seems to have been, ultimately, a kind of martyrdom. And sure enough, in the period from the second century, when Thecla's cult began to spread, to the fifth century, when Theodoret, the bishop of Cyrrhus, wrote up the lives of the ascetics he had met in his travels around Syria, Christian believers journeying into the desert increasingly thought of themselves as martyrs. The Greek word *askēsis* means training, practice, or profession, and these pioneers in holy asceticism were artists of martyrdom, professionals in the daily practice of dying to this world. They offered the ordinary people around them a picture of something that seemed central and indispensable, a live connection to the surprise, and the power, of the cross.

But that's only part of the picture. Thecla's story also has the first whispers of something else, a kind of personhood that would come fully into view in the lives of the fools who followed her. Her refusal to marry and to enter into the structures of ordinary life suggests a citizenship in some other life, a kingdom on the other side of martyrdom. That citizenship is key to the lives of the vagrants and mischief-makers who invented holy folly, and it will be key to the lives of the many hilarious figures who have followed them. Its distinctive contours are especially clear in the life of Symeon of Emesa, the strangest saint of them all.

*

Pretty much everything we know or imagine about Symeon comes from an account written in the 640s by Leontius, the bishop of Neapolis (modern-day Limassol) in southern Cyprus. *The Life of Symeon the Fool* was, as far as anyone knows, the first full-length biography ever written about a holy fool, and in its opening paragraphs Leontius throws down a gauntlet, pushing to the foreground the question pretty much any sane person is bound to ask upon reading about a wacko like Symeon. I know, Leontius says, that "to those more impassioned and more fleshly he seemed to be a defilement, a sort of poison, and an impediment"; and I know, he says, that most of you, my readers, will dismiss this man as an affront to your standards of virtue. But what if? What if Symeon was such a consummate artist of holiness, so minutely disciplined and developed, that the respectable citizens of the present age were bound to miss the meaning of his act? And what kinds of deaths would you have to die, my respectable reader, Leontius asks, to see this holy shock artist—who "spat upon all the softness and sentiment of life as on a spider"—with eyes wide open?[32] Can you follow where Symeon went?

That's Leontius's opening move, more or less. Clearly whatever comes next isn't going to be easy.

It all began when Symeon was twenty-two years old, a pampered boy who still slept with his mother every night. The two of them traveled to Jerusalem that year to celebrate the Feast of the Exaltation, a Christian holiday observed on September 14. In the holy city Symeon met a young guy called John, who was traveling with his new wife and his father, and the two of them became fast friends. When the feast was done, the two families decided to travel back to Syria together, and one day on the road, in a weird moment of mutual awakening, Symeon asked John if it was possible to see the "angels of God" who lived in the monasteries they passed along the Jordan River. John replied that yes, it was possible, "if we become like them."[33] So the two friends pretended they needed to find a place to poo, sneaked away from their group, took the road back toward Jerusalem, wandered into a monastery that had its front door open, and came under the care of a monk named Nikon, who spent just two days instructing and outfitting them before the pair was ready to begin their ascetic life.

Symeon and John learned in new ways, in that monastery, to regard themselves as children—"remember how we are orphaned," they implored Nikon before they set out—and they fared forward from there with no idea of where they were going, a couple of wayward innocents exposed to the world.[34] They walked until they hit the Dead Sea and stumbled upon a place where a holy hermit had died just a few days before. There they set up shop, and for twenty-nine years they practiced the interior disciplines of holiness, praying in silence for days on end, doing battle with the devil in their thoughts and dreams, and receiving gifts of mystical insight and miracle-working power. Both had visions in which they spoke with the loved ones they had left behind—Symeon accompanied his mother as she made the passage through death—and both endured such deprivations, agonies, and ecstasies that they came to transcend the laws of mortal life.[35] When Symeon spoke to his mother in the moment of her death, he assured her that she could "go to the King" because, he said, "I have asked him for help, and he has prepared for you a lovely place."[36] It was as if that other place was his own native country already. After twenty-nine years of establishing his citizenship in that far-off kingdom, Symeon had become so other to this world, Leontius says, that he "perceived himself fearing neither suffering, nor cold, nor hunger, nor burning heat, but rather nearly exceeded the limit of human nature."[37] He was fifty-one now, and he had achieved the anti-gravity, the miraculous untouchability, of the martyr.

That's when the calling to folly came.

The vocation seems to have hit Symeon like a lightning bolt. One day he got to his feet and said to John that he had to leave the desert. It's time, he said, to let our light shine before men. John objected strenuously, but Symeon spoke with the authority of a man who could see the road laid out before him: "I will go in the power of Christ," he said. "I will mock the world."[38] It's hard to know exactly what he meant by that promise, and in his movements from this point there's something shrouded, something strange. He went to Jerusalem and visited the holy places there; he headed north at a determined clip with John trailing sadly behind him; and finally he forced John to go back to the desert and then approached, alone, the Syrian city of Emesa. Why this particular city? How did he determine what his mission there would be? And what *was* his mission there? No one would ever really be able to say.

Somewhere outside the city, with some new intention stirring to life within him, he made his way to a dung heap. There he found a dead dog, tied his rope-belt around its foot, and sprinted into the city through a gate near a children's school, the stinking carcass dragging behind him. The kids had seen crazy people come in from the desert before—they knew what to do. As if on cue, they shouted, "Hey, a crazy abba!" and then they mobbed him, chasing him through the streets and trying to beat him around the ears. It must have been, from his perspective, a pretty successful first day on the job.

The next day was the Sunday of his grand public entrance, when he burst into the church and got himself beaten up by the pastry sellers, and from there he would go on to his many feats of bean eating, street pooping, and rule-breaking mayhem. In time, his whole life became a citywide spectacle, and though there's no indication that he ever stepped on a stage, he managed to become a celebrity entertainer, Emesa's highest-profile, lowest-budget mime. The most striking thing about Symeon's career in folly, though, is how much of his work took place in private, in encounters that happened in back alleys and behind bedroom doors. When one of the great men of the city fell desperately ill, Symeon appeared to him in a dream and told him he would die if he didn't stop defiling his wife's bed with unfaithfulness. When a young man secretly fornicated with a married woman and was possessed by a demon, Symeon caught him in private, punched the demon out of him, and declared, "Commit adultery no more, wretch."[39] In one particularly bewildering episode, Symeon went to a mime show, heard one of the performers saying scurrilous things, secretly threw a pebble that caused the man's hand to wither, and then appeared to him in a dream to call him to repentance. We might have thought he would regard this dirty-talking performer as a colleague; but Symeon, in secret, was here to do another kind of talking.

Stories like these pile up in Symeon's life, in encounter after encounter. Underneath the public antics, the core of his act turns out to have been intensely interpersonal. He had a way of looking into people's inward thoughts, stalking the back alleys of their dreams and fantasies. He taunted and teased and brought secrets to light. In one particularly unsettling incident, a servant girl got knocked up by a circus performer and told everyone, in her panic, that the fool Symeon had raped her. It was just the kind of charade he loved. He played along with leering glee, pampering the pregnant girl with meat and pickled fish, calling her "my wife" and enduring abuse from everyone who knew her. At the climactic moment, when the baby wouldn't come to birth, the fool danced and clapped his hands, proclaiming, "By Jesus, by Jesus, wretch, the child won't come out from there till she says who its father is."[40] She said who it was; and the baby came; and everyone was astonished, unsure whether this man was a demoniac or a prophet.

In each of these personal encounters, the sinners Symeon confronted began to understand his power, which meant that they came to see that he, too, had a secret. His covert holiness was not for the world to know about, and he charged everyone who caught a glimpse of it to say nothing. In some cases, whistleblowers and skeptics actually tried to find him out and expose him, and Symeon fought back with extreme force, striking them mute, confusing their senses, and threatening them into silence. Once he grabbed a hot wine jug and burned the lips of two monks so that they couldn't talk. Another time, a man who had spent time watching Symeon and "seen what was in his heart" miraculously lost the use of his tongue every time he tried to tell anyone about it.[41] Leontius, who tells all these stories in his seventh-century biography, regards Symeon's secrecy as more or less a functional explanation for his wild behavior. "And his every prayer," Leontius says, "was that his works might be hidden until his departure from this life, so that he might escape human glory, through which human arrogance and conceit arises"—which is to say that his folly and his secrecy were both just ways of staying humble.[42]

Maybe. But the stories Leontius tells about Symeon also suggest that his folly was something more profound than a ruse designed to avoid human glory. There was both a prophetic quality and a tender intimacy in Symeon's encounters with the people of Emesa.

He spoke their secrets to them, they spoke his to him, and both were bound in a relationship of mutual knowing. It's no accident that the confessions Symeon orchestrated so often revolved around sexual infidelity and sexual desire, and it's no accident, either, that he so often showed up in the dreams of his victims, stalking them like a holy Freddy Krueger. He did his work in the most intimate places of human life, places the respectable citizens of Emesa couldn't talk about at parties. When he danced with the girls in the circus, Leontius says, "the disreputable women threw their hands into his lap, fondled him, poked him, and pinched him," through all of which "the monk, like pure gold, was not defiled at all."[43] He had, in the desert, been freed from bodily desire partly for the sake of this very intimacy. He could draw close to the desires and bodies of others as no one else dared. In one of his secret ministries, he would pay dancing girls to be his girlfriends, on the condition that they had to be faithful to him; if they cheated on him, he somehow *knew*, eerily and immediately, and would ask the virgin Mary to strike them down with demons and diseases.

So let's just say there wasn't a lot of cheating, not by his girlfriends, and not by the countless others from whom he extracted promises to stop beating servants or performing in scurrilous shows or fornicating with neighbors. One by one, the people of Emesa became his faithful intimates, bound to him by a knowledge that they couldn't have guessed their neighbors also shared. When they danced with him in the streets or ate sausages with him in church—when they consented to laugh along with him—they helped to perpetuate his fool's disguise and became part of the act. And they also, in this feigning, expressed something true, a giddy fellowship rooted in a shared subterranean life. Around the acts of this fool, Emesa became a city with a secret, a knowledge swelling to strength in the hearts of many and waiting for the day of revelation to arrive.

Throughout his time in Emesa, Symeon's one real friend was a guy called John the deacon (not to be confused with the other John, Symeon's friend in the desert), who understood his antics and talked frankly with him about his mission and his methods. In his private moments with John, Symeon offered hints about the secret at the heart of his career, the thing that provoked his holy laughter. When John asked Symeon how it felt to storm the women's bathhouse, Symeon replied, "I felt neither that I had a body nor that I had entered among bodies, but the whole of my mind was on God's work."[44] It was for the same reason, Leontius adds, that Symeon would drop his pants right in the middle of the marketplace: because "he was above the burning which is from the Devil," a man living already beyond the realities of sexual desire or bodily shame.[45] He could, in other words, do the things he did because he had traveled already, through his living martyrdom, to a world on the other side of death. No surprise, perhaps, that Symeon burned with a particular vitality when death came near. In one chilling set of encounters, just before the outbreak of a plague, Symeon went around to the children of the city, kissing certain of them and telling their teachers to go easy on them, "for they have a long way to go."[46] It was funny, sort of, and the kids and teachers ridiculed and beat him for his weirdo antics. But sure enough, when the plague came, death took every one of the children he had kissed. He had, it seemed, been on watch the whole time along the borders of mortal life, bearing in his kisses both the grace of blessing and the power of death.

Because he came as the emissary of a kingdom beyond death, Symeon's laughter was always tinged with a distinctive sort of violence, both apocalyptic and oddly childish. He addressed pretty much everyone, from schoolteachers and civic officials to his old desert comrade John, as "idiot." In one gloves-off cage match with a bunch of rude schoolgirls, he made several of the girls go permanently cross-eyed. In another he started smashing the wares of a Jewish glassblower until the guy agreed to make the sign of the cross. It all looks like toddler-grade mayhem, except that Symeon also brought to these encounters a genuinely powerful prophetic fury. He took a special interest in those possessed by demons, and he would sometimes spend time with them outside the city, doing battle with their invisible oppressors until the demons cried out, "O violence, fool, you jeer at the whole world. Have you also come by to give us trouble?"[47] And of course he had. He was God's little angel, come to give everyone trouble.

That's the key thing about Symeon's theater of folly: it came from the same place, and belonged to the same disciplines of ascetic violence, as his long silence in the desert. As he fondled prostitutes and took beatings, Symeon entered into a shame, a daily practice of death, very close to the "mortification" that Leontius says he perfected during his desert sojourn. He got close with those who had to endure humiliation in the moral economy of sixth-century Emesa—the prostitutes, the hypocrites, the Jews, the demoniacs, the beggars, the idiots, the bad employees—and he blurred the boundaries between these suffering sinners and his own suffering self. By meeting the people of Emesa with both blistering confrontation and bouncing hilarity, he somehow managed to offer these sinners a little piece of the innocence that he knew, prophetically, to be his. He embodied, right before their eyes, the transfigurations of an age to come.

It's an absurdity, or a miracle: one minute he's streaking in the streets, and the next he's praying with such passion that balls of fire shoot from his hands and demons run screaming. Somehow those two lives were one, and he really did mean it when he said his naked romp in the women's bath was not naughtiness but prophecy, a sign of his citizenship in a kingdom beyond the desires of the body. The whole premise of his fool's career was that the bawdy dances and freaky pronouncements were themselves disciplines of the desert, the work of the same fool for Christ who shivered in his hut night after night, "drenching the ground with his tears," as Leontius says, and journeying into the deep places of spiritual knowledge and need.[48]

*

Symeon's gonzo antics contain the blueprints for much of what has happened in the long history of mischief-making comedians. He's the ancestor of a line of put-on artists that includes modern performers such as Pat Paulsen, Andy Kaufman, Sacha Baron Cohen, Diane Morgan, and Kate Berlant. When Paulsen announced his first presidential run in 1968, or when Kaufman started a brawl on the set of *Fridays* during a live broadcast in 1981, the laughter they provoked was laced with bewilderment: *What did we just see? Was it real?* Kate Berlant orchestrates a similar play of layered illusions in much of her stand-up work, where she tends to perform herself performing and leaves us with no certainty about whether or where the real Kate Berlant is to be found. In her 2022 special *Cinnamon in the Wind*, she has a bit near the end where she reveals that she has a very big secret—"My name is Megan, redacted for my privacy, but I'm actually the chief research analyst for behavioral science at Cornell University"—and then reaches up to pull off her Kate Berlant mask, which of course does not come off because it's not a mask, except that maybe, really, it is. Symeon's artistry is remarkably similar to a comic act like this one, with its layers of misdirection, its blurring of the boundaries between the comedian and her masks, and its hints that under all this performing there is a secret child, wide-eyed and frightened. And he also has kinship with a wide range of modern performers who have made comedy by fashioning their own faces into masks. His "Symeon Salos" persona is like Lincoln Perry's "Stepin Fetchit," Steve Martin's "Wild and Crazy Guy," or Stephen Colbert's Comedy Central–era "Stephen Colbert," an alter ego who expresses something of the performer's own manic identity. It's like Sarah Silverman being "Sarah Silverman" or Dave Chappelle being "Dave Chappelle," saying unbelievable things and leaving us to wonder whether that was really Dave talking? Or was it "Dave" talking? And what, exactly, is the difference?

Like these other performers, Symeon provoked laughter by acting out his most extreme possible selves, journeying out to the points at which the extremes of corruption converge with extremes of innocence. In his highwire act of demented holiness he performed much of the conventional material of comedy, ancient and modern: the abusive rants, the troglodytic rudeness, the pokes in the eye, the farts in church, the flabby nakedness, the over-indulgences, the displays of sheer mystical weirdness. Leontius reports at the end of his biography of Symeon that after the great fool had died, his body vanished from its grave (the dead Charlie Chaplin would replicate this final flourish of stage magic many centuries later). But he has also never entirely gone away. His folly connects the lived martyrdom of Thecla and her first imitators to the lives of prophets, hermits, healers, minstrels, vagrants, and visionaries across a wide cultural expanse in the centuries that follow. His charism of sacred laughter is there in Russian fools such as Procopius, who wandered naked in the regions around thirteenth-century Ustyug looking for a mysterious "homeland," and Italian fools such as the sixteenth-century priest Philip Neri, who once showed up at a ceremony in his honor with half his beard shaved off. It's there in the wild people and holy wanderers who proliferate around the margins of Irish monasticism, living in trees, licking the noses of lepers, and standing in frigid water to pray.[49] It's there in the revels of the boy bishops and lords of misrule who presided over the later medieval festivities of Christmas and Carnival, enacting pageants of eschatological reversal and renewal. And it's there in the career of a religious insurgent such as Francis of Assisi, who translated his identity as a fool for Christ into surprising forms of holy laughter.

Some historians of Christianity have observed that figures and movements such as these tend to flourish at times when the church is politically and economically ascendant, and when the interests of the Christian community converge with the interests of empire.[50] I might add that holy fools have flourished most of all in moments when the logic of holiness gets entangled with the logic of war, and when the church exercises power in accordance with the laws of scarcity, competition, and exclusion. Against the imperatives of security and strength, the holy fools proclaim a kingdom of and for the weak, in which littleness is strength and outcasts turn out to be children of the Most High. Because their enactments of this upside-down world make for such good and hilarious theater, these holy innocents have a close family relationship with whole traditions of comic performers: with the jugglers, minstrels, ballad-mongers, and "naturals" who built the culture of professional clowning in medieval Europe; with the entertainers who journeyed from those motley ranks into the theaters of early modern London, Venice, Naples, and Paris; with the minstrel-show and vaudeville clowns of the New World; and with all the comedians who have taken up the work of enacting a childhood that makes the grown-up world look strange.

Interlude
Rites of Renewal

The theatrical art form that the Greeks first called "comedy" came, in time, to be called "Old Comedy." The ancient Greeks gave this name to the comic plays of Aristophanes and his fifth-century contemporaries because in the following century, in the hands of the playwright Menander, another sort of comic drama began to develop. The Greeks called this sort of drama "New Comedy."

It's easy to see the links between Old Comedy and the ritual culture of ancient Greek religious festivals. Old Comedy is wild and weird, raucous and discontinuous, full of dancing and phalluses and wild provocations. It smells like folk festivity, and its plots and gags are closely connected to old practices of ritual mockery and Dionysian ecstasy.

New Comedy is a different story. Unlike Old Comedy, this new sort of drama is organized not around episodes of rambunctious clowning but around a single plot. It is urban and domestic in its values, often concerned with family conflicts, with lovers trying to get together, with the schemes and antics of clever slaves. It also happens to be immensely important for the later development of comic literature and drama. The history of New Comedy is, to a large degree, the history of theatrical comedy at large. Menander's artistic descendants include not just his many Greek and Roman imitators but also Shakespeare and Molière, Jane Austen and Oscar Wilde, *Ferris Bueller's Day Off* and *When Harry Met Sally*. It probably goes without saying that New Comedy is a more secular artistic medium than Old Comedy. Ferris Bueller lives a long way from the ancient world of religious ritual and apocalyptic vision.

Or so it seems. But New Comedy has its own ritual shape and its own tremors of religious longing. If you know where to look, you can find them in unexpected places. Since New Comedy is built around plots, and since those plots are always more or less the same, let's consider a textbook specimen. Here's the ritual anatomy of a comic drama.

Our specimen is *A Midsummer Night's Dream*; the setting is the Athens of the ancient hero Theseus. In its opening scene, the play establishes this city as a world of law and order, presided over by authority figures possessed of age, status, and rigorous moral sensibilities. Prominent among these authority figures is a father, Egeus, who refuses to allow his daughter to marry the man she loves. The play begins with Egeus asking Theseus to pronounce a severe sentence upon his daughter—death, or a nunnery—if she does not bend to her father's will. This is how comic plots tend to begin: with someone, usually young, who possesses vitality and desire, and with someone else, usually older, who enacts a law that obstructs desire and suppresses the young protagonist's vitality. (The great literary critic Northrop Frye calls this person the "blocking character.")[1] Think about Shakespeare's comic plays. *As You Like It* begins with a decree of exile; *The Merchant of Venice* begins both with the signing of a legal bond and the oppressive terms of a dead man's will; *Measure for Measure* and *Comedy of Errors* both begin with the handing down of a death sentence; *Twelfth Night* and *Love's Labours Lost* both begin with young people who enforce their own celibacy for a fixed number of years. Here, in *Midsummer*, the young lovers Hermia and Lysander have their celibacy enforced for them. In every case, a law is established, and it is a law that opposes life, a law that knows nothing of eros, innocence, or youthful longing.

So Hermia and Lysander run into the forest. Their ostensible destination is the home of his dowager aunt, but as soon as they get into the forest they seem to forget that fact. Instead, the forces of magic begin to stir. Night falls. The fairies come out. Other humans have come into the woods as well—Hermia's suitor Demetrius and her friend Helena, a group of tradesmen rehearsing for a play—and they all get drawn together into a web of world-inverting spells. Before long, the tradesman Bottom has been transformed into a donkey, the fairy queen Titania into his lover, and the admirers of Hermia into admirers of Helena. Identities and allegiances have been flipped: it's a season of tipsy, enchanting misrule.

This season of misrule is the core of the comic plot. In this play, as in many comedies, the misrule often involves an inversion of social roles. Here Bottom the Weaver becomes both an animal and a fairy king. In other comedies, parents change places with children, bosses with their employees, monarchs with their subjects. Humans are bewitched into alternate versions of themselves; men dress up as women and women as men. Quite often this churn of identities corresponds with a change of location from the places of ordinary social life to places far-off and strange. Here it's a forest, but it might also be a tropical island, a wild party, a vacation house, a road trip, a day off in Chicago. In that place of enchantments and inversions, a lord of misrule, a bustling Puck, holds sway. Often that presiding spirit has a prank or a con game to sustain for as long as the midnight madness lasts.

As the hours of the night and the acts of the comedy roll by, the revelry lurches toward exhaustion, and often toward the possibility of real trouble. In *Midsummer*, the conflict between Lysander and Demetrius becomes increasingly murderous and dangerous and finally comes to a head in their abortive duel. Puck intervenes by confusing the would-be combatants in the dark and amending the mislaid spells that have set them at odds. And then, at dawn, comes the real conclusion of the misrule, with the arrival of the Athenian authorities and a scene of reckoning in which Egeus calls for judgment, Demetrius relinquishes his claim to Hermia, and Theseus pronounces that all is forgiven and that it's time for a feast.

The misrule of comedy tends to end in just this way, with a new scene of judgment, a recasting of the judgment with which the drama began, often involving the disclosure of some new and crucial fact. It's one of the most familiar formulas of comedy: Mom and Dad come home just as the wild party ends; Lady Bracknell arrives from London with a secret to tell; the school headmaster hauls the pranksters in to answer for their crimes. Sometimes, in a common variation on this formula, the whole season of misrule has revolved around some competition—a football tournament, a talent show, a battle of suitors for a potential mate, a madcap race to a stash of money—and the culminating doom involves simply the climax and adjudication of the competition. Either way, the reckoning signifies that the sun is on the horizon and the misrule at its end. It's time for the tipsy world to be set back on its axis.

The end of misrule means a return to rational social life, and to the law-governed world of the comedy's opening scenes. But somehow, through all this disorder, the world of order has been renewed. The law will no longer obstruct healthful desires. Old relationships will be reconciled and new ones blessed. The time has come for weddings, and plenty of them. In Shakespeare's theater, *Midsummer*, *Twelfth Night*, and *The Merchant of Venice* all end with three weddings, promised or performed. *As You Like It* ends with no fewer than four, consecrated all together on stage, and *Love's Labours Lost* ends with a whopping five, though it ironically delays them by a year and a day so that the grooms can get their acts together. Quite often there is a feast to which all the persons of the play are invited, and quite often it is to this feast, just offstage or offscreen, that the characters make their final exit. The feast, with the weddings, celebrates and ratifies a renewed social order. In this renewed order, the blocking characters are either defeated or reconciled. The Egeus of *Midsummer* hovers ambiguously between these two fates, present in the play's final scenes but strangely silent, especially at the moment of doom when Demetrius relinquishes his claim on Hermia and so frees her to pursue her desires. It seems that Shakespeare doesn't really know what to do with him. But he no longer holds the power in this world.

He no longer holds the power because the social world of Athens has passed from his hands. If the old, the rich, and the titled held sway over the social world at the beginning of story, the movement through disorder and back to order has enacted a kind of passage, a handing of the torch to the young. The marriages that conclude so many comedies signify this transition. Literary critics have noticed for centuries that comedies end with weddings but never follow the happy couples into married life. What will the marriages of Hermia and Lysander, or of Jack Worthing and Gwendolen Fairfax, look like? Sometimes we shudder to ask. But comedy doesn't care about the answer, and its grammar of generational passage helps to explain why. The concern of comedy is with renewal. Once the renewal is accomplished, comedy is content to head off to the wedding reception and call it a night. Rosalind and Orlando have taken their place together at the heart of the social order; they won't be of interest to comedy again until, in about eighteen or twenty years, they tell their daughter she can't get married or prohibit their son from pursuing his love of dance, and the spirits of regeneration begin to stir once more.

The stories derived from New Comedy, in other words, follow the pattern of the Saturnalia. This festival involves a departure from the ordinary world of law and order into a magical enactment of the golden age. Then it ends, and we come back from that age of Edenic simplicity to the complicated realities of ordinary life. And then we find that before long, spring begins to stir. The movement of the festival is cyclical. Spring must come every year, if the world of green and growing things is to stay alive. The world needs to be renewed and rediscovered again and again. Comedy, in its movement from order to misrule and then back to order, enacts that cyclical movement.

At the same time, it also seems to follow the linear movement written into the Jewish and Christian festivities such as the Sabbath and the Eucharist. If a feast such as the Eucharist is founded on the eschatological promises of God—"behold, I make all things new"—comedy founds its own ritual movements on the folk-eschatological promise of Puck: "Jack shall have Jill, / Naught shall go ill; / the man shall have his mare again, and all shall be well."[2] So it is. Every player in the game is paired off, sent to her rightful reward, returned to his proper senses. In the progress from order to disorder and back to order, there is the quality almost of a dance, a graceful movement through discord toward a total harmony. Think about *Midsummer*, where the initial configuration—Hermia goes with Lysander, Helena goes with Demetrius—gives way to an ordered set of variations: Demetrius goes over to Hermia, and Helena stands alone; Lysander goes over to Helena, and the couples are thus inverted; Demetrius goes over to Helena, and Hermia stands alone; Lysander goes over to Hermia, and the couples are thus restored.[3] The whole thing bends toward the moment when everything is made right.

It turns out, then, that our familiar comic plots have their own ritual shape. They enact a process of renewal, in which an old world is made young again. They link that renewal to the processes of justice, in which the pieces of a broken world are put back in place. They offer glimpses of a golden world, revealed in midsummer dreams of reversal and misrule. And they suggest that comic misrule, when it expresses longing for Eden, might itself be an exercise in innocence.

IV

INNOCENTS

7

THE CHILD EVERLASTING
CHARLIE CHAPLIN

On the day *City Lights* had its worldwide premiere, there was chaos in downtown Los Angeles. Newspapers the next day estimated the crowds up and down Broadway at 25,000 people. The press of human bodies shattered department store windows and brought traffic to a halt. The police threatened to use tear gas. The brand-new Los Angeles Theater, which was also having its grand opening on this momentous day, seemed to be at the epicenter of some sort of cultural storm.[1]

It was January 30, 1931, a Friday. As the evening came on, the glitterati of Hollywood began to arrive, fighting their way through the crowds and into the theater. The Warners, the Zanucks, the Barrymores, and the De Milles were there. Mary Pickford and Douglas Fairbanks, Gloria Swanson and King Vidor, Marion Davies and Hedda Hopper were there. Albert and Elsa Einstein, by special invitation, were there. And of course this new movie's producer, director, writer, composer, editor, and one and only star, Charles Spencer Chaplin, was there, shuffling into the lights of this bright evening like a man going to his doom. He had expended three years of backbreaking work and well over a million and a half of his own dollars trying to get *City Lights* right, and he felt in his bones that it just wasn't right. In the years since he had begun working on this film, Hollywood had leapt headlong into the sound era and the world had entered into the Great Depression, and here was Charlie Chaplin, visibly older than the boyish tramp who had become a global icon fifteen years before, presenting a silent movie produced at vast expense. "I don't think it's going to go over," he fretted to Georgia Hale, his date for the evening, as they drove into Los Angeles; "I don't think they're going to like it."[2] He was, she later remembered, "like a shy little kid," a fragile creature stepping into a great big world.[3]

In the story that unfolded onscreen that evening, Chaplin's Tramp character gets tangled up with two people who can't really see him: a destitute blind girl who tries to sell him a flower on a street corner, and an alcoholic millionaire whom he saves from a suicide attempt. The Girl (none of these characters have names) becomes the Tramp's friend but wrongly thinks he's an affluent gentleman. The Millionaire welcomes the Tramp as his confidant, but only when he's drunk; sober, he doesn't recognize the Tramp as anything more than an anonymous beggar. The Tramp plays along with the delusions of both his new friends—he drives around in the Millionaire's Rolls-Royce and tries to impress the Girl with fake displays of wealth—and so spends the bulk of the movie living two lives, divided between his Rich Man and Poor Man personae. And this split in his identity, it turns out, is just the beginning. Over the course of the movie, the Tramp gets mistaken for, poses as, or tries to become a lot of things: an art connoisseur, a prizefighter, a dung-shoveler, a peeping Tom, a boxing referee, a homosexual flirt, a marble monument, a spool of yarn, a bush. Along the way, something in his feelings for the Girl deepens, and he tries to use his various disguises to raise the money she needs for a sight-restoring operation. Finally, in a culminating episode of mistaken identity, the Tramp gets taken for a criminal, via a sequence in which he convinces the Millionaire to give him money for the Girl, fights off armed robbers who have invaded the Millionaire's mansion, and then gets arrested himself by the arriving police. Rather than attempt to clear his name, the Tramp dashes off with the money and gives it to the Girl, and as a result of this mad flight he lands in prison, where he languishes for months, with all his layers of aspiration and disguise stripped away.

That's pretty much the whole of *City Lights*, down to the last six minutes. Decades after the premiere, Chaplin recalled in his autobiography that the crowd in the Los Angeles Theater that night was rapt, utterly engrossed in the Tramp's silent journey through his maze of identities. He himself was on edge, waiting for what he knew was coming. And then it came: the final sequence, the moment for which Charlie Chaplin had made this film. Some calendar pages fly onscreen to mark the passage of time, and we see the Girl, her sight restored, presiding over an elegant flower shop but wondering sadly whether her mysterious savior will ever return. And then we see the Tramp, released from prison and wandering the streets, more ragged than he ever has been before—he doesn't even have a shirt now under his ripped and tattered jacket. As he passes by the open window of her flower shop, the Girl sees this shabby little man and laughs, and he, looking up, stops stone-still, amazement in his face.

Now it happens. She offers him a flower and a coin. He shrinks away in shame but then reaches out to accept the flower. She takes his hand to press the coin into it. And in that moment, somehow, she knows. Stopped mid-sentence, she feels his hand with both of hers, lingeringly, her eyes fixed all the while on his. She touches his shoulder, and then her own face, as if only her hands can tell her what she needs to know. "You?" she asks, in a title card bearing that single word. The Tramp nods: "You can see now?" "Yes," she says. "I can see now." And what she sees now, most of all, is what no one else has seen: she sees *him*. Somehow, in choosing to expose his own shabbiness, the Tramp has given sight to the blind. The camera lingers for a last moment on her face, her eyes glistening, and then on his, as something like joy or release begins to break across it. And then the image fades to black, and it is finished.

The film critic James Agee, writing in 1949, called this scene "the greatest piece of acting and the highest moment in movies."[4] That's an exaggeration, no doubt—but the crowd that night in Los Angeles seems to have known that something special was happening. The applause was rapturous. It was if they had all come to see this man of many disguises as he most wanted or needed to be seen. In his old age, Chaplin recalled that as the final scene played he cast a glance over at Albert Einstein, seated right beside him. The great theorist of the quantum universe was wiping tears from his eyes.[5]

*

That rapture was nothing new. By 1931, in fact, it was getting old, and wouldn't last much longer. But for fifteen years, Charlie Chaplin had been enveloped in a charisma that seemed almost shamanic. He had begun developing his Tramp persona in 1914, and the character had quickly become a global sensation, a cult of celebrity unlike anything the entertainment world had seen before. When Georgia Hale first saw Chaplin onscreen in 1916, many people were already coming to experience his onscreen presence as a power beyond human accounting. Hale, as a depressed sixteen-year-old, felt that power. The other kids were hooting and screaming at the gags, she later recalled, "but I saw something different, something invisible. I felt something beautiful. A gentle beam of light had stolen into my dark world. 'What was it?' I was silent.... I wanted to hold it closely. Charlie Chaplin had spoken directly to me."[6]

It seems almost a conspiracy of the universe that Chaplin, eight years later, saw this girl from Chicago in an obscure film at just the moment when he had ruined his relationship with his latest leading lady and needed to be enchanted by someone new. But at the time, everything about Charlie Chaplin seemed a conspiracy of the universe. The Reverend Frederick E. Heath of Boston preached in a sermon that "had Chaplin lived in the old Puritanical days they would have believed him a witch and taken his life."[7] An essayist writing in 1915 called him "the Mob-God," an opiate of the masses, "the incarnation of the latent, imperfect, and childlike genius that lies buried under the flesh of his worshippers."[8] The image of Charlie-as-Tramp became, for his global audiences, something like a religious icon. When the Chaplin hysteria first got going in 1915, that iconic image began to appear everywhere. There were Tramp statuettes, Tramp dolls, Tramp buttons, Tramp lapel pins, Tramp posters, Tramp squirt rings, Tramp hats and ties and socks. The Ziegfeld Follies dancers dressed up like the Tramp for their number, "Those Charlie Chaplin Feet." A Mexican actor named Charles Amador changed his name to "Charles Aplin" and started producing eerily exact imitations of the Tramp figure. Men by the thousands began growing Chaplinstaches—even Marcel Proust grew one—and in the summer of 1915 there was a craze of Tramp impersonation. Theaters and cities across the US hosted look-alike contests. Thousands of people at a time gathered to make Chaplin's alter ego their own. The winner of one of these contests, in Cleveland, was a young man named Leslie T. Hope, later known to the world as Bob. Some said that the third-place runner-up at another of these competitions was the man himself, Charles Spencer Chaplin, who came unto his own, and they knew him not.

Where did this power come from? The Reverend Heath's comment about Chaplin as a witch expresses the bewilderment that many observers felt at the time. Observers a century later aren't much better off, but we have come to suspect, over the years, that Chaplin's charisma was connected with his vulnerability, his gift for spinning the sufferings and longings of his own life into myth. In the fifteen years between the first film he made as the Tramp character and the premiere of *City Lights*, Chaplin projected his shape-shifting, cane-twirling creation into many worlds and many forms. The Tramp, across fifty-odd films, was a salesman, a waiter, an immigrant, a cop, a soldier, a husband, a drunk, a firefighter, a wallpaper hanger, an escaped convict, a gold prospector, a circus clown. But in all these iterations, he seemed to bear within himself the image of his creator. His perennial destitution seemed to reflect the agonies of Chaplin's own childhood in the slums and workhouses of London, and his magical powers of metamorphosis and survival seemed inseparable from the acrobatic arc of Chaplin's own life. The Tramp in many of his films was called "Charlie," and audiences had no trouble understanding the connection. The crowd at the Los Angeles theater in January 1931 would have understood it themselves: *City Lights* wasn't just the story of a tramp playing a rich man. It was the spectacle, they all knew, of a rich man playing a tramp playing a rich man, or, deeper down, of a tramp playing a rich man playing a tramp playing a rich man. Somewhere at the center of it all was Chaplin himself, the Ur-Tramp. In his films, he promised to bring that core identity to light, to open our eyes to the personhood of this small, suffering creature. And even as those films had grand premieres in great cities like Los Angeles, he was playing the frightened child, shivering in the cold and asking Georgia Hale to tell him that this time it's going to be all right.

This could be the beginning of a clue to Chaplin's charisma. He had a secret self, a core of wounded innocence, that he only teasingly revealed. When Georgia Hale, Chaplin's date at the *City Lights* premiere, commented years later that the man she fell in love with in the 1920s was in fact two men (she called them "Charlie" and "Mr. Chaplin"), she got at the experience of that secrecy.[9] Everyone who spent more than a little time with Chaplin described him as an enigma, a labyrinth of shadows and shifting identities. The side of Chaplin that Georgia called "Charlie" was graceful and sensitive, a thoughtful listener and vibrant companion, a child-bright porcelain doll of a man. The illustrator Ralph Barton, who spent quite a bit of time with Charlie in the early 1920s, described him simply as "the most marvelous person on earth," and the poet Hart Crane, after a long night spent in intimate conversation with Charlie in 1923, gushed that "I am happy in the intense clarity of spirit that a man like Chaplin gives one if he is honest enough to receive it."[10] Chaplin provoked responses like these from men and women, from young children and distinguished intellectuals. He seemed to have an almost supernatural way of making others fall in love with him.

Look at his face in the right light, though, and there were always other faces just visible. The writer Thomas Burke spent time with Chaplin in London in 1921 and later published an essay describing that other Chaplin: "Catch him in repose," he wrote, and "you will catch a drawn, weary mouth and those eyes of steel."[11] This other Chaplin, Georgia's "Mr. Chaplin," disappeared into impenetrable silences for days or even weeks on end. He romanced friends and lovers with ardent passion and then turned ice-cold, as if he had become a different person. He could be tyrannically needy and viciously cruel ("probably the most sadistic man I'd ever met," Marlon Brando once said).[12] It seemed that, as his early boss Mack Sennett commented, "he *liked* to be lonely"; and at the same time, he was ravenous for attention, pathological in his need for the affection and loyalty of others.[13] Those who knew him best always suspected that under all the charm and performative vitality, Charlie Chaplin was curled up tight around some sort of pain.

What was the nature of that pain? There is of course no one answer to that question, but Chaplin himself spent much of his adult life reflecting on what he had inherited from his mother. In his autobiography, he recalled that she would play theatrical roles at home for him and his older brother Sidney, putting on face after face "until she was breathless and exhausted." She had failed in her career as a music-hall performer, but her boys watched wonderingly as she impersonated Napoleon or Nell Gwyn or Jesus on the cross in little one-woman living-room dramas. Clearly the man who later spent years dreaming up his own Napoleon biopic knew he had inherited his shape-shifting mother's powers of impersonation. But Hannah Chaplin wasn't just a gifted actor: she was also clinically schizophrenic, and the magic show of her whirling identities was a sign not just of her theatrical charisma but also of her sickness. Chaplin always feared that he had inherited that sickness, too. His powers of impersonation didn't seem to have an off switch—his own son once called him "the man who was so many men in one"—and he sometimes confessed in private his fear that his mother's insanity would one day come for him. Meanwhile, in his films, he gave himself fully to the exercise of those powers, using them to tell the very story of family anguish in which they had their roots.

"Who is this man?" the Millionaire in *City Lights* asks, when he awakens from his final drunken stupor and sees the Tramp in his house. That's more or less the question Chaplin spent his career trying to answer. As much as any performer in the history of comedy, he relentlessly mythologized his past, chronicling his own lost innocence and spinning fantasies about the child he imagined himself to be. The story of his comedy begins with that child, and with that innocence.

*

Biographers have never succeeded in finding Charlie Chaplin's birth certificate, and the exact circumstances of his birth, like much else in his early life, are hard to make out, confused by the haphazard documentary evidence and the often blatantly false accounts of the people involved. Chaplin always celebrated his birthday on April 16, and somewhere close to that day, in 1889, he was indeed born, in south London, the second son of parents who were already on their way to splitting up. His father, Charles Chaplin, was a music hall performer who had occasional contact with his children before his drinking killed him in 1901. But Hannah, Charlie's mother, was the one who really mattered in his life. She had been born to an underemployed father and a mentally unstable mother and had run away from home when she was sixteen. She later claimed (as did Charlie, in his autobiography) that after leaving home she played a leading role with an Irish touring troupe and then eloped to South Africa with a rich bookmaker.[14] But there's no record of any of these activities, and some of Chaplin's biographers have noticed that in the 1952 film *Limelight*, where he tells a version of her story, he seems to entertain the possibility that the sixteen-year-old Hannah had to make her way as a prostitute.[15]

At age nineteen, in March 1885, Hannah gave birth to a son, Sidney, and three months after that she married Charles Chaplin, a neighbor in her London lodging house, who claimed not to be the father but gave the boy his name even so. She made some forays into musical theater, but her career had fizzled by the time Charlie was born four years later. Not long after that, the elder Charles was gone, and Hannah and the two Chaplin boys were left destitute.

It isn't entirely clear how the trio scraped by for much of Charlie's early childhood: his father, certainly, didn't do much to support them. When Charlie was six, his mother was hospitalized for the first time, and for the next three years, the boys bounced, often separately, in and out of workhouses, Poor Law schools, the homes of relatives, a training ship in Essex (that was Sidney), and rented back rooms, sometimes in the care of their mother, sometimes not. When Charlie was nine, his mother was hospitalized again after a severe mental collapse, and the authorities pressured a reluctant and now severely alcoholic Charles Chaplin to give his sons a place to stay. Charlie later remembered that when they were told about his mother's collapse, he felt "that she had deliberately escaped from her mind and deserted us."[16] He stayed with his father and a hostile woman named Louise for a few unpleasant weeks (unpleasant enough that on one occasion the Society for the Prevention of Cruelty to Children came to inquire), but it wasn't long before his father came up with an alternative arrangement, in the form of a clog-dancing troupe called the Eight Lancashire Lads.[17] Charles knew the manager of the group, who judged that Charlie had potential as a dancer and took him on. And so, at nine years old, young Charlie Chaplin hit the road as a touring theatrical professional.

He was well advanced by now in his first education, a schooling in poverty, displacement, and abandonment. Later in life, he emphasized that the humiliation was the thing that gave his boyhood poverty its sting. He wrote in his autobiography about a time at the Poor Law School at Hanwell when, infected with ringworm, he had his head shaved and iodined and tried to keep from being seen by the other boys as he looked out the window of the sick ward.[18] That humiliation didn't dissipate easily. In one of the first press interviews he gave, in 1915, he responded to questions about his childhood by dishing out one lie after the next. He said that his father had died when he was seven (actually he was twelve), that he never had any schooling (he did have *some* schooling), that his mother was a "highly cultivated" woman (not exactly), and that she too had died in England when he was young (she was, in 1915, still very much alive).[19] That last falsehood is particularly striking: it's as if he didn't have the will or the language, at age twenty-six, to talk about who his family actually were and what they had endured. How did he account for himself at age nine?

He might not have been asking that question at the time, but on the road with the Eight Lancashire Lads, he began to discover an answer. The two years he spent touring with the Lads were grueling—he later recalled that at times "we would almost fall asleep on the stage," the demands were so exhausting—but they also marked the beginning of a second education for young Charlie Chaplin.[20]

In the music halls where he clogged away night after night, there was a rich ecosystem of popular performance, a world of singers, jugglers, acrobats, clowns, mummers, mesmerists, impersonators, escape artists, living statues, dramatic monologuists, exotic animals, mnemonic prodigies, and entertaining weirdos of every kind.[21] The competition was fierce and the crowds were merciless, but for any young performer willing to endure and survive, every night was a festival of possibility, a kaleidoscope of illusions and theatrical enchantments. Charlie took it all in, storing this world of masks and human images within himself, the materials for a life still far off in the future.

The Lads let him go around the time he turned twelve, and he went back to his mother in London. It was often just the two of them now: Sidney had joined the Union Castle Mail Steamship Company and went to sea for weeks at a time. Not long after Charlie came home, he saw his now shockingly ill father for the last time and then, a few weeks later, attended his funeral. Over the next couple years, he picked up a remarkable array of jobs to help his mother make ends meet. He worked as a barber's boy, a chandler's boy, a doctor's boy, a page boy, a glass factory laborer (this one lasted a single day), a printing press operator, a street-hustling clothes-monger, and a self-employed maker and vendor of toy boats. In May 1903, just after Charlie had turned fourteen, Hannah had her most catastrophic mental collapse yet, and he had to take her to the hospital himself, as she raved about dead people looking out of windows and screamed out prayers and profanities. When they arrived at the hospital, she said that the floor of the examining room was the Jordan River and refused to cross it. Charlie then went home, alone, to their little rented room, where he suffered in solitude until Sidney returned from sea a few weeks later.

*

From the moment of Hannah's hospitalization that day in 1903, Charlie Chaplin's adult life began. He registered with a theatrical agency and before long had landed roles in a couple of touring dramatic productions, where he enjoyed decent work and respectable pay for a couple of years. After slogging it out for another two or three years in third-rate comedy troupes and unsuccessful one-man endeavors of his own, he finally signed in early 1908 with the company where his brother Sidney was now performing, the comedy outfit run by the legendary Fred Karno, a.k.a. "The Guv'nor." Karno's show was a raucous, vigorously physical, and by all accounts hilarious theater of mayhem, and his sketches were famous for ending in what was known as the "Karno picnic," in which every performer flooded the stage in an unhinged anarchic melee. But what looked to audiences like barely controlled chaos in fact depended on an almost balletic or scientific precision. Karno spent months training every new performer in the minutiae of timing, gesture, body control, stunt-work, and acrobatics. His troupes performed only a small handful of sketches, but every one of those sketches was a marvel of orchestration, refined and rehearsed down to the last detail. The effect seems to have been tremendous. Stan Laurel, who joined the company a couple years after Chaplin did, called Karno's company, and in particular their famous sketch *Mumming Birds*, "one of the most fantastically funny acts ever known—probably the greatest ensemble of the century."[22]

Karno didn't think much of his new recruit at first, but Charlie surprised him by excelling under his regime of perfectionist discipline. Under Karno, the young performer learned how to move and to mime. He learned how to fall off ladders and land in somersaults like a human cat. And he came to share his boss's belief in the power of carefully refined details to create theatrical illusion. Before the year was out, the nineteen-year-old Charlie had a major role in a London run of *Mumming Birds*, and in the years following, as a member of Karno's touring companies, he took the show to Paris (1909), the US (1910–1912), and then to the US again (1912–1913). It was good for a while, but by the time Chaplin got into his second American tour, he was increasingly unhappy. The other performers didn't care for his solitary and complicated temperament, and Chaplin never was suited for the unpredictability and exposure of live performance. He was too reserved, too much in need of control, to enjoy the presence of a live audience.

Even so, reviewers and audiences began to notice him, and in the spring of 1913, a whole new kind of opportunity came calling. Adam Kessel and Charles Baumann, the owners of New York Motion Pictures and of its subsidiary, the Keystone Film Company, sent a telegram to Karno's American tour manager that read as follows:

> IS THERE A MAN NAMED CHAFFIN IN YOUR COMPANY OR SOMETHING LIKE THAT IF SO WILL HE COMMUNICATE WITH KESSEL AND BAUMANN 24 LONGACRE BUILDING BROADWAY NEW YORK.[23]

"Chaffin" took a train to New York thinking that Kessel and Baumann might be lawyers and that perhaps his great-aunt in New York had died and left him some money. Instead they surprised him by asking if he'd like to work in motion pictures. He signed in July, and at the end of that year, when his contract with Karno had ended, he headed off to Hollywood and the studios of Mack Sennett, the presiding spirit of the Keystone comic universe.

Sennett's crews and comedians at Keystone churned out two films every week (these were one-reelers, about ten minutes long). His films were known for their breakneck energy, for their delight in kicks to the arse, bricks to the head, and wild chases at vicious speed. Keystone film crews never did retakes, and Sennett's star comedians weren't known for their subtlety. The films hurtled along so fast that subtlety didn't have time to matter. Chaplin arrived on this scene as a veteran of stage productions that took months of work to perfect, and he began to suspect right away that this arrangement was a terrible mistake. Sennett shared his suspicion and made him sit around idly for several weeks (an eternity, in Keystone time) before he finally gave Chaplin a role, as a street swindler with a handlebar moustache in the film *Making a Living*, shot in late January 1914 and released on February 2. It was Charlie Chaplin's first time on screen. The universe didn't exactly shudder. A perceptive reviewer for *Moving Picture World* did mention favorably "the clever player who takes the part of a nervy and very shifty sharper," but Chaplin and his bosses at Keystone all hated the picture.[24]

The months that followed, though, were one of those seasons when something in an artist awakens, and a whole new field of possibilities comes into view.[25] In his second film for Sennett, Chaplin improvised a costume involving a derby hat, a little square moustache, and pants that were a bit too baggy. In his fifth film for Sennett (released exactly one month after the first), Charlie hit on the idea of making his derby-hatted character a panhandler. By the time he was shooting his tenth film, a month after that, Chaplin's bosses got word that theaters all over the country were booking every picture with the little guy in the derby hat. And by the time he began making his eleventh film (released on April 20, two days after the tenth), the little guy in the hat was not just the star but also the writer and director of the show. He had first stepped in front of a camera barely three months before, but already he had a sure enough sense of himself to know that he was dissatisfied with Keystone's other directors and eager to make films in his own distinctive style. Before the year was out, he would write, direct, and star in another eighteen pictures, and along the way would also co-star in *Tillie's Punctured Romance*, regarded by many film historians as the first feature-length cinematic comedy.

In the context of Chaplin's total career, the Keystone films look primitive, crude first drafts of the delicate artistry he would cultivate in his later work. But the signs of this comedian's difference are already emerging. In Chaplin's productions, the manic Keystone pace slows just a little. The shots get longer; the camera lingers on small interpersonal exchanges. The Tramp of these films is for the most part a vicious demon-dervish, inflicting pain on others out of greed or lust or the sheer sadistic pleasure of it. But there's also, from the beginning, a kind of poetry in his movements, a penchant for absurdist flourishes and touches of wry awareness. When, in his very first film, Chaplin as the "sharper" kisses the hand of a woman he's flirting with, he pauses for just a moment and smacks his lips appraisingly, as if judging the taste of food. Even more significantly, Chaplin begins, in these films, to suggest that the action originates not outside the principal characters, in a scenario that sets them moving, but rather inside them, in their motives and desires. In a couple of films he even brushes against the idea that his trickster-demon Tramp might be human, and capable of good. In *The New Janitor*, produced in September, the little guy actually does something selfless, stopping a robbery at the company that just fired him and rescuing a woman in the bargain.

Audiences in 1914 saw the difference. By the time *Motion Picture Magazine* ran the November edition of its "Great Cast Contest," Charlie Chaplin won the voting in the male comedian category, just edging out the Vitagraph star John Bunny.[26] At the end of the year he moved from Keystone to the Essanay Film Manufacturing Company and essentially became his own studio head, slowing his pace to roughly one film a month and overseeing more and more details of his productions, from directing to casting to styling his leading lady's hair. The twelve films he released with Essanay in 1915 were mainly two-reelers (about twenty minutes long), and in them Chaplin began feeling his way more deeply into the possibilities of the Tramp as his own alter ego. Especially in *The Tramp*, released that April (and the film that once and for all gave the derby-hatted character his name), Chaplin did something that would have been nearly unthinkable at Keystone: he made the Tramp really and truly vulnerable, a man with desires and a capacity for suffering. In this film, when the Tramp defends a farmer's house from robbers and gets blasted with a shotgun, he falls down, not in the butt-to-the-sky backward somersault that was Chaplin's slapstick standard, but in a wincing collapse, as a wounded person would fall. And when he discovers, later, that the farmer's daughter has a handsome fiancée, he suffers real heartbreak, wiping his eyes as he pens his farewell note and then disappearing down a dusty road as we watch from behind. The final shot of this film is the first instance of the shuffling-into-the-sunset finale that would become a Chaplin signature, and there's an exquisite pathos in the image. The Tramp has exchanged his life at the farmer's house, with its warm bed and hot meals, for a life exposed on the open road, in part because his broken heart compels him, and in part, we know, because the road is where he belongs. In films like this one, as his audience watched, the mischief-making Tramp was undergoing a metamorphosis, changing from a grotesque comic mask into the icon of a humanity that longs for something good.

It was just as the Tramp took his first steps into that new life that Chaplinitis erupted across the US and Europe. By the time his contract with Essanay expired at the end of 1915, Chaplin had become a phenomenon with no real precedent in the cinema world, and the Mutual Film Corporation shocked everyone, including

Chaplin himself, by offering him a one-year contract at $10,000 dollars a week, plus a $150,000 signing bonus. The jaws of the world dropped. Journalists fell over themselves to capture the scale of this sum: Charlie Chaplin's pay for the year would be 93 percent of the entire US Senate's payroll, more than five times the combined earnings of the entire Supreme Court, enough money for a cab fare every two seconds, all year long, even while sleeping. No public person outside royals, emperors, and possibly the president of US Steel had ever earned this much money in a year. No singer, actor, or artist had even come close.[27] And all this for guy who two years before had been an obscure music-hall clown. How could it have happened? It was in response to this outrageous news, in a sermon called "Charlie Chaplin's Half Million," that Frederick E. Heath, the Boston minister, made his comments about burning Chaplin as a witch.[28]

Over the next eighteen months, in the dozen two-reel films he made for Mutual in 1916 and 1917, this unlikely magician worked one miracle after the next. His films were marvels of inventiveness and perception, beautiful in their panoramic comedy of human life. And his Tramp character passed into a phase in which he seemed almost an angelic being, overcoming the uniformed bullies, corrupt institutions, and constraining physical laws of this present world with his aerodynamics of grace. Some film historians have observed that the iconic performers in the silent era often seemed to possess some sort of magical power: W. C. Fields's juggling, Buster Keaton's acrobatics, and Fred Astaire's dancing were almost supernatural in the way they defied the usual limits of gravity and embodiment.[29] In his Mutual films, Chaplin came fully into his own wonder-working charisma, not exactly as an acrobat or dancer—though he had plenty of skill in both those areas—but as a man around whom the physical world seemed to turn pliable and stir into life. He could make his hat tip itself, could lift himself up by the seat of his own pants, could twirl bread dough like a lasso. He could zoom down a staircase like a bobsled and bounce off the floor like a ball—and on roller skates, as his performance in *The Rink* demonstrated, he was nothing less than a god. He seemed to be made of rubber or water or atomic energy, and there was an electric sort of charge in the movements of his body. It was as if this little clown, who would later make Albert Einstein his special guest at the premiere of *City Lights*, had his own special access to the secret laws of the physical universe.

These weird powers, for the Tramp of the Mutual films, made possible a comedy of strength in littleness and survival against all odds. Chaplin was built small, and in these films he made himself seem even smaller by surrounding himself with imposing antagonists such as Henry Bergman and the mountainous Eric Campbell, who glower and bully and enforce the rules of whatever institution they happen to represent. The street bully played by Campbell in *Easy Street* is so absurdly and hilariously strong that he sends entire battalions of police officers fleeing in terror. Only the tiny manipulator of physical laws manages to overcome him, by maneuvering his head into a street lamp and turning on the gas. In some of the films—*The Vagabond*, *The Adventurer*, *The Immigrant*—Chaplin identified this tiny hero explicitly as a figure on the margins of American society: a street musician, a felon on the run, an immigrant on a ship bound for Ellis Island. He took the Tramp into slums and drug dens, charity institutions and rehab hospitals. As he represented these dark corners of the world, he asked what it's like to be at the mercy of respectable civic institutions that dehumanize and demean vulnerable people. And he seemed to know the answer all too well. In one particularly biting scene in *The Immigrant*, the ship comes into view of the Statue of Liberty, an intertitle reads "The arrival in the land of liberty," the ragged passengers stare in reverent wonder, and then—here's the bite—an official comes charging in with a rope and corrals them like cattle.

*

After he left Mutual, Chaplin's films began to get longer and his imaginative scope larger, and in 1919, under contract with the First National Exhibitor's Circuit, he began working on his first feature-length production, the movie that would be released in 1920 as *The Kid*. The film was a moment of emergence for Chaplin. Here, at the threshold of his great feature films of the 1920s, Chaplin began to make audacious new experiments in presenting his comic persona as a projection out of his own interior. He seems to have discovered, in the process, that the comic hilarity and spiritual charisma of the Tramp derive from his core of vulnerability, his special innocence. Over the next decade, the lives Chaplin lived onscreen and the lives he lived offscreen would become harder and harder to tell apart.

He started work on *The Kid* in the immediate aftermath of an agonizing ordeal in his own life. In the summer of 1918 he had met and become infatuated with a young woman named Mildred Harris. (Her age at the time has never been entirely clear, but she was probably around fifteen.) In the fall she told Chaplin she was pregnant, and he married her, very reluctantly, that October, before finding out the pregnancy was a false alarm. The year that followed was utterly miserable. Chaplin's creative work plummeted, in his view because of the unhappy marriage. Mildred soon became pregnant for real, giving birth to a baby boy, Norman Spencer Chaplin, on July 7, 1919. Three days later, the baby died, and Chaplin was shattered. Mildred much later said, "That's the only thing I can remember about Charlie… that he cried when the baby died."[30] Within a few months of that cataclysm, Mildred would initiate a divorce proceeding that turned very ugly before the couple finally reached a settlement in November 1920.

It's impossible to know how the dots of these events connect. But it's a fact that ten days after his infant son died in early July, Chaplin was auditioning babies at his studio, and by August he had abandoned his other projects and hurried *The Kid* into full-steam production. In this film, Chaplin went places he had never gone before. The movie begins with a woman emerging from the iron gates of a charity hospital, clutching a baby to her chest. An intertitle appears—"The woman—whose sin was motherhood."—and we know that her child is illegitimate. The two stern-faced attendants who have ushered her out of the hospital padlock the gates behind her, and she begins to walk forward toward the camera, fear and determination mingling on her face. Just as she turns and walks offscreen to our right, the film cuts, jarringly, to a still image: it's Christ in silhouette, facing the same direction, dragging his cross. It then cuts back to the Woman with her child, and there's no room for doubt: this woman, too, is carrying a cross. Who will take it up for her?

The answer to that question arrives in the person of the Tramp, who stumbles upon the baby in a trash heap after a series of events in which the Woman abandons the child in the back seat of a limousine and some car thieves dump it in an alley. The Tramp, too, tries several times to abandon the baby, but their meeting has been ordained by some providence or fate, and his attempts all comically fail. When at last he finds a scrawled note in the baby's swaddling clothes—"Please love and care for this orphan child"—his heart softens, and he takes the baby home to his ramshackle attic apartment. Five years pass, an intertitle tells us, and the film then devotes itself to portraying the shared life of these two castoffs, the Tramp and the five-year-old Kid. They cook together, eat together, and hustle for money together, a beautifully harmonized and endearing pair. In the meantime, the disgraced mother becomes a wealthy movie star, and she happens to befriend the boy while doing charity work in the slum where he and the Tramp live. In time, the authorities discover this orphan living in poverty and try to snatch him away, precipitating some drama in which the two castoffs go on the run and the boy finally gets caught and hauled off to an institution. That's the low point of the plot. It doesn't last long, though, because soon the Woman tries to pay the boy a visit in the Tramp's now-empty apartment, and there she sees the note she had scrawled five years before. At that moment, in a flash, she knows the truth. She knows who this child is. And she knows, in another way, who this Tramp is. He is her Christ, the messiah who came to take up her cross.

The meanings of this movie were of course complex for Charlie Chaplin. Watching the efforts of the Tramp to keep himself and the boy together, it's hard not to think of the episode, which Chaplin later wrote about in his autobiography, when Hannah Chaplin pranked the Poor Law school that housed her boys by pretending she was taking them into her care, all so that she could take them to the park for a single day. The life he portrays in the attic room that the boy and the Tramp share is remarkably like his descriptions of the room he shared with his mother in London when he was a young teenager. No surprise, perhaps, that throughout the film, the identities of the Tramp and the Kid seem to be interchangeable: the Tramp is an orphan and the Kid a tramp. The merging selves of these two little waifs can be hilarious, as in the scene where the Tramp tries to save money in a boarding house by passing himself and the boy off as a single person. But in the end, their interchangeable identities suggest a shared vulnerability, and in the last scene of the movie the Woman takes them both into her care, the mother not of one lost child but of two.

With these collapsing identities, Chaplin found his way into the terrain his comedy would explore over the next decade, at the junction of his own tender vulnerability and his messianic charisma. In his next feature-length production, the remarkable four-reel film

The Pilgrim (1923), he maps that terrain further. The film opens with a shot of iron gates that explicitly recalls the opening of *The Kid*—he's constructing, with more and more care, a cinematic myth-world of icons and images—but this time the gates belong to a prison, and the Tramp isn't there: he's already escaped, a convict on the lam. By the time we lay eyes on him, he has already stolen the clothes of a man—a minister, as it happens—swimming in a river, and so it is that, for the rest of the movie, Chaplin's hero lives in doubleness, a criminal disguised as a man of God. The layering grows more complex as he goes. He gets mistaken for the new minister in a small Texas town and does his bravest best to be good and do good, enduring the abuse of an obnoxious child with saintly patience, trying earnestly to join this society of respectable people, and finally saving the widow he is boarding with from a vicious robber. But neither his apparent goodness nor his real goodness can save him from his real, or apparent, criminality. The sheriff of the town finally sees his face on a wanted poster and arrests him, and in a stunning final scene the holy criminal's double identity becomes more iconically vivid than ever. The sheriff brings the Tramp down to the Mexican border and leaves him on the other side, where American law can't reach him, and as the lawman rides off, the Tramp rejoices in his freedom for about two seconds before bandits run out from behind the hills and start shooting at each other. The little escapee then runs back to the border, not sure which side to choose, and at last, as the camera directs our gaze down the line of the border, he shuffles off toward the horizon. It's his iconic into-the-sunset exit, but this time he has his legs splayed wide, and one foot on either side of the border.

Chaplin now knows and has named it: his Tramp is an amphibious being, a citizen both of this world and of others, far off. He is a criminal and a priest, a vagrant who is also a pilgrim, a cosmic traveler whose strangeness is the key both to his miracle-making and his funniness. In *The Pilgrim*, the collision of his two identities is the engine that drives his comedy: handed a Bible when it's time for him to preach in church, he places his left hand on it and raises his right, as if on trial; when he looks over at the twelve-member choir, he sees, for a shuddering moment, a jury. But he is also an apocalyptic entity, in whose presence that which was hidden is made known. He is himself a walking secret, waiting to be disclosed, and with his arrival the secret sins of others become visible and drain away, like the liquor from the bottle the deacon is hiding in his pants before he and the Tramp fall down together and shatter it. With each small disclosure, the audience laughs, and waits for the bigger revelation of which of these little apocalypses are a promise, when the man himself will be revealed and everyone will see the truth at last.

With the release of *The Pilgrim* in early 1923, Chaplin fulfilled his contract with First National, and he now embarked on a string of ambitious feature-length productions under the auspices of United Artists, which he formed along with Mary Pickford, Douglas Fairbanks, and D. W. Griffith. In these films, the Tramp suffers more profoundly than he did in any film before: he endures near-starvation in *The Gold Rush* (1925), the humiliation of failing in front of crowds in *The Circus* (1928), the complex pains of anonymity and unrequited love in *City Lights*. Chaplin was himself suffering profound and often self-inflicted miseries in those years. From the middle of 1924 to the end of 1926, he was at the center of yet another atrocious spectacle of seduction, forced marriage, and much-publicized divorce, this time involving Lita Grey, who had played a minor role in *The Kid* at age twelve and who was just fifteen when Chaplin started pursuing her. In January 1926, as the divorce proceedings were getting ugly, the federal government froze Chaplin's assets and demanded nearly a million and a half dollars in back taxes. In November 1926, the sets for *The Circus* were devastated by a fire in Chaplin's studio. In October 1927, *The*

Jazz Singer was released, introducing to the world the technology of cinematic sound and prompting widespread speculation about the sudden obsolescence of the world's greatest silent clown. In August 1928, Chaplin's mother, Hannah, died. And Chaplin carried the fear, shame, and furious hysteria of all these events into the comedy of these self-mythologizing films. It was just as Lita announced her second pregnancy and Charlie descended into an emotional breakdown that he told an associate he wanted to do a gag "placing me in a position I can't get away from for some reason. I'm on a high place troubled by something else, monkeys or things that come to me and I can't get away from them."[31] Is that comedy? Is it sheer, naked despair? Whatever it is, he did develop the gag, and it became *The Circus*, with its climactic scene of the hapless Tramp trying to do a tightrope dance with the covert help of a safety harness attached to his belt. The harness pops off; the Tramp shimmies on for a few more seconds in ignorant bliss; the loose harness dangles, exquisitely, into his line of sight. He freezes. And then the monkeys come.

This is comedy, for Charlie Chaplin: a man in danger, hounded by hunger on the one hand and chaos on the other. And this is the comedian, Edenic and innocent, goaded onto the tightrope of life in this wicked world. But the Tramp in these great films is not just a suffering child, and not just an agent of apocalypse, but also a redemptive and life-renewing force. In *The Gold Rush*, his presence helps to redeem a dance-hall girl from her dissolute life in the northern territories. In *The Circus*, he helps to redeem a young acrobat from the tyranny of her stepfather. His innocence is alchemical, turning everything around him to gold, and even his pranks have the effect of transfigurations, as when, in *The Gold Rush*, he turns two dinner rolls into a pair of elegant dancing legs, the stuff that dreams are made of. In the final scenes of *City Lights*, the harmonic interplay between pranking and transfiguration rises to its highest pitch, as comedic unmasking opens into ecstatic vision. The streethustler of Chaplin's very first Keystone film is still here in the Tramp of *City Lights*, trying to survive from one lie to the next. But his games of disguise and disclosure, his hunger and resourcefulness, have been translated into forms of longing that nothing in this world can answer. Though the man behind the greasepaint is, in this later film, beginning visibly to age, his alter ego seems more than ever like a child, a little creature looking for rescue, refuge, and love. Chaplin has transfigured the Mob-God, the trickster demon who leapt out of him the first time he stepped in front of a camera, into an image of innocence, exiled from an Eden that he will never stop trying to find.

*

Chaplin made films for another three and a half decades after *City Lights*. But that film marked the end of something. It marked the end, for one thing, of Chaplin's silence, which had been for him much more than a matter of technological necessity. Silence was the atmosphere in which he always breathed easiest, a protective sheath. It was the condition that enabled his eloquent language of movement and gesture. In the final minutes of his next film, *Modern Times* (1936), Chaplin broke the spell, making his Tramp sing aloud and then sending him off down the highway for the last time.

He went on from there to make a number of talking films, from *The Great Dictator* (1940) to *A Countess in Hong Kong* (1967), and some of these films are striking in their ambition and audacity. But something of Chaplin disappeared along with his comic alter ego. Because it was linked with his Edenic nature, his comedy had always depended on his agelessness. After he put the Tramp aside, he allowed his onscreen selves to age, and he crossed from the miracles and myth-worlds of comedy over to the secular ordinariness of melodrama. At times, his later films seem like eulogies for the comedian he once was (this most explicitly in *Limelight*, the 1952 film in which he played his final scenes alongside Buster Keaton). In certain moments, they seem like attempts to understand the secret, still elusive, of that otherworldly creature's charism of life.

In the early 1940s, Chaplin spent some months working on a screen adaptation of Paul Vincent Carroll's 1937 play *Shadow and Substance*, about an Irish girl who has visions of Saint Brigid, her namesake. He never made the movie, but at the end of his script he included a lyric that resonates back through his lives as the Tramp. The lyric might almost be a hymn to that ever-suffering, ever-surviving figure. "Ecce homo," it begins, "Ecce homo / His crown / Just a barren wreath of thorns." And then, in its spare way, it makes a turn and shows us something more: "A rose / So red / Blooming on his crown of thorns."[32]

Ecce homo: behold the man. We're back, with these words, to the moment of glory when the once-blind woman took the Tramp's hand and the eyes of the crowd glistened with tears. The poem is touched with the transfiguring lyricism of much of Chaplin's best work: he sees a crown of thorns and remembers that branches of thorns can also put forth roses. The woman in *City Lights* was a flower girl for a reason, perhaps. She sees the man under the crown of thorns at just about the moment when she reaches out to hand him a rose, an image of the beauty that blossoms, like resurrection itself, even in the midst of death.

Chaplin's career always pointed forward, into a future in which the world would experience much of its comedy on screens, and the comedians who loomed into life on those screens would spin cults of laughter out of their personal wounds and transgressions. It's an odd coincidence that Lenny Bruce moved from New York to Los Angeles in the spring of 1953, at pretty much exactly the moment that Chaplin, under pressure because of his communist affiliations, surrendered his US re-entry permit and abandoned Los Angeles for good. It's as if a torch was passed. Lenny's idioms were of course different, but much of what he did could be read as another version of Chaplin's comedy of wounded innocence and Edenic criminality.

But Chaplin also looks backward, to Francis receiving the wounds of Christ into his own body, and to the little poor man touched with prophetic innocence. He inhabited that enchanted life from the moment he first got transfigured into light and projected onto a screen, a figure who lived, as Federico Fellini later said of him, "in two aspects," both a vagabond and something stranger than a vagabond: "the solitary aristocrat, the prophet, the priest and the poet."[33] He still had an uncanny charisma even in death, and his last joke was very much like the last prank of Symeon Salos, whose body was miraculously spirited away. Not long after Chaplin's death on Christmas Day 1977, the superintendent of the Vevey Cemetery arrived for work one morning and found that this great fool's body, too, had vanished. It was a wonder and a mystery; the global press buzzed with speculation about Charles Chaplin's empty tomb.

But this miracle was also all too human. The thieves got busted a few weeks later, after failing to extort a ransom from the Chaplin estate. They were, it turns out, just a couple of tramps, trying to survive in a hungry world.

8

APOCALYPTIC COMEDY

This should be said: dogs, too, make good comedians. Consider Pluto, Chaplin's canine heir. Consider Scooby-Doo. Consider Marmaduke. Consider Petey, of *Our Gang* fame, or the *All Barkie Dogville Comedies* that MGM produced right at the beginning of the cinematic sound era. Consider all those YouTube videos you've seen.

Or consider Snoopy the beagle. What is he, this high-flown, round-snouted spirit? He is what gods would be if gods were also children. He is what children would be if children were also gods. He's what a dog would be if a dog were also a hippo. He's Joe Cool. He's a dance man. He's the World War I Flying Ace, dealing death from his doghouse in the sky.

Dogs make good comedians because dogs are a subspecies of children, and children, too, make good comedians. The children's troupes that gave Shakespeare a run for his money in the first era of modern professional theater were full of good comedians, and those child performers were nothing new. They carried memories of Christmastide boy bishops, children's carnival pageants, the carousing gangs of young people with whom Francis of Assisi honed his antic art. The first great comedians of the film era, Chaplin and Buster Keaton, started as boy acts in British music halls and American vaudeville houses, and after them came the little mayhem-makers of *Our Gang*, the little philosophers and freedom-fighters of *Peanuts*, the little improv artists of *Kids Say the Darndest Things*, the little serialized everypeople of *Leave It to Beaver*, *Webster*, *Diff'rent Strokes*, and *Full House*, the little action heroes and miniature grownups of family films from *The Shaggy Dog* to *Home Alone*.

There's something of the holy fool in these tiny adventurers. The paradigmatic holy fool, Symeon of Emesa, was himself a schoolyard cut-up, constantly getting in scuffles with mischievous boys and girls. His childlikeness was a gospel imperative—"unless you turn and become like children, you will never enter the kingdom of heaven"—and he understood, as many other saints also have, that the little ones of the present age possess something from beyond the present age.[1] The child clowns of comedy come bearing that something from beyond. They are atoms of innocence in an all-too-grown-up world. They see things grown-ups can't see, and they speak with a wisdom beyond the wisdom of adulthood. Sometimes they seem to belong, like Peter Pan's Lost Boys or Alice's Tweedledum and Tweedledee, to an upside-down order, a magic kingdom in which littleness is the highest form of strength.

That kingdom is the kingdom of comedy, and comedians at a certain level are always playing their infant selves. Chaplin's male counterparts in early comic cinema—Harold Lloyd, Stepin Fetchit, Curly Howard—were often man-child amphibians, and plenty of others have played the same role since. I began with these figures in my introduction. They prance around as little people in big bodies. Sometimes they play actual children, or grownups regressing into childhood. Sometimes—as Gallagher, Robin Williams, or Jim Carrey—they tear through gag props and silly faces with hyperactive abandon, as if fueled by red Kool-Aid or too many cartoons. Sometimes—as Ernest P. Worrell, Bob Wiley, or Ted Lasso—they play grown people blessed or cursed with perpetual childhood. Vanessa Bayer often plays an overgrown child, with her colossal-cute smile and her preschool-teacher enunciation. "Weird Al" Yankovic's special form of genius is the way he gathers into himself a whole iconography of pop stardom, a cultural universe predicated on badness and cool, and reimagines it all as a playground of goodness and innocence. Diane Morgan projects her own bent innocence in her Philomena Cunk persona, channeling both a frowning toddler and a sullen tween as she subjects world-class scholars and experts to conversations like this one, with gramophone expert Dr. Aleksander Kolkowski, from the "Rise of the Machines" episode of *Cunk on Earth*:

> *Philomena Cunk:* If I speak into this trumpet bit, can I ask the person a question about what it's like where they are?
>
> *Dr. Kolkowski:* No you can't, because the recording was made over a hundred years ago.
>
> *Philomena Cunk:* But it's a *phon*ograph. Doesn't it work like a phone?

Even taboo-breaking stand-up comedians, as I said in the beginning, have something in them of the overgrown child. Richard Pryor wasn't just channeling his lingering Bill Cosby envy when he told stories about his childhood and his own children. Stand-up comedians always tell a lot of stories about their childhoods and their children. That infant universe is where they live. Their vulnerability is part of their power. The story goes that when Nina Simone hired the young Pryor to open for her at the Village Gate in 1963, he trembled so pitifully before every performance that she took him in her arms, night after night, and rocked him like a baby.

*

To be an infant is to be naked: innocent, unashamed, possessing nothing. "Naked I came from my mother's womb," the biblical Job says, "and naked shall I return."[2] We might be tempted to misunderstand the frequent nakedness of comedians. Did you think all their stripping was a sign of their knowledge of good and evil?

They do strip a lot. Lenny Bruce walked naked onto the stage when he was working strip clubs in the 1950s. Pryor appeared naked, made up to look like his man-parts were gone, in the first episode of his 1977 television show. (It was his commentary on what had been done to him by his NBC handlers, who of course removed the scene from the actual broadcast.) Tig Notaro performed topless in 2014 after her double mastectomy. In comic films, it's conventional for the comedian to end up inconveniently naked: audiences of cinematic comedy have seen Alan Partridge's bum in a hilarious climbing-through-a-window debacle, Borat brawling naked with his producer in a hotel-room debacle, Brian Cohen standing naked before a giant crowd in a morning curtain-opening debacle. We've seen Key and Peele stripped to their bare torsos as slaves at auction, in a wickedly funny sketch about human flesh as a consumable good. (They're indignant about being sold as property; and then, increasingly with each round, they're indignant that no one's buying *them*.)

These strip shows are anti-erotic. They are spectacles of adipose flesh, meant more to mock than to arouse erotic desire. They acknowledge that these bodies of ours are frail and farting things, not entirely our own, subject both to jiggly decay and to the power of others. Think about how humiliating exposure can be. A keynote speaker goes to the bathroom wearing a hot lapel mic: humiliation. Some junior police officers lift the outer shell off a porta-potty where their commandant is doing his business, right in the middle of a sports arena: howling, skull-clutching humiliation. In scenes like these (from *The Naked Gun* and *Police Academy 4*, if you really want to know), the fig leaves of respectability are torn away and someone proud is brought low. There's no desire, in these scenes of nakedness, but the desire to hide. And even when the stripping of the comedian has a tremor of erotic energy—when Donna Reed's character ends up naked in the bushes in *It's A Wonderful Life*, or when a thousand female comedians after her find themselves accidentally locked out of the shower—there's an innocence in her predicament of nakedness. She's without guile in this moment of maximum exposure. When the laughter does turn leering and lewd—when, in other words, the dynamics of power tilt toward the men who might catch a glimpse of her—it's generally a sign that the comedian in the room is not the person who's been stripped.

But in the anti-eros of these stripped comedians there's also another kind of desire, a different and deeper sort of eros. Think again about naked saints such as Symeon of Emesa, bursting into the women's bathhouse and recounting afterward that it was as if he didn't have a body, or Francis of Assisi, stripping himself in order to die in communion with the dust of the earth. In these strip shows, the uncovering is an apocalypse in the very basic sense that it reveals. When Francis stripped for the last time, the early legends report, he uncovered his hidden stigmata and so revealed his union with the crucified Christ. His secret self was laid bare, and the invisible kingdom to which he belonged became visible. Your secret self is laid bare, too, when your expensive trousers snag on a nail and your flabby bum greets the crowd you wanted to impress. In this stripping, the question of who you really are is answered.

There is a kind of eros, a desire to know, in these scenes of exposure. Comedians create an effect of striptease when they hide behind layers of disguise and dare audiences to ask who's really here. Kate Berlant did this when, at the end of *Cinnamon in the Wind*, she reached up to strip off her mask and show us the real face underneath. Andy Kaufman turned this sort of comic teasing into a complex theater of illusion, shape-shifting in and out of his identities as Tony Clifton, Foreign Man, Elvis impersonators, impersonators of Elvis impersonators, Andy the wrestler, Andy the naïf, Andy the screaming jerk, Andy the mumbling failure, and Andy full stop, the "real" Andy, who isn't like—or is he like?—all those other Andys.

He could whirl through all these identities in the course of a single performance, teasing his audience into a growing desire to rip away the layers of costuming and get to the real Andy Kaufman underneath it all. Symeon of Emesa played this game of antic misdirection, too, and the more his audience watched his act, the more they came to believe that he had a secret, a hidden identity no one could map out. They followed him, worked at his riddles, tried to make sense of what they saw him doing when no one else was looking.

In some of their performances, these saints and comedians tease us with the promised revelation not just of one person's naked selfhood but of larger human realities, things we share in common. They are like Shakespeare's Mad Tom, whose stripped body shows King Lear a vision of humanity in all our ridiculous abasement. "Thou art the thing itself," Lear cries, staring at Mad Tom's nakedness: "unaccommodated man is no more but such a poor bare, forked animal as thou art." And then, with the cry, "Off, off, you lendings," he himself starts to strip, trembling with desire for the primal human condition that the abject wild man represents.

But Lear doesn't get naked after all, because his Fool stops him. And we know what Lear does not: that even the nakedness of this madman is an elaborate disguise. The showman billed as The Thing Itself turns out to have his own secrets. He's like Symeon in the bathhouse and Andy in his costumes, laughing at our lust and keeping the eschaton of fulfilled desire out beyond our reach.

*

The festivities that have occasionally come into view in this book—Saturnalia, Sabbath, Eucharist, Carnival—all depend on what Charles Taylor calls "higher times," on realities that exist beyond ordinary time and that nevertheless break into ordinary time and give it a new shape.[3] The fools and lords of misrule who preside over these festivals enact a golden age, an Edenic innocence or eschatological future. They embody orders of being larger than the laws that govern our ordinary social existence, and they invite the citizens of the ordinary present to inhabit those higher times, to become children in the garden of Eden and lovers at the wedding supper of the Lamb. In their miracles of community and their enactments of a world without scarcity, these festivals are apocalypses, prophetic disclosures of a kingdom that both undergirds and upends the world of the present. They celebrate the spiritual eros—the aching desire—that reaches all the way out toward the consummation of all things.

Even now, centuries after many of them have had cultural salience, these festivals are the homeland of comedy. It's no accident that at the beginning of the modern era, Shakespeare's comedies derived so much of their form and their energy (and their titles) from rituals such as Christmas, Twelfth Night, and Midsummer. And the festive core of comedy helps to explain why so many comic plots still revolve around the occasions of weddings, funerals, Christmas celebrations, frat-house keggers, family reunions, camping trips, exotic vacations, sports tournaments, and trials by jury. These observances are our own Saturnalian festivities, the places where we enact our apocalyptic visions of a world made new.

I once saw Kirk Fox open a stand-up set by promising that if the world out there ended while he was on stage in this comedy club, he would take care of us. He would pair us up like Adams and Eves to begin repopulating the earth. He would send scouts out to look for any relatives we think might still be alive. He would stand at the ready to do a little CPR. I don't exactly know how to do CPR, he said—not too clear about the R—but others can fill in, and we'll be a family. The effect of the set was that the world outside this windowless room came to seem spectral and far off, and we, huddled together around our tables, seemed the beginning of a new human community, both a little Eden in the wasteland of the ordinary and an image of something on the other side of this life.

Stand-up comedy offers more of these visions than we tend to notice. Marc Maron's 2021 special *End Times Fun* ended with an apocalyptic vision in which Jesus returns to an ecologically wasted earth. Lenny Bruce's famous "Christ and Moses" bit imagined those two figures visiting contemporary New York and Los Angeles, wreaking havoc and exposing hypocrisy everywhere they went. Richard Pryor had a bit in which God comes to the earth for a visit, asks to see Emmett Till, Bobby Kennedy, and Jesus, and learns that we murdered them all. There are no gags or punchlines in this little fantasy; it's simply a scene of reckoning.

All these bits express a prophetic indignation about the wrongs of the world, but they all point also toward something bigger, a spiritual or moral order that exposes and outlasts those wrongs. At a moment in the fall of 2016 that felt apocalyptic to many people, Dave Chappelle closed his election-week monologue on *Saturday Night Live* by offering his own attempt at apocalyptic vision. He told of a party he once attended at the Obama White House, in which the past, the present, and the future seemed to gather in a single moment of revelation:

> I saw the bus stop, or the corner where the bus stop used to be, where I used to catch the bus to school and dream of nights like tonight… and at the end of the night everyone went into the West Wing of the White House, and there was a huge party, and everybody in there was Black… and on the walls were pictures of all the Presidents of the past… and I looked at that room, and I saw all those Black faces… and I saw how happy everybody was… and it made me feel hopeful, and it made me feel proud to be an American, and it made me very happy about the prospects of our country.

His vision was not just a vision of one night at the White House. It was a vision of what America has been, is, and might be, and of what happens when the exiled children of Eden join together in hopeful celebration. It was an apocalypse. He might almost have added: *And I saw the holy city, new Jerusalem, coming down out of heaven from God... and I heard a loud voice from the throne saying, "Behold, the dwelling of God is with men. He will dwell with them, and they shall be his people..." and he who sat upon the throne said, "Behold, I make all things new."*[4]

This vision is not out of place in the context of comedy. Comic plots, too, tend to end with scenes of apocalyptic doom, with Keystone Cop brawls and banjo-music chases, with the crashing of parties and the stripping of disguises, with decisions by juries and long-resistant love interests, with Slim Pickens riding his H-bomb to the Great Rodeo in the Sky. The comic climax is the breaking or boiling point, the cataclysmic crash through which everything is revealed. And then, after the cataclysm, comes the feast, and the flickering image of a world made new: weddings, dancing, scenes of resolution and celebration. At the center of these apocalyptic scenes stands the comedian, looking for a language weird enough to convey something of that other world. Comedians often find themselves speaking the sort of gorgeous nonsense that Shakespeare's Bottom the Weaver does after he's lost his ass's head and awakened from his midnight-mad enchantment:

> I have had a most rare vision. I have had a dream past the wit of man to say what dream it was. Man is but an ass, if he go about to expound this dream. Methought I was—there is no man can tell what. Methought I was, and methought I had—but man is but a patched fool if he will offer to say what methought I had. The eye of man hath not heard, the ear of man hath not seen, man's hand is not able to taste, his tongue to conceive, nor his heart to report what my dream was. I will get Peter Quince to write a ballad of this dream. It shall be called "Bottom's Dream," because it hath no bottom....[5]

He's doing his best and silliest Paul of Tarsus impression here. There's no point in asking whether this is mystical vision or whimsical comedy. In Bottom's universe, you can't have one without the other.

*

I've said throughout this book that the charisma of both saints and comedians is connected to their suffering, their exile from the economy of power in the present age. But their distinctive vitality depends even more on their embodiment of an alternative economy, a kingdom that turns the laws of the present age upside down. "I can levitate birds," says Steven Wright, "but nobody cares." Both sides of the equation are here. *Nobody cares*: this is a person destined for abjection. And at the same time: he can *levitate birds*.

We've met all sorts of figures whose weakness or abjection becomes the source of their power, from little spiritual warriors like Thecla and Francis, to little sufferers like the Chaplin of *City Lights* and the nebbish J of *Awkward Black Girl*, to the little prophets and CPR-class dropouts who bring tidings of the apocalypse. It's no accident that, in American culture, one of the most resonant representations of the paradigmatic little warrior, the Christ child, comes in the person of Linus van Pelt, clutching his blanket and speaking to an empty auditorium: "And this shall be a sign unto you: you shall find the babe wrapped in swaddling clothes, and lying in a manger." The unlikely victors of all these comic performances overcome the world of temporal power by affirming the things temporal power chronically fails to acknowledge: faith, hope, love, *shalom*, the grace of forgiveness, the promise of resurrection, the possibility that those birds aren't flying but levitating, because there are miracles all around.

And then there are the three hermits who couldn't remember the part about the daily bread. They scratch their heads and walk on water, and they, too, belong to this army of unlikely messiahs. They are a joke, foolish enough to forget the Lord's Prayer; and they are a revelation, foolish enough also to forget the laws of gravity. Around them, the kingdom of heaven is already breaking through. Like all tellers of good jokes, they disclose in the apocalyptic *boom* of this *click-boom* scene the secret of who they really are. They are, it turns out, citizens of a kingdom beyond gravity, and their walk across the water enacts a future that makes the present look strange. In their wonder-working innocence, they belong to a history that stretches from the image of the boy Isaac sitting puzzled on the altar of sacrifice to the image of Linus on stage, an impromptu stand-up artist, declaring that the kingdom is at hand.

So the comic performance of the water-walkers is a festive occasion, an enactment of the miraculous life at the center and the end of all things. Who are they? They are mere mortals, no doubt, ignorant, failing, and frail. But out on the water, they are prophets of the eschaton. They are holy fools. They are Joe Cool. They float free of the earth, birds being levitated, while the people down below look up from their striving and the sound of an everlasting laughter begins to be heard.

Notes

INTRODUCTION

1. Berger tells the story in *Redeeming Laughter: The Comic Dimension of Human Experience* (De Gruyter, 2014), 193. I've retold it here in my own way.

2. Matt. 18:3. Unless otherwise indicated, all biblical quotations come from the *Revised Standard Version*, ed. Herbert G. May and Bruce M. Metzger (Oxford, 1973).

3. It was, she said, "probably why he retained that marvelous child-like wonder and innocence." Quoted in Kenneth Lynn, *Charlie Chaplin and His Times* (Simon & Schuster, 1997), 51.

4. Kliph Nesteroff tells a big part of this story in *The Comedians: Drunks, Thieves, Scoundrels, and the History of American Comedy* (Grove Press, 2015).

5. Aristotle, *Poetics*, trans. Stephen Halliwell (University of North Carolina, 1987), 37.

6. *Poetics*, 36.

7. This interview, with Larry Siegel, was first published in *Playboy* (October 1966) but has become famous and circulated around fairly widely.

8. This one, with Brad Darrach, again first appeared in *Playboy* (February 1975).

9. Ezek. 12:18.

10. Isa. 6:5.

11. Goldman, *Ladies and Gentlemen: Lenny Bruce!* (Random House, 1971), 452.

12. I quote Gleason from his liner notes for the 1975 album *The Real Lenny Bruce*, now anthologized in *Music in the Air: The Selected Writings of Ralph J. Gleason*, ed. Toby Gleason (Yale, 2016), 221; and Merton from David Belcastro, "Thomas Merton and the Beat Generation: A Subterranean Monastic Community," in *The World in My Bloodstream: Thomas Merton's Universal Embrace* (Three Peaks Press, 2004), 86.

13. On Jewish humor, though, the place to start is Jeremy Dauber's *Jewish Comedy (A Serious History)* (Norton, 2017).

14. G. K. Chesterton, *Heretics*, in *Collected Works*, vol. 1 (Ignatius, 1986), 166.

15. Quoted in Simon Critchley, *On Humor* (Routledge, 2002), 17–18.

CHAPTER 1

1. I cite all early *vitae* of Francis from the great collection of documents gathered in the three volumes of *Francis of Assisi: Early Documents*, ed. Regis J. Armstrong, J. A. Wayne Hellmann, and William J. Short (New City Press, 1999), here qtd. at 1.113-14. I cite by volume and page number.

2. *Early Documents* 2.186.

3. *Compilatio Assisiensis*, ed. Marino Bigaroni, vol. 2 of *Pubblicazioni Della Biblioteca Francescana Chiesa Nuova—Assisi* (Porziuncola, 1975), 236.

4. *Early Documents* 2.186. The Latin for "minstrels," again here, is *ioculatores*.

5. *Early Documents* 2.209. The text of the *Assisi Compilation*, in which this story appears, reads, "I, a breviary! I, a breviary!" In modifying the English translation, I follow André Vauchez, *Francis of Assisi: The Life and Afterlife of a Medieval Saint* (Yale, 2012), 123.

6. *Early Documents* 3.491. This last one, like many of the more outlandish stories about Francis, appears in a fourteenth-century Latin text called the *Deeds of Saint Francis and His Companions*, very popular

(especially in its Italian translation, *The Little Flowers of Saint Francis*) but often of questionable veracity.

7. *Early Documents* 2.318.

8. *Early Documents* 2.318.

9. See, e.g., Vauchez, *Francis of Assisi*, 78–80, 99–100.

10. *Early Documents* 2.560.

11. *Early Documents* 1.283, 280; and see also 1.254, 260. Here and in my quotations from Bonaventure's *vita*, I've omitted line breaks that appear in the versified text.

12. On these markets and Pietro's career, as on much else, Arnoldo Fortini's *Francis of Assisi*, trans. Helen Moak (Crossroad, 1980), is dizzying and magnificent (and sometimes fanciful) in its detail; see 39–40.

13. *Early Documents* 2.68.

14. These Italian terms I take, respectively, from Fortini, *Francis of Assisi*, 131–42; and Vauchez, *Francis of Assisi*, 15.

15. *Early Documents* 2.69.

16. Vauchez, *Francis of Assisi*, 10.

17. *Early Documents* 2.243.

18. See Fortini's account, *Francis of Assisi*, 154–55.

19. *Early Documents* 2.70.

20. *Early Documents* 1.185.

21. *Early Documents* 2.271.

22. *Early Documents* 2.70.

23. *Early Documents* 2.71.

24. *Early Documents* 2.532.

25. *Early Documents* 2.71.

26. Says Paul, "What shall I do, Lord?" (Acts 22:10).

27. *Early Documents* 2.74.

28. They were "hunted like dogs," says Fortini in his harrowing and vivid account; see *Francis of Assisi*, 206–11, qtd. at 211.

29. *Early Documents* 2.249.

30. *Early Documents* 2.74.

31. *Early Documents* 1.124.

32. *Early Documents* 2.80.

33. *Early Documents* 2.80.

34. *Early Documents* 2.538; and see also Thomas of Celano's nearly identical comment, *Early Documents* 1.193.

35. *Early Documents* 1.194.

36. *Early Documents* 1.166–67.

37. *Early Documents* 2.133.

38. As before, *Early Documents* 2.186.

39. Matt. 3:2; *Early Documents* 3.508, 1.275.

40. The wolf of Gubbio story, like the jumping-in-the-fireplace story, appears among the more questionable narratives of the *Deeds of Saint Francis and His Companions*, in *Early Documents* 3.482–85, qtd. at 483.

41. *Early Documents* 1.126.

42. *Early Documents* 1.250.

43. *Early Documents* 2.642.

CHAPTER 2

1. 1 Sam. 16:1–13.
2. 1 Sam. 16:6.
3. Job 19:21.
4. Esther 4:14.
5. 4 Macc. 11:12.
6. 2 Macc. 7:33–34.
7. 2 Macc. 7:38.

8. Van Henten, "Jewish and Christian Martyrs," in Marcel Poorthuis and Joshua J. Schwartz, *Saints and Role Models in Judaism and Christianity* (Brill, 2004), 165. Note that Youval Rotman records the Hebrew phrase as *kiddush hašem*, *Insanity and Sanctity in Byzantium* (Harvard, 2016), 93.

9. I've learned a lot about this idea from Yair Furstenberg, "The Changing Worlds of the Ten Rabbinic Martyrs," in *Martyrdom: Canonisation, Contestation and Afterlives*, ed. Ihab Saloul and Jan Willem van Henten (Amsterdam, 2020), 55–77; and from Daniel Boyarin, *Dying for God: Martyrdom and the Making of Christianity and Judaism* (Stanford, 1999). See also Rotman, *Insanity and Sanctity in Byzantium*, 106–8.

10. This is the *Story of the Ten Martyrs*, which circulated in various forms in late antiquity, on which see Furstenberg, "The Changing Worlds of the Ten Rabbinic Martyrs."

11. *Yerushalmi Berakhot* 9.3, in *The Talmud of the Land of Israel*, vol. 1, trans. Tzvee Zahavy (Chicago, 1989), 346.

12. It's in episode 16.

13. These digital platforms, though, have also changed the nature of the exchange. Jesse David Fox discusses this perceptively in *Comedy Book: How Comedy Conquered Culture—And the Magic That Makes It Work* (Farrar, Straus, and Giroux, 2023).

INTERLUDE: A JOKE IS A PROPHECY

1. Eccl. 7:24.

2. Dan. 2:28.

3. Freud, *Jokes and Their Relation to the Unconscious*, trans. James Strachey (Norton, 1960), 13–14; in the first quoted bit, Freud is himself quoting the German philosopher Kuno Fischer.

4. *The Dialogue of Solomon and Marcolf: A Dual-Language Edition from Latin and Middle English Printed Editions*, ed. Nancy Mason Bradbury (Medieval Institute, 2012), 4.10.

5. Blake's Proverbs of Hell are part of his poem, "The Marriage of Heaven and Hell," in *The Complete Poetry and Prose of William Blake*, ed. David Erdman (Berkeley, 1982).

6. *The Dialogue of Solomon and Marcolf*, 4.71.

7. I quote this from Richard Zoglin, *Comedy at the Edge: How Stand-up in the 1970s Changed America* (Bloomsbury, 2008), 220.

8. I quote from his 2017 Netflix special *Louis C. K*, 2017.

9. Charles M. Schultz, *A Peanuts Treasury* (MetroBooks, 1968).

CHAPTER 3

1. There might be a joke here about the Elizabethan penalties for certain sorts of public-speech violations: printers who fell afoul of government censors really did sometimes lose their ears. But still.

2. There are some good biographies of Armin, including Charles Feltner, *Robert Armin, Shakespeare's Fool: A Biographical Essay* (Kent State University Bulletin, 1961) and the relevant chapters in David Grote, *The Best Actors in the World* (Greenwood, 2002), Andrew Gurr, *The Shakespeare Company, 1594–1642* (Cambridge, 2004), Bart van Es, *Shakespeare in Company*, and David Wiles, *Shakespeare's Clown* (Cambridge, 1987).

3. Keir Elam and Leslie Katz, "Armin/Shakespeare Collab: 'you must allow vox,'" *Journal of the Wooden O Symposium* 19 (2019): 51–69.

4. On Kempe's jigs, see Wiles, *Shakespeare's Clown*, esp. 43–60.

5. I have found Grote's comments about the difference of the Kempe-era plays useful: see *The Best Actors in the World*, 93–97.

6. On which see Millicent Bell, *Shakespeare's Tragic Skepticism* (Yale, 2002).

7. See, for instance, Catherine Henze, *Robert Armin and Shakespeare's Performed Songs* (Routledge, 2017).

8. Every scholarly account tells a slightly different story about the chronology of Armin's arrival. To say that Touchstone was written for Armin in 1599 is to follow majority opinion; but dating Kempe's final public break to spring 1600, as I do, makes that claim complicated. Some scholars, such as David Grote, claim that Armin came later and that Touchstone was in fact written for Kempe. See *The Best Actors in the World*, 83–93.

9. *As You Like It* 5.1.56. All quotations of Shakespeare's plays come from *William Shakespeare: The Complete Works*, second edition, ed. John Jowett, William Montgomery, Gary Taylor, and Stanley Wells (Oxford, 2005). I'll occasionally make small changes to punctuation and orthography.

10. *Twelfth Night* 3.1.34.

11. *Troilus and Cressida* 5.8.8–9.

12. *The Tempest* 3.2.146.

13. *King Lear* 3.4.100.

14. *King Lear* 3.4.33–34.

15. *King Lear* 1.4.144.

16. *King Lear* 3.2.79–80.

17. On John in the Hospital, see Sandra Dahlberg and Peter Greenfield, "'To stirre vp liuing mens minds to the like good'": Robert Armin, John in the Hospital, and the Representation of Poverty," *Medieval & Renaissance Drama in England* 29 (2016): 46–67.

18. *King Lear* 2.2.259–60.

19. Armin, *Fool upon Fool* (London, 1600).

CHAPTER 4

1. For the details of Pryor's life, I'm indebted to Scott Saul, *Becoming Richard Pryor* (Harper, 2014), and to David Henry and Joe Henry, *Furious Cool: Richard Pryor and the World that Made Him* (Algonquin, 2013).

2. On this detail, see Henry and Henry, *Furious Cool*, 212-213.

3. See Saul, *Becoming Richard Pryor*, 471.

4. Henry and Henry, *Furious Cool*, 82.

5. On these traumas see Saul, *Becoming Richard Pryor*, 39-40, 48; and Henry and Henry, *Furious Cool*, 25-26.

6. Quoted in Carpio, *Laughing Fit to Kill: Black Humor in the Fictions of Slavery* (Oxford, 2008), 95.

7. Carpio, *Laughing Fit to Kill*, 15.

8. Carpio, *Laughing Fit to Kill*, 75.

9. Carpio discusses these renunciations, and Pryor's responsibility for his performances, in *Laughing Fit to Kill*, 95-100.

10. Henry and Henry, *Furious Cool*, 156. Saul describes some other scenes of the screenplay, which survives in fragments, in *Becoming Richard Pryor*, 260-61. It's wild.

INTERLUDE: COMEDY IS A CARNIVAL

1. George Thompson, *Aeschylus and Athens* (Grosset & Dunlop, 1968), 226.

2. Many of these facts I glean from the fifth-century writer Macrobius. See his dialogue *Saturnalia*, trans. Robert A. Kaster (Loeb Classical

Library, 2011), 1.10.1, 1.6.2. On mock combats involving women and dwarves, see Statius, *Silvae*, trans. D. R. Shackleton Bailey (Loeb Classical Library, 2003), 1.6.51–56. There's a remarkable representation of a slave's reckless Saturnalian speech in Horace's second book of satires, where the poet's slave Davus attacks his master with incendiary moralizing fury. See Horace, *Satires*, trans. H. Rushton Fairclough (Loeb Classical Library, 1926), 2.7.

3. Horace, *Satires*, 2.3.1–10.

4. *The Metamorphoses of Ovid*, trans. Allen Mandelbaum (Harvest, 1993); see 1.89–112.

5. Gen. 2:25; Isa. 65:25.

6. Heb. 4:9–10.

7. Matt. 26:29.

8. Rev. 21:5.

CHAPTER 5

1. That's my paraphrase; see Prudentius, *Crowns of Martyrdom*, trans. H. J. Thompson (Loeb Classical Library, 1953), 2.401–4.

2. Henry George Liddell and Robert Scott, *An Intermediate Greek-English Lexicon* (Oxford, 1997); Plato, *Gorgias*, ed. G. P. Goold (Loeb Classical Library, 1925), 471e. The English translation is mine.

3. Aristotle, *Rhetoric*, ed. J. H. Freese (Loeb Classical Library, 1982), 1.15.13.

4. W. H. C. Frend, *Martyrdom and Persecution in the Early Church: A Study of a Conflict from the Maccabees to Donatus* (Baker, 1981), 87–91.

5. I offer here the traditionally accepted dates. Some (Perpetua, Lawrence) bear up under critical scrutiny; some are harder to establish. Candida Moss argues, for instance, that the *Martyrdom of Polycarp* is a third-century text, *Ancient Christian Martyrdom: Diverse Practices, Theologies, and Traditions* (Yale, 2012), 62–75.

6. *The Martyrdom of Polycarp*, in *Ante-Nicene Fathers*, vol. 1, ed. Alexander Roberts and James Donaldson (Hendrickson, 1994), 39.

7. *The Martyrdom of Polycarp*, 41. That last quotation is my paraphrase.

8. That account appears in Prudentius' poem *Crowns of Martyrdom*. The persecutions of 258 are attested in historical records, but the details of Prudentius's legend of Lawrence are impossible to verify.

9. *Crowns of Martyrdom* 2.173–76.

10. *Crowns of Martyrdom* 2.272–76, 282.

11. *Crowns of Martyrdom* 2.318–20, 324.

12. *Crowns of Martyrdom* 2.401–3. I've amended the Loeb translation—"let's try what your hot god of fire has done"—to capture the more specific language of the original: *tuus Vulcanus ardens*.

13. *Crowns of Martyrdom* 2.394.

14. See Ambrose, *Duties of the Clergy*, in *Nicene and Post-Nicene Fathers*, vol. 10, ed. Philip Schaff and Henry Wace (Eeerdmans, 1979), 65.

15. For Akiva's laughter under torture, see, again, *Yerushalmi Berakhot* 9.3, in *The Talmud of the Land of Israel*, 346. For the fox and Akiva's merriment, see *The Babylonian Talmud: Seder Nezikin: Makkoth*, trans. H. M. Lazarus, ed. Rabbi Dr. I. Epstein (Rebecca Bennet, 1959), 24a–24b.

16. *The Martyrdom of Perpetua*, in *Ante-Nicene Fathers*, vol. 2, ed. Alexander Roberts and James Donaldson (Hendrickson, 1994), 704.

17. *The Martyrdom of Andrew*, in *Ante-Nicene Fathers*, vol. 8, ed. Alexander Roberts and James Donaldson (Hendrickson, 1994), 515.

18. *The Acts of Sharbil*, in *Ante-Nicene Fathers*, vol. 8, 691.

19. *The Letter of the Churches of Vienna and Lugdumum*, in *Ante-Nicene Fathers*, vol. 8, 782.

CHAPTER 6

1. 1 Cor. 4:9.

2. L. L. Welborn, *Paul, The Fool of Christ: A Study of 1 Corinthians 1-4 in the Comic-Philosophic Tradition* (T & T Clark, 2005), 50–54; Liddell and Scott, *An Intermediate Greek-English Lexicon*.

3. 1 Cor. 4:10.

4. See Liddell and Scott, *An Intermediate Greek-English Lexicon*, for the full range of meanings.

5. Welborn, *Paul, The Fool of Christ*, 32–39.

6. For a general account of mime and its popularity, see Welborn, *Paul, The Fool of Christ*, 3–10.

7. 1 Cor. 4:10, 11, 13.

8. 1 Cor. 1:23.

9. 1 Cor. 1:28.

10. 1 Cor. 3:18. See also John Saward, *Perfect Fools: Folly for Christ's Sake in Catholic and Orthodox Spirituality* (Oxford, 1980), 1-7.

11. Prudentius, *Crowns of Martyrdom*, 317-18; I've tweaked the translation here, from "art" to "trick."

12. Rotman, *Sanity and Insanity*, 12. I've slightly amended the punctuation here.

13. On which see Peter Brown, "The Rise and Function of the *Holy Man* in Late Antiquity," *The Journal of Roman Studies* 61 (1971): 80-101.

14. For Isidora and Sarapion, see Saward, *Perfect Fools*, 14-15. For Symeon, see Theodoret of Cyrrhus, *A History of the Monks of Syria*, trans. R. M. Price (Cistercian Publications, 1985), 160-76.

15. Theodoret, *A History of the Monks of Syria*, 170.

16. John of Ephesus, *Lives of the Eastern Saints*, trans. E. W. Brooks (Firmin-Didot, 1923), 513.

17. Saward suggests "crackpot," *Perfect Fools*, 15

18. *Acts of Paul and Thecla*, 487

19. Mark 12:25.

20. *Acts of Paul and Thecla*, 588

21. *Acts of Paul and Thecla*, 488.

22. *Acts of Paul and Thecla*, 489.

23. *Acts of Paul and Thecla*, 489.

24. *Acts of Paul and Thecla*, 491.

25. *Acts of Paul and Thecla*, 490–91.

26. Gal. 3:28.

27. *Acts of Paul and Thecla*, 492. Some manuscripts say she then went to Rome searching for Paul (who would have been well past 100), learned he was dead, and there died herself. Not all contain the passage I've quoted.

28. Frend, *Martyrdom and Persecution*, 158.

29. Frend, *Martyrdom and Persecution*, 158.

30. See Stephen Davis, *The Cult of Saint Thecla: A Tradition of Women's Piety in Late Antiquity* (Oxford, 2001).

31. Davis, *The Cult of Saint Thecla*, 4.

32. Leontius of Neapolis, *The Life of Symeon the Fool*, in Derek Krueger, *Symeon the Holy Fool: Leontius's Life and the Late Antique City* (Berkeley, 1996), 133.

33. *The Life of Symeon the Fool*, 134.

34. *The Life of Symeon the Fool*, 142.

35. *The Life of Symeon the Fool*, 146.

36. *The Life of Symeon the Fool*, 146.

37. *The Life of Symeon the Fool*, 148.

38. *The Life of Symeon the Fool*, 148.

39. *The Life of Symeon the Fool*, 154.

40. *The Life of Symeon the Fool*, 156.

41. *The Life of Symeon the Fool*, 157, 160.

42. *The Life of Symeon the Fool*, 150.

43. *The Life of Symeon the Fool*, 159.

44. *The Life of Symeon the Fool*, 154.

45. *The Life of Symeon the Fool*, 153.

46. *The Life of Symeon the Fool*, 155.

47. *The Life of Symeon the Fool*, 165.

48. *The Life of Symeon the Fool*, 168.

49. On Philip Neri, see James Martin, SJ, *Between Heaven and Mirth* (HarperOne, 2011), 77–78. On Procopius and many other figures from Russia to Ireland, see Saward, *Perfect Fools*.

50. Saward, *Perfect Fools*, 16.

INTERLUDE: RITES OF RENEWAL

1. Frye, *Anatomy of Criticism* (Princeton, 1957), 164–65.

2. Rev. 21:5; *Midsummer* 3.3.45–47.

3. On the dancelike choreography of this play, see C. L. Barber, *Shakespeare's Festive Comedy: A Study of Dramatic Form and Its Relation to Social Custom* (Princeton, 1959), 128–29.

CHAPTER 7

1. For much of what I know about the events of Chaplin's life, I'm indebted to David Robinson, *Chaplin: His Life and Art* (McGraw-Hill, 1985), Kenneth Lynn, *Charlie Chaplin and His Times* (Simon & Schuster, 1997), and Chaplin's own *My Autobiography* (Melville House, 2012). Many of the details of the *City Lights* premiere I glean from Robinson, *Chaplin*, 414–15, and from press clippings gathered at the Charlie Chaplin Archive: www.charliechaplinarchive.org. Chaplin himself tells the story in *My Autobiography*, 326–27.
2. Robinson, *Chaplin*, 414.
3. Robinson, *Chaplin*, 414.
4. Quoted from Lynn, *Charlie Chaplin and His Times*, 337. Chaplin's own "it was beautiful" comments are quoted in Robinson, *Chaplin*, 410.
5. Chaplin, *My Autobiography*, 327.
6. Lynn, *Charlie Chaplin and His Times*, 296.
7. Robinson, *Chaplin*, 160.
8. Lynn, *Charlie Chaplin and His Times*, 162.
9. Lynn, *Charlie Chaplin and His Times*, 297.
10. Lynn, *Charlie Chaplin and His Times*, 301, 276.
11. Lynn, *Charlie Chaplin and His Times*, 259.
12. Lynn, *Charlie Chaplin and His Times*, 516.
13. Lynn, *Charlie Chaplin and His Times*, 125.
14. Chaplin, *My Autobiography*, 16–17.
15. Lynn, *Charlie Chaplin and His Times*, 35.
16. Chaplin, *My Autobiography*, 33.
17. Robinson, *Chaplin*, 27.
18. Chaplin, *My Autobiography*, 32.
19. Lynn, *Charlie Chaplin and His Times*, 19–20.
20. Chaplin, *My Autobiography*, 44.
21. On which see Lynn, *Charlie Chaplin and His Times*, 60; and Robinson, *Chaplin*, 31–32.
22. Lynn, *Charlie Chaplin and His Times*, 87.
23. Robinson, *Chaplin*, 102.

24. Charles Maland, *Chaplin and American Culture: The Evolution of a Star Image* (Princeton, 1989), 7.

25. I've learned a lot about these early films from Dan Kamin's books *The Comedy of Charlie Chaplin: Artistry in Motion* (Scarecrow, 2008) and *Charlie Chaplin's One-Man Show* (Scarecrow, 1984), and also from Jeffrey Vance, *Chaplin: Genius of the Cinema* (Harry N. Abrams, 2003) and Kyp Harness, *The Art of Charlie Chaplin: A Film-by-Film Analysis* (McFarland, 2008).

26. Maland, *Chaplin and American Culture*, 8.

27. Maland, *Chaplin and American Culture*, 26–27; Robinson, *Chaplin*, 159–60.

28. Robinson, *Chaplin*, 160.

29. See Kamin, *The Comedy of Charlie Chaplin*, 55.

30. Robinson, *Chaplin*, 252.

31. Robinson, *Chaplin*, 360; Lynn, *Charlie Chaplin and His Times*, 307.

32. Robinson, *Chaplin*, 514.

33. Robinson, *Chaplin*, 632.

CHAPTER 8

1. I quote Jesus's words from Matt. 18:3.

2. Job 1:21.

3. Charles Taylor, *A Secular Age* (Harvard, 2007), 54.

4. Rev. 21:1-5.

5. *A Midsummer Night's Dream*, 4.1.198–213. As usual, I quote from *The Oxford Shakespeare*, but I here amend the punctuation in a couple of places to conform to modern American usage.

Index

Abasement   105, 135
  self-   41, 97
  stereotypes and   102
Abraham   52
absurdity   64, 66
  of Chaplin, Charlie   177
  martyrdom, relation to   120, 125
  Symeon, of Emesa, relation to   151
The Acts of Paul and Thecla   139–43, 212 n.27
addiction   104–5
Admonitions (Francis of Assisi)   45
Agee, James   166
The Age of Spin (comedy special)   102–3
Agur   63–4
Ahasuerus (King)   51
Akiva (Rabbi)   53, 124
Aladdin Hotel and Casino, Las Vegas   98
Alan Partridge (fictional character)   194
Allen, Woody   54
"All-Women-Going-Through-Perimenopause-and-Menopaue" Comedy   60
al-Malik al-Kamil   41
alter ego
  of Chaplin, Charlie   167–9, 178, 187
  of Symeon, of Emesa   152–3
Altman, Robert   9

Amador, Charles   167
Ambrose, of Milan   124
American culture, myths of   101
Ancient Christian Martyrs (Moss)   210 n.5
Andrew, martyrdom of   125
anger   28, 126
Antioch   140, 142
Antiochus IV Epiphanes   52–3
anti-wisdom   66–8
apocalypse   2–3, 5
  anti-wisdom and   67–8
  comedy, relation to   13, 18
  jokes and   65–6
  prophecy of   198–201
  Saturnalia, relation to   110
apodeiknynai (to put on a show)   132–3
apokalyptein (to disclose or uncover)   65
Aristophanes   43, 109, 155
Aristotle   11–13, 116
Armin, Robert   73–5, 77
  as Blue John   88–9
  in *Hamlet*   84
  in *King Lear*   85–6
  Lord Chamberlain's Men and   79, 82
  natural fools and   76
  physiognomy of   87
  Pryor, R., compared to   106
  Quips upon Questions   78–9, 86
  as Touchstone   82–3, 208 n.8

Arrested Development (television series)   54
asceticism, martyrdom and   143
ascetic violence   151
askēsis (training)   143
Astaire, Fred   179
As You Like It (Shakespeare)   156
   Touchstone in   82–4, 87, 208 n.8
   weddings in   158
Atkinson, Rowan   54
atrocities   128
Auden, W. H.   21
Augustus (Emperor)   134
authority, relation to laughter   123

Baby J (film)   96
The Babylonians (Aristophanes)   109
bad faith   83
Ball, Lucille   91
Bamford, Maria   4
   self-disclosure of   77
   weakness and   58–9
Barbie (fictional character)   4, 42
Bargatze, Nate   57–8, 77
Barr, Roseanne   57
Barton, Ralph   169
Battle of Collestrada   33–5
Baumann, Charles   175
Bayer, Vanessa   192–3
beatitude   20–1
Berger, Peter   1
Bergman, Henry   180
Berlant, Kate   58, 152, 195
Berle, Milton   11
Bernardone, Francesco. *See* Francis, of Assisi
Bernardone, Pica   29
Bernardone, Pietro   29–30, 40
Berra, Yogi   9
Birbiglia, Mike   59
The Bird Revelation (comedy special)   102
Birds (Aristophanes)   43
Blackness   100, 103–4

Blake, William   67
Blandina   116, 118, 127, 129
Blazing Saddles (film)   48
blocking character   156
Blue John (fictional character)   88–9
Bob Wiley (fictional character)   192
Bonaventure, of Bagnoregio   29, 40, 41
Bonifazio   33–4
Borat (fictional character)   194
Bottom the Weaver (fictional character)   48, 79–80, 157, 199–200
boundaries, morality and   17
Brand, Jo   63–4, 67
Brando, Marlon   169
Brennan, Neil   58, 77
Brian Cohen (fictional character)   49
Brooks, Mel   12–14, 55
Bruce, Lenny   4, 8, 10–11
   "Christ and Moses"   198
   burlesque of   77, 78
   Chaplin, Charlie, relation to   188–9
   Christianity, relation to   19
   free speech and   104
   as moralist   16–17
   nakedness of   194
   obscenities of   101
   postlapsarian stand-up set of   91–2
Buddy the Elf (fictional character)   4, 5, 42
buffoon (*mōros*)   133–4
Bugs Bunny (fictional character)   119
Bunny, John   177
Burbage, Richard   83–4
Burke, Thomas   169
burlesque   77, 78

C. K., Louis   68, 96
"Cain Kills Abel"   74, 75
Caliban (fictional character)   85, 87
Campbell, Eric   180

Candy, John   57
"Canticle of the Creatures"   26–8
Carlin, George   101
Carnival   111
Carpio, Glenda   100
Carrey, Jim   58, 192
Carroll, Paul Vincent   188
Carthage   115, 118
cataclysm   199
celebration   20–1
censors   76, 207 n.1
Chaplin, Charles   170–2
Chaplin, Charlie   3, 4, 8–10, 91, 191
    alter ego of   167–9, 178, 187
    Bruce, relation to   188–9
    charisma of   166–8, 179, 189
    in *The Circus*   186
    City Lights and   163–6, 168, 170
    in Eight Lancashire Lads   172–3
    in *The Great Dictator*   48
    Karno and   174–5
    Keystone Film Company and   78, 175–7
    The Kid and   181–3
    Mutual Film Corporation and   178–80
    in *The Pilgrim*   184–5
    suffering and   76–7
Chaplin, Hannah   169–71, 173–4, 183, 186
Chaplin, Norman Spencer   181
Chaplin, Sidney   171, 173
Chapman, Graham   43
Chappelle, Dave   17–18, 58
    Clayton Bigsby and   104
    Pryor, R., compared to   105
    recklessness of   102–3
    on *Saturday Night Live*   198–9
Chappelle's Show (television show)   17, 104
charisma
    of Chaplin, Charlie   166–8, 179, 189
    of Francis, of Assisi   28–9, 45

of Marx   9
    spiritual   5
    suffering, relation to   200
    of Thecla   142
    vulnerability and   183
charisms
    "Charlie Chaplin's Half Million"   179
    laughter as   127, 153
    of natural fools   76
Chesterton, G. K.   20–1
children   5
    "Christ and Moses"   198
    as comedians   191–2
    innocence of   4
    vulnerability of   193
Christ's Hospital   88
Christianity   6
    Bruce, relation to   19
    festivals of   110–11
    Lawrence, relation to   123–4
Christmas   6, 111
Churchill, Winston   9
Cinnamon in the Wind (comedy special)   152, 195
The Circus (film)   185, 186
City Lights (film)   163–6, 168, 170, 180, 185–8
civil war, in Italy   32–3
Clayton Bigsby (fictional character)   104
Cleese, John   43
click-boom structure   65
Clouds (Aristophanes)   109
clowns, comedians compared to   9
Coen brothers   54
Cohen, Brian   194
comedians   10. *See also specific comedians*
    children as   191–2
    clown compared to   9
    personae of   19–20
comedy. *See specific topics*
Comedy of Errors (Shakespeare)   156

The Comedy Store 58, 93, 101
comic theater, at Greek festivals 5
communal political order 32
confession, forgiveness and 95–6
"confraternities of youth" 30–1, 33
conjure 100
Conrad, of Spoleto 32
consciousness, culture and 19
Corinth 132–3, 135
Cosby, Bill 102–3, 193
A Countess in Hong Kong (film) 187
Cracking Up (film) 54
Crane, Hart 169
Critchley, Simon 65–6
crucifixion
  farce and 134
  paradox and 135
cruelty, relation to empathy 87
culture
  American 101
  consciousness and 19
  Jewish 53–4
  pop 2–3
culture war 5, 8
Cunk on Earth (television show) 193
Curtain Theater 73–5, 82
Cyprus 144
Cyra 143

d'Arce, Lazzaro 39
Dangerfield, Rodney 54
Daniel 65
David (King) 49–50, 52
David, Larry 77
death 13, 150, 151
defiance and hope 129
DeGeneres, Ellen 96
dehumanization, relation to laughter 127
Demetrius (fictional character) 157–60
denial, relation to laughter 127
Dionysos 107–9

to disclose, or uncover (*apokalyptein*) 65
disorder 158, 159
Doctor Faustus 78
Dogberry (fictional character) 79–80
dogs, as comedians 191
Dr. Lahiri (fictional character) 59–60
drama 108, 109
  martyrs, relation to 116
  melodrama 76–7, 187–8
  New Comedy and 155
dumbness 58

Easter 111
Easy Street (film) 180
Ebony (magazine) 92
Ecclesiastes 64–5, 69
Edenic age 110
Edessa 118
Edmund (fictional character) 85
Egeus (fictional character) 156, 158, 159
Egypt 136
Eight Lancashire Lads 172–3
Einstein, Albert 166, 180
Eli'ab 49–50
Emesa 149–51. *See also* Symeon, of Emesa
empathy, relation to cruelty 87
enchantment 5
End Times Fun (comedy special) 198
entertainment 122
Ernest Goes to Jail (film) 48
Ernest P. Worrell (fictional character) 48, 192
eros 195, 197
erotic desire 194–5
eschaton 111
Essanay Film Manufacturing Company 177–8
Essays (Montaigne) 81
Esther 51–3
Eucharist 111, 160
Ezekiel 14

farce   119, 134
Farley, Chris   57
the Fat Boys   57
Fat Comedy   57–8
"Fat Girl"   56–7
Feast of the Exaltation   145
Feimster, Fortune   57
Fellini, Federico   189
Felton, David   105
Ferrell, Will   4
fertility dances   5–6
Feste (fictional character)   83–5
festivals
    of Christianity   110–11
    Eucharist   111, 160
    Feast of the Exaltation   145
    Greek   5, 107–9
    higher times and   196–7
    Old Comedy at   155
    Saturnalia   109–10, 118, 159–60
Fetchit, Stepin   58, 192
Fields, W. C.   179
Fifth Crusade   41
First National Exhibitor's
        Circuit   181, 185
folly
    holiness, relation to   132, 137, 143–4
    humility and   148
    martyrs and   135–6
    as spiritual path   138
Fool upon Fool (Armin)   87–9
forgiveness   95–7
Fox, Kirk   197
Foxworthy, Jeff   59
Francis, of Assisi   15, 153–4, 189
    "confraternities of youth"
        and   30–1, 33
    charisma of   28–9, 45
    children and   191
    illness of   25–7, 34–5
    on joy   42–3
    leprosy and   38–40
    nakedness of   195

Paul compared to   37
self-abasement of   41
strangeness of   44
Walter, of Brienne and   36
worms and   45–6
free expression   101
free speech   104
Friars Minor   25, 28, 29
Fridays (television show)   152
Frye, Northrop   156

Gadsby, Hannah   17–18
    in *Nanette*   104
    pain of   127
    Pryor, R., compared to   105
    self-disclosure of   77
Gaffigan, Jim   11, 57, 59
Gallagher   192
Gambini, Vinny (fictional
        character)   119–20
the Girl (fictional character)   164–6
Gleason, Ralph   19
Gloomy-on-Thursday-Morning
        Comedy   60
The Gold Rush (film)   177, 185, 186
Gorgias (Plato)   116
"Great Cast Contest"   177
Great Depression   164
The Great Dictator (film)   48, 187
Greater Dionysia   108–9
Greccio   35
Greek festivals. *See also specific festivals*
    comic theater at   5
    Dionysos and   107–9
Gregory, Dick   16
Grey, Lita   185, 186
grief   126
Grote, David   208 n.8
Gubbio   45
Gwendolen Fairfax (fictional
        character)   159

Habib   126
Hagia Thekla   143

Hale, Georgia   164, 166–9
Hamilton, Argus   6
Hamlet (Shakespeare)   81–4
Hangry-In-Traffic Comedy   60
Hanks, Tom   49
Han Solo (fictional character)   49
Hardy, Oliver   57
Harris, Mildred   181
Heath, Frederick E.   167, 179
heaven, kingdom of   44–5
Hebrews, New Testament   110–11, 116
Hebrew tradition   64, 110–11
Hedberg, Mitch   63–4, 68
Helena (fictional character)   157, 160
Henry V (Shakespeare)   79
Herbert, George   63–4
Herman, Pee-Wee   4
Hermia (fictional character)   156–60
higher times, festivals and   196–7
hilarity
    festivals of   111
    suffering, relation to   86, 88
Holes (Sachar)   54
holiness   52, 145
    folly, relation to   132, 137, 143–4
    innocence and   52
    laughter and   150
    martyrdom, relation to   142
    mime, relation to   136
    of Symeon, of Emesa   148
    war, relation to   154
Hollywood   163–4, 175
holy fool (*salos*)   138
Hope, Bob   49
Hope, Leslie T.   167
hope
    defiance and   129
    laughter, relation to   111
Horace   109
Hosea   14, 106
Howard, Curly   11, 57, 192
Hughes, John   9
Hugolino (Cardinal)   43

humiliation   41
    Fat Comedy and   57
    of poverty   172
humility, folly and   148
humorists, comedians compared to   9
Huntington Library   6

Iago (fictional character)   85
Iglesias, Gabriel   57
Ignatius, of Antioch   118–19, 126
ignorance   2, 65
illness
    pain of   25–7
    in prison   34–5
The Immigrant (film)   180–1
impersonation   169–70, 195
innocence   18, 55, 160
    alter ego and   153
    of Chaplin, Charlie   186
    of children   4
    holiness and   52
    ignorance and   2
    of Philomena Cunk   193
    Saturnalia, relation to   109–10
ioculatores Domini (the minstrels of the Lord)   27, 44
Irish monasticism   153
irony   64
Isaac   50–1
Isadora   137
Isaiah   15, 106
Isidora   136–7
Is It Something I Said? (album)   47–9, 55, 61, 97–8, 102
It's a Mad, Mad, Mad, Mad World (film)   54
It's a Wonderful Life (film)   194–5
Italy
    "confraternities of youth" in   30–1, 33
    civil war in   32–3

J (fictional character)   55–6, 59–60, 200
Jackass crew   58

Jaques (fictional character)   82
The Jazz Singer (film)   185–6
Jefferson Smith (fictional
    character)   48, 52
Jeremiah   14, 15, 106
Jerusalem   146
Jerusalem Talmud   53
Jesse   49–50
Jesus, of Nazareth   29, 198
    martyrs for   116–17
    Pryor, R., relation to   105–6
    worms and   45–6
Jewish culture   53–4
Job   50, 54, 64, 193
Joe vs. The Volcano (film)   49
John   111
    of Amida   138
    the deacon   150
jokes
    anti-wisdom in   67–8
    apocalypse and   65–6
jongleurs   27, 34, 44
Joseph   52
joy   42–3
Julius Caesar (Shakespeare)   79
Justin Martyr   116

Kaling, Mindy   57, 59–60, 77
Karno, Fred   174–5
"Karno picnic"   174
katharsis   11
Kaufman, Andy   4, 152, 195–6
Keaton, Buster   179, 191
    Armin, relation to   76
    in *Limelight*   187–8
Kempe, Will   78, 208 n.8
    Armin, relation to   82–3
    in Lord Chamberlain's Men
        79–81
Kennedy, Bobby   198
Kent (fictional character)   88–9
Kessel, Adam   175
Key and Peele   194
Keystone Film Company   78, 175–7

The Kid (film)   181–3, 185
kiddush hašem ("the sanctification of
    God's name")   53
Kids Say the Darndest Things
    (television show)   192
kingdom, of heaven   44–5
King Lear (Shakespeare)   88–9
    Armin in   85–6
    nakedness in   196
Kolkowski, Aleksander   193

Larry Gopnik (fictional character)   54
Las Vegas, Aladdin Hotel and
    Casino   98
Laughing Fit to Kill (Carpio)   100
laughter   13–14, 18–20, 87, 201
    alter ego and   153
    authority, relation to   123
    confession and   95–6
    of Francis, of Assisi   44–5
    holiness and   150
    hope, relation to   111
    of Lawrence   128–9
    martyrdom and   118–20, 124–7
    prayer compared to   21
    of recognition   60
    shame and   97
    strangeness and   46
Laurel, Stan   174
Lawrence   116–17, 120
    Christianity, relation to   123–4
    laughter of   128–9
    pain of   127
    prank of   121–2, 136
    in Rome   115
    suffering of   125
    Thecla compared to   141
The Legend of the Three Companions
    (*vitae*)   31
Leo (Brother)   42
Leontius   144, 146, 148–9, 151–2
leprosy   38–40
Lewis, Jerry   54, 58, 91, 98
Life of Brian (film)   49

The Life of Symeon the Fool
  (Leontius) 144
Limelight (film) 171, 187–8
Live from the Sunset Strip (film) 96
Lloyd, Harold 192
Lord's Prayer 1
Lord Chamberlain's Men 79–82
Los Angeles Theater 163, 165, 168
Love's Labours Lost
  (Shakespeare) 156, 158
Lyons 118, 127
Lysander (fictional character) 156–8, 160

Maccabees 52–3
Mad Tom (fictional character) 196
Major Legend (Bonaventure) 40
Making a Living (film) 176
Mama Cass 57
mania 107–8
Marana 143
Marcolf, Solomon and 66–7
Margareton (fictional character) 85
Maria 7, 137–8
Maron, Marc 198
Martin, Steve 54
martyrdom 43
  asceticism and 143
  holiness, relation to 142
  laughter and 118–20, 124–7
  mayhem and 117
The Martyrdom of Polycarp 117–18, 210 n.5
martyrs 7, 115, 146. See also specific martyrs
  folly and 135–6
  mayhem of 141
  mischief of 119–20
  pain, relation to 126–7
  in Rome 116–17
  suffering, relation to 120, 123, 128–9
  Ten Rabbinic 53

Marx, Groucho 10, 119
  anti-wisdom and 67
  charisma of 9
  Pryor, R., and 98
māšîaḥ (messiahs) 51–2
Maximilla 143
mayhem 109
  Karno and 174
  martyrdom and 117
  of martyrs 141
  of Symeon, of Emesa 150–1
McCarthy, Melissa 57
Measure for Measure
  (Shakespeare) 156
melodrama 76–7, 187–8
Menander 155–6
The Merchant of Venice
  (Shakespeare) 156
Merton, Thomas 19
Merv Griffin Show (television show) 98
messiahs (*māšîaḥ*) 51–2
Metamorphoses (Ovid) 109–10
The Metamorphosis (film) 54
MGM 191
Mia Thermopolis (fictional character) 48
A Midsummer Night's Dream
  (Shakespeare) 79, 156–60
the Millionaire (fictional character) 164–5, 170
mime 133–4
  holiness, relation to 136
  Symeon, of Emesa as 147
The Mindy Project (television show) 57
the minstrels of the Lord (*ioculatores Domini*) 27, 44
Miracle on 34th Street (film) 49
The Mis-Adventures of Awkward Black Girl (comedy series) 55–6, 58–60, 200
Mischief
  of martyrs 119–20
  of the Tramp 178

misdirection   196
misery   26
misrule   158, 160
Modern Times (film)   177, 187
Monroe, Marilyn   58
Monty Python and the Holy Grail (film)   43
Mooney, Paul   99, 101
moral catastrophe   12–13
moralists   14–17
morality
    boundaries and   17
    revulsion, relation to   103
morality tales   96
moralization   103
moral judgment   11
moral order   17
moral recognition   12–13
Mordecai   51
Morgan, Diane   58, 67, 193
mōros (buffoon)   133–4
mortification   43, 151
Moss, Candida   210 n.5
Motion Picture Magazine   177
Moving Picture World (magazine)   176
Mr. Portakalos (fictional character)   3
Mr. Smith Goes to Washington (film)   48
Much Ado About Nothing (Shakespeare)   79
Mudbone (fictional character)   99, 100
Mulaney, John   96
Mumming Birds (sketch)   174–5
Mutual Film Corporation   178–80
My Cousin Vinny (film)   49
myths, of American culture   101

nakedness   193
    of Francis, of Assisi   195
    in *King Lear*   196
    of Pryor, R.   194
Nanette (comedy special)   104

natural fools   76, 84, 88
nebbish   53, 200
    observational comedy and   60
    suffering of   54–6
negative wisdom   65
Negri, Pola   4
Neri, Philip   153
New Comedy
    drama and   155
    ritual of   156
    Saturnalia, relation to   159–60
The New Janitor (film)   177
New Testament
    Hebrews   110–11, 116
    Revelation   125
New York Motion Pictures   175
Nikon   145
See No Evil, Hear No Evil (film)   103–4
Notaro, Tig   194

obscenities   99–101
observational comedy
    nebbish and   60
    of Seinfeld   68
Old Comedy   155–6
Onesiphorus   139
order   158
Orlando (fictional character)   159
Othello (Shakespeare)   85
otherworldly visitors   2–3
Our Gang (film series)   191
outrage artist   28
Ovid   109–10

P, Christina   6
Pacifico (Brother)   27
pain
    of Chaplin, Charlie   169–70
    of illness   25–7
    laughter, relation to   129
    martyrs, relation to   126–7
    of nebbish   54
    shame and   104

paradox   21, 45, 127–8, 135
Paul   41–2, 132–5
    Bottom the Weaver, compared
        to   200
    Francis, of Assisi, compared to   37
    Thecla and   139–41, 212 n.27
Paulsen, Pat   152
Peanuts (comic)   68–9, 191–2
Peisetairus (fictional character)   43
Pelt, Lucy van   63–4
Perpetua   115, 116, 118–19, 122,
    126–7
    laughter of   125
    Lawrence compared to   128
    Thecla compared to   141
personae, of comedians   19–20. *See
    also* alter ego
Perugia   33–5
Pesci, Joe   119–20
Peter (Brother)   43
Peter Pan (fictional character)   192
Philomena Cunk (fictional
    character)   4, 8, 193
physiognomy   87
The Pilgrim (film)   183–5
pilgrims   2–3, 136
Plato   116
Poetics (Aristotle)   11–12
Polycarp   116–18, 120, 122, 135–6,
    210 n.5
Poor Law School   172, 183
Poor Tom (fictional character)   86
pop culture   2–3
populist movements   32
Poseidon   43
postlapsarian stand-up set   91–7,
    104–5
poverty   38, 172
Povitsky, Esther   6
pranks   121–2, 126, 127, 136
prayer, laughter compared to   21
The Princess Bride (film)   3
The Princess Diaries (film)   48
Priscilla   143

prison   34–5
Procopius   153
professional clowning   76
prophecy   124
    of apocalypse   198–201
    Symeon, of Emesa, relation to   151
prophets, moralists compared to
    14–16
Proust, Marcel   167
proverbial wisdom   63–4
"Proverbs of Agur"   64
Proverbs of Hell (Blake)   67
Prudentius   121–3
Pryor, Deborah   92, 93
Pryor, Richard   4–5, 10, 198
    Blackness, relation to   103–4
    Is It Something I Said?   47–9, 55,
        61, 97–8, 102
    Jesus, relation to   105–6
    nakedness of   194
    pain of   127
    postlapsarian stand-up set of
        91–7, 104–5
    racist slurs and   99–101
    shame and   77
    Simone, relation to   193
public execution   134
public shame   95
public-speech violations   207 n.1
Puck (fictional character)   48, 157–8,
    160
Purity and ignorance   2
to put on a show
    (*apodeiknynai*)   132–3

Qohelet   63–4, 66, 67, 69
Quips upon Questions (Armin)   78–9,
    86

racist slurs   99–101
Rae, Issa   8
    Blackness, relation to   104
    in *The Mis-Adventures of Awkward
        Black Girl*   55–6, 58–60

rage   99
recklessness   102–3
recognition, laughter of   60
Redneck comedy   59
Reed, Donna   194–5
religious faith   18–19
renewal, festivals of   111
renunciations   44–5
Revelation, New Testament   125
revulsion, morality relation to   103
Rhetoric (Aristotle)   116
Richard Pryor (film)   93
righteous anger   28
The Rink (film)   180
"Rise of the Machines"   193
ritual
   of New Comedy   156
   sacred   5–7, 19
Rivers, Joan   11
The Road to Bali (film)   49
Robbie, Margot   4
Rome   37
   Lawrence in   115
   martyrs in   116–17
   Sarapion Sindonites in   136–8
   Saturnalia in   109–10, 118, 159–60
Rosalind (fictional character)   159
Russia   1, 153
Ryan, Meg   49

Sabbath   110–11, 160
Sachar, Louis   54
sacred ritual   5–7, 19
Sahl, Mort   16, 104
saint (*sanctus*)   41, 52, 61
salos (holy fool)   138
Samuel   49–50, 52
sanctus (saint)   41, 52, 61
San Damiano   30, 40
Sanders, Melani   60
Sarah   52
Sarapion Sindonites   136–8
satire   14
Satires (Horace)   109

Saturday Night Live (television show)   104, 198–9
Saturnalia   109
   apocalypse, relation to   110
   Ignatius at   118
   New Comedy, relation to   159–60
Sayings of the Desert Fathers   136
"second illumination"   65
Seinfeld, Jerry   9, 11, 63–4, 68
Seleucid Empire   52–3
self-abasement   41, 97
self-caricature   77
self-disclosure   77
self-exposure   87
Sennett, Mack   169, 175–6
serious topics   20
Servant of the People (television series)   48
setup-punchline structure   65–6
shabbiness   60–1
Shadow and Substance (Carroll)   188
The Shaggy Dog (film)   54
Shakespeare, William
   Armin and   73, 77, 84
   festivals, relation to   197
   Kempe and   80–1
   Lord Chamberlain's Men and   79–80
   otherworldly visitors and   3
   weddings and   158–9
shalom   45, 110, 124
shame   99, 150
   Fat Comedy and   58
   laughter and   97
   pain and   104
   postlapsarian stand-up set and   96
   Pryor, R., and   77
   public   95
Sharbil   116, 118, 126
the *Shema*   53
Shore, Pauly   6, 58
Silverman, Sarah   4
Simone, Nina   193
A Simple Man (film)   54

Simpson, O. J.   102–3
sin, suffering and   53, 55
Singer, John   78
Sirach   63–4
skepticism   83
Slim Pickens (fictional character)   199
Smith, John   88
Smyrna   117–18
Snoopy (fictional character)   191
Snuff the Clown   73–5, 78, 86, 89
social division and culture war   8
social order   110
social transgression   102–3
Society for the Prevention of Cruelty to Children   172
Socrates   109, 116
Solomon   64, 66–7
Spanky (fictional character)   119
spectacle (*theatron*)   132–3, 137
spiritual charisma   5
spiritual path, folly as   138
Star Wars (film series)   49
stereotypes   100–2
stigmata   25, 46, 195
strangeness   44
  laughter and   46
  of natural fools   76
  of saints   52, 61
stylites   137
suffering   14, 151
  charisma, relation to   200
  festivals, relation to   111
  hilarity, relation to   86, 88
  laughter and   127
  of Lawrence   125
  martyrs, relation to   120, 123, 128–9
  in melodrama   76–7
  of nebbish   54–6
  in prison   34
  sin and   53, 55
  Symeon, of Emesa, relation to   146
  theatron of   137
surrealism   177

Symeon, of Emesa   138, 144, 149, 192
  alter ego of   152–3
  holiness of   148
  mayhem of   150–1
  as mime   147
  misdirection of   196
  nakedness of   195
  Nikon and   145
  suffering, relation to   146
  as Symeon Salos   15, 131–2, 189
Symeon Stylites (saint)   7, 137, 138
Syria   131, 136–7

taboos   10, 17
Talmud   53, 124
Tarlton, Richard   78
Ted Lasso (fictional character)   4, 48, 52, 192
Ted Lasso (television show)   48
The Tempest (Shakespeare)   85
Tennessee Kid (comedy special)   57
Ten Rabbinic Martyrs   53
Tertullian   143
Testament (Francis of Assisi)   39
Thamyris   139–40
theatron (spectacle)   132–3, 137
"The Canticle of Brother Sun"   26–8
Thecla, of Iconium   138–40, 143–4, 153, 212 n.27
  charisma of   142
  Lawrence, compared to   141
Theodoret   137, 143
Theophilus, Maria and   137–8
Thersites (fictional character)   85
"the sanctification of God's name" (*kiddush hašem*)   53
Theseus (fictional character)   156, 158
Thespis   108
This Can't Be Happening to Me (film)   105
Thomas, of Celano   29, 33, 35, 39, 44, 45
"Those Charlie Chaplin Feet"   167

Three Stooges 58
Till, Emmett 198
Tillie's Punctured Romance
 (film) 176–7
Titania (fictional character) 157
torture 53, 124
touched 14–15
Touchstone (fictional character)
 82–4, 87, 208 n.8
tragedians, comedians compared to 9
tragedy 11–13
 comedy compared to 61
 Greater Dionysia and 108
The Tragic Imagination (Williams,
 Rowan) 108
training (*askēsis*) 143
the Tramp (fictional character) 3,
 177, 179
 in *City Lights* 164–8, 170, 185–8
 in *The Kid* 182–3
 mischief of 178
 in *The Pilgrim* 184–5
The Tramp (film) 178
trauma of war 35
True and Perfect Joy (Leo) 42
Tucker, Sophie 56–7, 76
Turkey 136, 143
Twelfth Night (Shakespeare) 83, 156
The Two Maids of More-clacke
 (Armin) 82, 84, 88

Union Castle Mail Steamship
 Company 173
United Artists 185
Ustyug, Russia 153

Valerian (Emperor) 120–1
van Pelt, Linus (fictional
 character) 200

Vevey Cemetery 189
violence 74, 151
vulnerability 74
 charisma and 183
 of children 193

Walter, of Brienne 36
war
 civil 32–3
 holiness, relation to 154
 trauma of 35
Warren Nefron (fictional
 character) 54, 55
weakness 58–9
weddings 158–9
"We Do Not Care Club" 60
Wesley (fictional character) 3
"What Have I Lost?" 74
When-Will-My-Kids-Go-Back-To-
 School Comedy 60
Williams, Robin 192
Williams, Rowan 108
wisdom
 anti- 66–8
 negative 65
 proverbial 63–4
witness, martyrs as 116
Working It Out (podcast) 59
worms 45–6
Worthing, Jack (fictional
 character) 159
Wright, Steven 63–4, 67, 68, 200

Yankovic, Weird Al 193
Yorick (fictional character) 83

Zelensky, Volodymyr 48
Zeus 108
Ziegfeld Follies 167